T

?

Toussaint's Clause

TOUSSAINT'S CLAUSE

The Founding Fathers and the Haitian Revolution

Gordon S. Brown

UNIVERSITY PRESS OF MISSISSIPPI   JACKSON

An ADST-DACOR Diplomats and Diplomacy Book

www.upress.state.ms.us

The University Press of Mississippi is a member of the Association of American University Presses.

Copyright © 2005 by Gordon S. Brown

Manufactured in the United States of America

12 11 10 09 08 07 06 05   4 3 2 1

Library of Congress Cataloging-in-Publication Data

Brown, Gordon S., 1936–

Toussaint's clause : the founding fathers and the Haitian revolution / Gordon S. Brown.

p. cm.

"An ADST-DACOR diplomats and diplomacy book."

Includes bibliographical references and index.

ISBN 1-57806-711-1 (cloth : alk. paper)

1. United States—Foreign relations—1789–1809. 2. Toussaint Louverture, 1743?–1803.

3. United States—Foreign relations—Haiti. 4. Haiti—Foreign relations—United States.

5. Haiti—History—Revolution, 1791–1804. I. Title.

E310.7.B76   2005

327.7307294'09'033—dc22   2004010403

British Library Cataloging-in-Publication Data available

CONTENTS

FOREWORD

For nearly 230 years extraordinary men and women have represented the United States abroad under all kinds of circumstances. What they did and how and why they did it remain little known to their compatriots. In 1995 the Association for Diplomatic Studies and Training (ADST) and Diplomatic and Consular Officers, Retired (DACOR) created a book series to increase public knowledge and appreciation of the involvement of American diplomats in world history. The series seeks to demystify diplomacy by telling the story of those who have conducted our foreign relations, as they lived, observed, and reported them. Former ambassador Gordon Brown's lively study of early American foreign relations and economic diplomacy, *Toussaint's Clause: The Founding Fathers and the Haitian Revolution,* advances these aims.

Brown relates how America's early leaders and their diplomatic representatives dealt with the politically sensitive issue of the 1790–1810 slave rebellion in Haiti led by Toussaint Louverture. Founding fathers Washington, Adams, Hamilton, Jefferson, and Madison struggled with the dilemma of how to protect America's highly profitable trade with the rich French colony while ensuring America's national security and maintaining its beneficial position of neutrality between the warring European powers. The leaders' policy toward the revolt was consistent on only one point—the need to protect America from what they saw as Haiti's radicalism. America's diplomats contributed significantly to resolving the controversy. Although communications were often slow, insecure, uncertain, and frequently overtaken by events, this left room for a degree of improvisation unthinkable today.

Before turning to historical and analytical writing, Gordon S. Brown spent thirty-five years in the Foreign Service, mainly in the Middle East and North Africa. He served as political advisor to General Norman Schwarzkopf in the first Gulf War and as ambassador to Mauritania. His previous publications include *Coalition, Coercion and Compromise: Diplomacy of the Gulf Crisis, 1990–1991* (Institute for the Study of Diplomacy, 1997) and *The Norman Conquest of Southern Italy and Sicily* (McFarland, 2003).

In *Toussaint's Clause*, Gordon Brown vividly recounts how, from the nation's earliest days, fiercely partisan politics, congressional constraints, the pressure of economic interest groups, bureaucratic ambition, and larger foreign and domestic goals shaped, and then reshaped, critical foreign policies.

—KENNETH L. BROWN, President
Association for Diplomatic Studies and Training

—ROBERT L. FUNSETH, President
Diplomatic and Consular Officers, Retired

PREFACE

The formation of foreign policy is not a tidy, nor a linear, process. A career spent in the American diplomatic service served to show this author how apparently lucid considerations of national interest can be influenced, and sometimes even perverted, by the impact of personality, bureaucratic considerations, and, above all, domestic politics. Our founding fathers lived in what seems to us today a much simpler world, yet it was nonetheless one where many of those same considerations had great weight. Our policy toward revolutionary Haiti—St. Domingo in the parlance of the time—was no exception.

This book had its origin in a fit of curiosity. I wanted to know more about Toussaint Louverture, that iconic figure about whom most Americans have, at best, only a shadowy knowledge. I began to read the record. There, I learned for the first time how closely the Haitian revolution had touched early American politics, and how crucially the American and Haitian stories were intertwined during the exciting decade that saw the United States take its first foreign policy initiatives, and make the fateful Louisiana Purchase. The book flowed easily from the drama that I saw in this often overlooked story, and from the desire to dissect it as a sort of case study as to how American foreign policy was made.

I am most appreciative for the two superb institutions that house most of the information on which this book is based: the Library of Congress and the National Archives. Helpful staff and comfortable,

even inspiring working conditions have made the research a pleasure. Our tax dollars are well spent.

Several notes are necessary to explain spelling and other features of
the text that may give readers pause. First, the use of archaic spellings
in the quotations. I have tried to preserve the original spellings wherever possible, both to give a greater sense of authenticity to the pieces
and to avoid creating my own template of grammatical or ortho-
graphic correctness. I did, however, alter the original grammar on
those few occasions when the document otherwise would have made
little sense to a modern reader. For documents translated from the
original French, on the other hand (primarily Turner and the items
from the French archives), I used modern spellings, but stuck as
closely as possible to the original grammar. Any errors in translation
are mine alone.

I have chosen to spell the folk religion of Haiti by its most com-
monly recognized form of "voodoo," although many specialists pre-
fer "vodou" or other variations that correspond more closely to the
local dialect.

Names can also create difficulty. The modern country of Haiti is
called St. Domingo in most of the text, because that is what it was called
by the Americans at the time. But the French name, St. Domingue, is
also used in situations or quotations that are purely French. And a third
name, Haiti, is even used toward the end of the book, after the colony
had taken the final step of independence and adopted that new name.
I hope there will be no confusion. I have, in a similar spirit of using contemporary nomenclature, referred to Toussaint Louverture exclusively
as Toussaint, without his surname. The surname, which he adopted
in the process of the anticolonial struggle, was used primarily in his
own country at the time. Elsewhere, he was generally known by his
given name, and that usage corresponds to the texts and quotations
employed here.

Finally, it should be noted that quotations from the *Annals of
Congress* are usually not direct quotes. As there was no verbatim

record taken of the debates at the time, the quotations represent paraphrases, or stenographic records of unknown completeness, that were used to compile the *Annals*. Still, they are contemporary recreations, more or less accurate in their tone, tenor, and phraseology, and they are as close as we can get to what was actually said. As reflections of the thoughts and emotions of the legislators, they lend immense color to the record even while we have to recognize that the quotations may not be entirely accurate.

If the typical reader gets only half the enjoyment from looking into this fascinating vignette of history as I got in exposing it, I will be gratified.

Toussaint's Clause

INTRODUCTION

It is indeed an animating thought that, while we are securing the rights of ourselves and our posterity, we are pointing out the way to struggling nations who wish, like us, to emerge from their tyrannies also. . . . Heaven help their struggle, and lead them, as it has us, triumphantly through them.

—Thomas Jefferson, March 11, 1790

Our democratic papers have for years past been puffing the French Revolution as exhibiting the grand and magnificent spectacle of a great people struggling for liberty. But now, similar efforts made by the blacks of Hispaniola are dubbed a wicked rebellion . . . why then are the brave, independent blacks now to be starved, or those to be treated as rebels who attempt to feed them? Does the difference in color make a difference in the rights of man?

—*Columbian Centinel*, April 3, 1802

Three revolutions reshaped western political thinking at the end of the eighteenth century. The first was the American war for independence, which began as a colonial rebellion calling for greater political liberty, and in time gave birth to the first modern republic. The new American state had scarcely established itself before the second, and then the third, revolution broke out.

The French Revolution pursued the same republican ideal, but went a step further: it encompassed revolutionarily social as well as political goals. Embracing the principle of equality in addition to that of liberty, the French not only threw off the country's old rulers, they broke the old ruling system.

3

And yet it was the third revolution, in Haiti, that turned out to be the most profound. Building on the revolutionary momentum of their French mother country, the Haitians transformed a colonial revolt into a thoroughgoing social revolution. In breaking the old political system, they also permanently overthrew the old social structure of the country, with the result that they, much more than the American rebels at Yorktown, truly turned their world upside down. Yet sadly, neither they nor the French succeeded at the time in achieving political liberty.

The three revolutions shared a common rhetoric of liberty and freedom. Then why was it that the Americans, who had been first to put those stirring slogans to practical use, found it difficult to accept the way they were applied in France, and then in Haiti?

To the Americans, liberty meant the freedom to make their own political decisions, on a national level as well as in their traditional local self-government. But there was little or no pretension to equality, either political or social. In fact, most of the founding fathers were profoundly distrustful of what they called the "leveling spirit." No wonder, then, that so many American patriots were dismayed when the French Revolution went beyond its liberal, constitutional beginnings to become a blood-drenched and radical social upheaval.

The Haitian revolution began as a colonial revolt, much like the American. But once revolution in the mother country of France turned in a radical direction, the instigators of the revolt in Haiti were unable to maintain control of what they had started. In a racist slave colony like theirs, Jacobin appeals to liberty and equality took on profoundly new and inflammatory meaning, and the local situation was far too combustible for gradual reform. Once the slaves realized that they had the power to demand changes, the brutally exploitative plantation regime was doomed. In over a decade of horrible and genocidal struggle, the slaves finally won their personal, if not much political, liberty.

Americans were horrified. If some of the more ardent republicans were slow to lose their initial enthusiasm for the French republican experiment, they could muster none at all for the Haitian revolution. To begin with, the Haitian revolt was egalitarian in the most blatant way, at a time when our founding fathers were unready for any leveling of class distinctions. And moreover, it was in no way republican. The American model of representative government did not succeed in taking any credible shape in Haiti, where a military autocracy took root instead. Americans could, in short, see little in the politics of Haiti's revolution beyond the fact of a slave revolt. Public opinion, North or South, saw no fellow constitutional republicans there with whom they could identify. And the day in which the "freedom fighter" would be lauded was far, far away.

Was there an element of racism in the American attitude? Of course; racism was pervasive in American society at the time. But many Americans, North as well as South, were simply appalled at the excesses of the French revolution, and it was the slaughter and disorder unleashed by proponents of the Rights of Man, as much as their skin color, that shocked. Americans would have turned away from any revolution in the neighborhood that was as bloody and destructive of property as was the Haitian one. That the implications of Haiti's slave revolt also posed a threat to public security in the fledgling and insecure United States (in all but the abolitionist New England states) made it doubly suspect. Most Americans had been frightened enough by the social upheaval and threat to order and property exemplified in Shay's and then the Whiskey rebellions. Few were prepared to laud a foreign rebellion that compounded the same threat of anarchy with the potential to serve as a model for domestic slave unrest.

That southerners, who lived in a slaveholding society and had the most to lose from a slave revolt, most feared the spread of radical egalitarian ideas from Haiti is obvious. Racism in this circumstance was mixed with economic interest, forming a most powerful combination. Three of the presidents who dealt with the Haitian revolution—Washington, Jefferson, and Madison—were slaveowners, and that was an economic and social fact that certainly influenced their personal approaches to the issue. Yet there is little room for generalization, and less (at least for this author) for psycho-political analysis about the role of racism in their decisions. Jefferson, whose views on slavery we know to have been famously complex and contradictory, seems to have been equally ambiguous in his attitude toward the Haitian revolution, at times accepting it and yet always apprehensive. But there was no way that he, the champion of republicanism, could see the Haitian rebels as fellow liberals. Nor did they, in all honesty, deserve to be so identified. It was, after all, a defense of republican ideals, not rebellion per se, that Jefferson had in mind when he addressed the good citizens of Alexandria (as quoted above) in 1790.[1]

The few Americans who did defend the Haitian revolution on ethical grounds came, surprisingly, from the ranks of the Federalists, who otherwise gave few indications of much dedication to democratic principles. As a matter of fact, those occasional defenses of the Haitian rebels (like the one quoted above), when looked at closely, look remarkably like rhetorical exercises, designed by their authors more to embarrass their Democratic-Republican adversaries than to champion black liberation. The authors' objectives in defending the Haitians, indeed, stemmed more from economic than political factors, as it was the highly lucrative commerce with the island that led them to take up Toussaint's cause to begin with.

Economic interests, in the author's view, determined the main lines of the debate over America's Haitian policy. Specifically, it was a clash between the shipping and merchant interests, largely from the North, and the slaveholding interests in the South, and it was an exemplar of the fundamental North-South divide that characterized the nation's politics at the time. Oversimplified, the maritime centers wanted to trade with the Haitian rebels, while the plantation owners wanted to isolate them or squelch them, and the direction of our fluctuating policy was determined by which of the groups had the current administration's ear. Successive American administrations supported first the French, then the Haitian rebels—even flirting with encouraging their independence—and then again (although with reservations) the French.

American policy toward the Haitian revolution was, of course, heavily influenced as well by the maelstrom of the long and desperate war between the European powers. But the same American economic interest groups were parties to that debate as well, and the nation's foreign policy considerations served more to inflect the tactics of our Haitian policy than to determine its fundamental direction.

The ambiguities of our policy toward the emerging state of Haiti were, in the end, a reflection of how closely balanced those competing interest groups were during most of the period under discussion in this work. It was only when the combined effects of Jefferson's embargo and the collapse of the Haitian export economy caused the maritime interests effectively to drop out of the political argument that an anti-Haitian policy became crystal clear.

JULY 1790

S ince the Fourth of July fell on a Sunday in 1790, the official celebrations were held on the following Monday. In New York, capital of the fledgling federal government, the citizens set aside their usual preoccupations and turned over the day, as a reporter put it, to "the little gods of festive mirth and conviviality."[1] There were good reasons for the festival atmosphere, too. Finally, years after the last battles against Britain, the full benefits of independence seemed attainable. The new general government, as many called the federal system created by the two-year-old constitution, had begun to organize the finances of the country and bring the economy out of its postwar slump. And even though the new republic was still weak, and its government very much a work in progress, the prospects were increasingly promising. It was a good time to commemorate the signing of the Declaration of Independence, and with a bit of real enthusiasm.

President Washington, on Monday, even gave up his usual dawn horseback exercise to prepare for the events of the day. Those events were, like the president, dignified, understated, and straightforward. In mid-morning, the New York militia mustered in the lower city, the pageantry of their parade heightened by bands and punctuated by gunfire salutes—thirteen rounds from cannon at the Battery, and rolling musket salutes, or *feux de joie*, from the infantry. Toward noon, the members of Congress, New York officials, "strangers of distinction" (there was as yet almost no resident diplomatic community), and the officers of the Society of Cincinnati paid their respects to the president at the City Tavern, and marched with him down Broad Street to St. Paul's Church. There, they listened to a "sensible oration," by Brockholst Livingston, which the president described as follows: "the tendency of which was, to shew the different situation we are now in, under an excellent government of our own choice, to what it would have been if we had not succeeded in our opposition to the attempts of Great Britain to enslave us; and how much we ought to cherish the blessings which are within our reach, & to cultivate the seeds of harmony & unanimity."[2]

Following the service, most of the assembled company retired to Burchin's Tavern, where they enjoyed a festive and considerably less sedate banquet, punctuated by numerous congratulatory toasts. It was a big day for New York, still a small town at the time, and the last such celebration for the city by the Hudson. By the end of the year, the federal capital was to move to the United States' only major city at the time, Philadelphia.

Similar commemorations were held in other American cities on that day. The prominent role played in the ceremonies by the militias, and the Society of Cincinnati, demonstrated that the day was, above all, a celebration of American success in the war for independence, and a commemoration of the role of the citizen-soldier in that effort. In New York city, however, Aaron Burr's new Society of St. Tammany gave a slightly more antiestablishment cast to the day by mounting a second celebration for its own membership, who were treated to a public reading of the Declaration as well as more solid fare. Everywhere, it can safely be assumed when considering the tippling customs of the time, much spirituous liquor fortified the patriotic sentiments of those on the street and in the banquet halls, where the toasts were numerous and enthusiastic.

"Hail to this festival, All hail the Day
Columbia's standard on the roof display
And let the people's motto ever be,
United thus, and thus United be."[3]

Of the many banquet toasts made that day, in Philadelphia, New York, and probably elsewhere, one stands out: to Louis XVI of France. This republican toast, to that royal ally, was undoubtedly sincere; French help had been crucial in winning the recent war. But, in light of the momentous and revolutionary events that were then unfolding in France, the toast may also have been deliberately double-edged— expressing thanks for the king's help in the past, while at the same time celebrating his present dilemma. After all, the king's royal privileges were being attacked by his own rebellious and republican-minded subjects, and the revolution was moving so fast that royal Louis, according to one observer, had just agreed, "with apparent cordiality," to accept a new constitution and other "measures which absolutely reduce him to the state of Lord Mayor of France."[4]

For most Americans, the events in France were a moving testimony to the virtues of their own revolt from the British monarchy. Most newspapers ran accounts of the stirring debates in the French legislature, and Americans were hopeful that the ancient French monarchy would complete its year-long revolution soon, transforming itself into a republic based on the same political ideals that had given birth to the United States.

In reality, however, what happened, or did not happen, in Paris was far from the daily concerns of most Americans in 1790. Much more immediate subjects were on their minds, ones that affected their hopes to carve out a decent future under the new system of government their representatives had chosen. The final state, Rhode Island, had reluctantly ratified the constitution only in May, but resistance to the broad powers assigned to the new federal government remained strong in most of the states. The ratification debate of the past two years had highlighted a great number of philosophical, pocketbook, political, and regional differences between the states and their different communities, but the compromises made by the delegates to the Convention had stood up and the constitution had been approved. The new government was in place, and a supplemental bill of rights was on the way to approval. Major differences persisted, however, and how well the new government would manage them was far from clear, or even if it could. The economy, too, was still weak. Even though the postwar depression was ending, national and state finances were askew, and trade remained low due to continued lack of money. Illustrative of the lack of confidence in the economy was the New York city lottery, which unblushingly advertised that its prizes were to be awarded in British Pounds Sterling. Finally, internal security was by no means assured. Five years earlier, the fiasco of Shay's Rebellion had badly shaken social stability, as well as confidence that the government could deal with domestic unrest. And in the promising but vulnerable western territories, European colonial officials in neighboring Spanish Louisiana and English Canada took every opportunity to destabilize the situation, either by trying to stir up separatism through prejudicing the settlers against their eastern coast colleagues, or by inciting the Indian tribes against them.

Nonetheless, the thirteen ex-colonies were being shaped, haltingly, into a new framework—not yet a nation, much less a union, but no longer a set of parallel sovereignties as they had been under the Articles of Confederation. The presence as president of solid, steadfast George Washington, with his great personal integrity and sense of mission, was an irreplaceable unifying factor in a country and government struggling with basic issues of organization. It was not easy to build a new, national, and republican system of governance, and the policy arguments were heated. Alexander Hamilton, the brilliant, assertive, and ambitious young secretary of the treasury, was pushing to build a truly national economy, but was opposed in the cabinet and Congress by those, headed by Secretary of State Thomas Jefferson, who aimed for a smaller, rural-based government. Gradually, though, Hamilton had brought the president to his point of view and was prevailing on the specific reforms: a uniform set of external tariffs, federal funding of the war debts at par, assumption of state debts, and other centralizing measures were passed. The country needed nothing more, Hamilton had argued, than a period of political stability and fiscal discipline that would allow it to build the foundations of future prosperity. A dominant federal role in finance would sort out the monetary chaos and solidify a national economy. That, in turn, would stimulate the growth of trade (principally with Great Britain, the country's greatest trading partner), which in its own turn would bring in the customs revenues that were the general government's main source of income, allowing the country to pay off its huge debt.

That summer, Washington wrote to his old comrade-in-arms, the Marquis de Lafayette, who had become one of the leading figures of the expanding revolution in France. Thanking his young colleague for the highly symbolic gift Lafayette had just sent, which was no less than the key to the Bastille, Washington carefully avoided comment on the uneven progress of the French experiment in revolution. Instead, he showed his own clear, postrevolutionary desire for stability and order:

> Gradually recovering from the distresses in which the war left us, patiently advancing in our task of civil government, unentangled in the crooked politics of Europe, wanting scarcely any thing but the free navigation of the Mississippi (which we must have and as certainly shall have as we remain a Nation) I have supposed, that, with the undeviating exercise of a just, steady, and prudent national policy, we shall be the gainers, whether the powers of the old world may be in peace or war, but more especially in the latter case. In that case our importance will certainty encrease, and our friendship be courted.[5]

Lafayette himself was to pay a commanding role in the upcoming July 14 celebrations in Paris. Infinitely more splendid than those in New York, they were designed to celebrate the storming of the Bastille at the beginning of the revolution a year earlier, and at the same time to mark the beginning of what Lafayette hoped would be a new, constitutional age. The day was to be celebrated as the Festival of the Federation, and was to highlight the king, embodiment as he was of centuries of despotism, as he accepted the novelty of a rule of laws created by others. The king was to join the militias and the National Assembly in pledging allegiance to the nation and to a new (and still unfinished) constitution—which would severely limit the powers that his ancestors had so assiduously extracted from their subjects. A dramatic ceremony had been planned, in a country that knew a great deal about opulent display. Preparations for the event had taken weeks. A decorated bridge of boats had been built across the Seine, the Champs de Mars had been emblazoned with flags and allegorical paintings, and a triumphal arch, a statue of liberty, and an amphitheater had been constructed, as well as a raised dais for the king's throne. The king himself had even joined in the preparations, wheeling three barrows of gravel into the works, according to the press.

The day of the festival itself, unfortunately, was dogged by a steady rain. But the half million citizens who had thronged to the event were undeterred. Cheers greeted the arrival of each element of the ceremony and its military escort: first the members of the National Assembly, then the delegates from each of the newly created Departments, then the Paris National Guard headed by Lafayette. Bands and drum corps vied with each other, punctuated by a salute of one hundred guns, while entertainment acts further enlivened the three-hour procession. Then came the climax of the ceremony: the pledges of allegiance. Led off by Lafayette, they progressed through the Departmental and National Assembly delegates, to climax with the oath of the king. "I, the King of France, swear to the nation to make use of the power that is delegated to me by the constitutional laws of the state, in maintaining the constitution, and putting the laws into execution. I swear it." As he pronounced the last phrase, with his arms extended, he was cheered wildly by the crowd, while the moment was defined by a second artillery salute, and a flourish of fifty thousand swords. The king's oath, so rich with symbolism and even hope, was followed by still another symbol of Lafayette's constitutional aspirations for his country—the entry into the amphitheater of the flag of the new

American republic, carried by those two icons of the revolution, John Paul Jones and Thomas Paine.

After the emotional scene, the happy but thoroughly wet crowd dispersed to their homes, or to the taverns, for material sustenance, while the dignitaries were treated to a grand state dinner in the illuminated city. As an American correspondent reported, "The naturally lively character of the French had excited some apprehension of tumult on this occasion—but the prudent precautions of the Magistrate or, perhaps, the fatigue and wetting the actors and spectators had undergone during the day rendered everything so very peaceable. . . . To see the representatives of a mighty Empire, with the sovereign at their head, emerging from the depths of slavery and darkness to light, liberty and happiness, impresses feelings on every philanthropic mind too great for utterance."[6]

This particular American may have let the enthusiasm of the day overtake him when he voiced his conclusions, for the festival, it would turn out, marked more the end than the beginning of the constitutional phase of France's revolution. The upheaval had unleashed primordial political and social passions, and violent differences, that the festival succeeded in masking only momentarily. A nation with deep and festering social differences, unfamiliar with either self-government or liberty, was suddenly experiencing intoxicating doses of both, in a revolutionary process with no governing mechanism. Anarchy warred with order on a daily basis; the peasants in many part of the countryside were rising against their hereditary lords, while in the cities—in Paris particularly—the mob and its radical leaders had begun to take violent measures that put serious pressure on the moderate reformers who still, but barely, controlled the weak Assembly.

Moreover, the revolutionary fervor and its attendant disorders had crossed the Atlantic into the French West Indies, where Americans enjoyed important trading contacts. No wonder that many Americans, whose political revolution had been largely free of social upheaval, looked on the growing excesses of the French—the murders of rural gentry, the storming of royalist citadels, the political murders, the civil war in some colonies—with apprehension. Washington, in writing that summer to another old comrade-in arms-from France, Count Rochambeau, noted his concerns in a light-hearted manner, but his choice of the word "licentiousness" to describe the social upheaval may best describe his fear of the possible consequences:

> The little anecdote which you recall to mind, My dear Count, of your Countrymen at Rhode Island who burnt their mouths with the hot soup, while mine waited leisurely for it to cool, perhaps, when politically applied in the manner you have done, has not less truth than pleasantry in its resemblance of national characters. But if there shall be no worse consequence resulting from too great eagerness in swallowing something so delightful as liberty, than that of suffering a momentary pain or making a ridiculous figure with a scalled mouth; upon the whole it may be said you Frenchmen have come off well, considering how immoderately you thirsted for the cup of liberty. And no wonder as you drank it to the bottom, that some licentiousness should have been mingled with the dregs.[7]

Thomas Jefferson, for his part, was apprehensive but not pessimistic. Deeply committed to individual liberty, and close to many of the French intellectuals and reformers whom he had known during his years as an American representative in Paris, he saw the revolution as an inevitably messy but profoundly positive process. Monarchy, aristocracy, the oppressive central government, all should and would be swept away, he thought. Although he, too, feared the mob, he trusted that the men of reason, the propertied class, would in the end bring about a moderate conclusion. The victory of republicanism in France, the thoughtful Virginian and his colleagues hoped, would solidify the republican cause in America against those who, they feared, hankered for a return to British monarchical practices.

Another founding father, on the other hand, felt that the French experiment in liberty was already slipping out of control. Gouverneur Morris of New York, a staunch patriot, also a Francophile, but concerned over a "leveling spirit" such as that which had animated Shay's Rebellion, distrusted both the French populace and its would-be leaders. In Paris on business but keeping his old colleague informed of the turns of events there, he sent a letter to President Washington at the beginning of the year in which he spelled out his fears with both wit and foresight:

> This Assembly may be divided into three parts; one, called the aristocrats, consists of the high clergy, the members of the law (note, these are not the lawyers), and such of the nobility as think they ought to form a special order. Another, which has no name but consists of all sorts of people, [are] really friends to good government. The third is composed of what is called here the *enragés*, that is the madmen. These are the most numerous, and are of that class which, in America, is known by the name of pettifogging lawyers; together with a host of curates and many of those persons who, in all revolutions, throng to the standard of change because they are not well. This last party is in close alliance with the populace here and derives, from the circumstances, a very great authority. They have already unhinged everything, and, according to custom on such occasions, the torrent rushes on irresistible, until it shall have wasted itself.

The king, Morris continued, was "a small beer character," who "little thinks how unstable is his situation." Morris's report to New York concluded by predicting, correctly if quite prematurely, that there would be a general war: "All Europe, just now, is a mine ready to explode."[8]

Americans knew that a war in Europe, which would inevitably pit those old antagonists the British and French against each other, would with equal inevitability spread across the ocean. Past wars between the great rivals had been fought in the New World as well as in Europe, and there was no reason to expect that a new struggle would not follow the same pattern. The ex-colonies were now on their own, an independent but virtually undefended country, bordered by colonies of England and Spain, and with intimate trading relations with the West Indian colonies of France and other powers. Their newly emerging security and economic prospects would be transformed by a war, for both good and bad. Washington, in his letter to Lafayette quoted above, had suggested that America's strategic situation would work to its benefit. But, as much as America's friendship, trade, and products would be in demand during a war, they would also be put at risk by the competition between the European powers. Each belligerent was sure to try to deny American favors to its opponents. America's trade would be transformed—its risks and rewards both magnified, and its government caught between the competing demands of the major powers, who were also neighbors.

American vulnerability to the wars of other countries, as well as its ability to seize any opportunities presented, came from the fact that the United States in 1790 was, to a large degree, a trading and maritime nation. Most of the population still lived on or near a navigable river or the sea, and the roads were so underdeveloped that, even in 1816, it cost as much to cart a ton of goods fifty miles overland as to ship it to London.[9] That meant that water was still the principal means of transport for any heavy or bulky products. And America mainly produced bulky agricultural and fisheries products; modern manufacturing had scarcely begun. Indeed, the country's first machine-driven factory, a textile plant in Pawtucket, had just opened during the year.

So America's bounty—the grain, tobacco, flour, wood and marine products, the livestock, fish, and other goods—reached their markets largely by water, as did the imports from Europe. Interstate commerce was still in its infancy, the disjointed trade regime under the Articles of Confederation having done little to wean the separate states from their dependency on trade with European countries and their colonies.

What little trade between the states there was also moved largely by water. All these factors, plus a ready availability of lumber, marine goods, and cheap, skilled labor, had promoted the growth of a vital and vibrant shipping industry. Shipowners, merchants, sailors, and trading houses formed an important interest group and provided many of the leading citizens, particularly in the main ports of Boston, Providence, New York, Philadelphia, Baltimore, and Charleston. More-over, the abundance of navigable rivers, and smaller ports, assured that almost every community near the Atlantic seaboard had a significant interest in the shipping business.

Independence had given American shippers and traders, as well as the producers of the export goods that they carried, a vital interest in free trade. Before the Revolution, the Americans had operated under the regime of the British Navigation Acts, which in those mercantilist days was a regime designed to maximize, even to monopolize, the trade between Britain and its colonies for ships flying the British flag. The colonists in many ways had benefited: their British flags, and the British Navy, had protected the American shippers and had allowed them to prosper. But the system also had its costs. One of those had been Britain's attempt to keep the American colonists out of the sugar trade with its West Indian colonies, and to monopolize it for Britain-based ships. The Molasses Act of 1733 and the Sugar Duties Act of 1764 were in fact so detested in the American colonies that they can be seen, well before the Stamp Act, as one of the grounds for the unrest that led to the events of 1775–1776. The Americans, of course, often refused to respect the Molasses Act, and the experience they gained in smuggling, making false papers, and other circumventions of its provisions gave them valuable experience which they put to good use during the revolutionary war and beyond.

After gaining their independence, the Americans were on their own. The French, in spite of their wartime alliance with the rebellious colonists, did little to broaden their commercial relationship with the States after the war, and American trade with France remained decidedly secondary to the dominant trade with Britain. American ships, now flying the Stars and Stripes, had to compete with the British, the French, and other European shippers for the trade with Europe. Luckily, American shippers were very competitive and could get their fair share of the business, but they were still handicapped by the mercantilist rules of the colonial powers, who sought to monopolize their colonial markets whenever possible. And in case of war, the Americans could expect to be treated by the powerful British Navy like the ships of any other power, and would get no protection.

In practice, the British agreed to let American ships compete freely in the bilateral trade, on a basis of equality with British ones. But, by an Order in Council of 1783, the British closed the trade to and from their West Indies colonies to American ships. This was a severe blow to American interests, almost worse than the hated Molasses Act, which had tried to limit only the sugar trade. In response, Congress sent John Adams to London on a mission—in the end unsuccessful—to try to soften the British trade restrictions.

America's trade with the Caribbean colonies of the European powers was crucial for a number of reasons. To begin with, it provided a dynamic outlet for American goods, since the monoculture systems in the island sugar colonies necessitated that they import large quantities of foodstuffs and building materials to keep the plantations running. As the Americans were highly competitive in both raw material and shipping costs, their products dominated the West Indies market wherever they were not frozen out by colonial regulations. Indeed, almost one-third of total American exports were sold into the region during the period 1790–1814,[10] and many producers as well as shippers in America were dependent on the island market. Moreover, American ships also carried out a robust indirect trade between Europe and the West Indies, landing the goods first in American ports and then re-exporting them.

The sugar trade with the West Indies had also produced a profitable transformation industry in American ports: rum distillation.

This was what the Molasses Act had been designed to crush, for it was a very lucrative business indeed. American traders bought the molasses cheap in the islands, distilled it at home—Massachusetts and Rhode Island between them had more that a hundred rum distilleries in the 1750s—and sold it to their bibulous countrymen. American-made rum also had become an important medium of exchange—it was traded for profit in Canada and on the Grand Banks for fish, and in West Africa for slaves.

The West Indian trade as a result provided employment for a great number of American seamen, port workers, and shipbuilders, while the flow of goods through American ports provided the new U.S. government with significant customs revenues. Finally, the West Indian trade was vital to the American economy in still another way—its earnings helped to pay for imports from Europe, and to ease substantially the balance of trade deficit America perpetually ran with the old continent.

Back in 1783, John Adams had written, "The commerce of the West Indies is a part of the American system of commerce. They can neither do without us, nor we without them. The Creator has placed us upon the globe in such a situation that we have occasion for each other. We have the means of assisting each other, and politicians and artful contrivances cannot separate us."[11] His implication, at the time, was that the American traders would find clandestine means to circumvent British and French efforts, or indeed any efforts, to regulate the trade. He would, not too many years later, have good opportunity to see how his prediction worked out in practice.

The French West Indies was a key area of American interest. Several things had attracted the Americans since the beginning of the century, when the French sugar plantations had entered their remarkable period of expansion. First, sugar was produced remarkably efficiently in the French islands of Guadeloupe, Martinique, and particularly in France's richest colony, St. Domingue. Low production costs led to low prices—often over 25 percent lower than the cost of sugar from British colonies.[12] And if that had not been incentive enough, the French had created a further reason for the Americans to come: they had decided to protect their brandy distillers at home by banning the import of molasses into France. The result was a molasses glut in the French islands, and extraordinarily low prices, which the savvy Americans were quick to take advantage of. Even during the wars, Yankee traders had figured out how to get around the various restrictions of the British and French, and had become adept at smuggling French molasses to their distilleries. Once the French allied with the colonists in the war of independence, the trade with the French West Indies was licit, and took on strategic importance as well. Admiral De Grasse's fleet was based there before the Yorktown campaign, as were a number of American privateers, and arms were smuggled to the Continental Army through St. Domingue and other French islands.

After their war of independence, the Americans were given yet another incentive to come to the French islands, prompted by the British ban of American trade with royal colonies. American merchants soon established a network of commercial allies on the French islands, where they found that the local planters resented their mother government's colonial trade restrictions almost as much as Americans had resented the British Navigation Acts. The planters, who wanted the cheapest possible food for their slaves and supplies for their mills, continually agitated for a relaxation of the import restrictions on American goods, and with considerable success.

From all these factors, the Americans had a good, and lucrative, market in the French West Indies, and they wanted to keep it going.

There was however one serious cloud on the horizon. The French revolution had spread to the islands, with increasingly disruptive effects. The newspapers and private correspondence that summer of 1790 reported the alarming developments from St. Domingue, with typical attention to the trading possibilities arising from the circumstances. "We now have a civil war throughout this island: citizens are fighting citizens, and trade is entirely at a stand, and unsafe; it is a very critical time, and a dangerous time to have debt out," said one. "Everything in that Island seemed in the greatest confusion," said another: "Several vessels had arrived from Philadelphia, but did not chose to trust their cargoes on shore. Flour was for $9 to 10."[13] "We are in the midst of a terrible crisis . . . the young people are greatly excited and gather at public places and at the theaters. . . . God grant that this disturbance may come to an end, for there is some fear that the negroes may revolt," worried an American resident.[14]

In the uncertainty of the revolutionary situation, two things at least were sure: that the island economies would continue to require American goods, and that American exporters and traders would do whatever was necessary to stay active in a market that had been so profitable.

ST. DOMINGUE

The Pearl of the Antilles, St. Domingue was the pride, and the richest, of France's colonies. An astonishing, half century-long boom on the island had spawned majestic fortunes, incomparable luxury, and dizzying profits, all based on sugar, and a brutal plantation system that produced it. Much of France, too, benefited from the island's prosperity. Merchant houses in the mother country—in Bordeaux in particular—waxed fat on the trade; the French merchant marine blossomed; French grain growers and consumer goods makers had full order books; and the tax collectors made sure the royal court got its share of the profits. At the court of Versailles, numerous mega-rich Creole planters flaunted their new and often astounding wealth, and "à la Creole" became a synonym for flamboyant consumption.

The island's boom had been fueled by a century of burgeoning demand in Europe for sugar, coffee, and other tropical products— sugar consumption per capita in England, for example, had risen from just one pound per year to twenty-five pounds during the century ending in 1770.[1] Consumption was still increasing in 1790, and there seemed to be no end in sight to the good times.

Some three centuries earlier, the whole island of Hispaniola had been claimed for Spain by Christopher Columbus on his first voyage to the New World. He returned there during his second voyage to

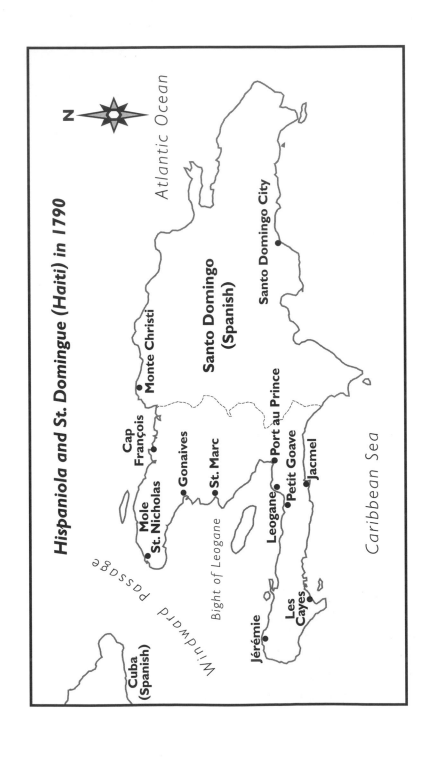

Hispaniola and St. Domingue (Haiti) in 1790

N

Atlantic Ocean

Windward Passage

Cuba
(Spanish)

Mole
St. Nicholas

Cap
François

Monte Christi

Gonaives

St. Marc

Santo Domingo
(Spanish)

Bight of Leogane

Jérémie

Les
Cayes

Leogane

Petit Goave

Port au Prince

Jacmel

Santo Domingo City

Caribbean Sea

set up a colony on the north shore, and eventually the island's main city, Santo Domingo, became the Spanish colonial capital. But the colony lost importance during the two centuries of Spain's ascendancy in the Caribbean, bypassed in favor of the richer colonies in Mexico and South America. It became a haven for buccaneers, a sleepy colony of cattle ranchers, colonial officials, and small merchants. Then, as a result of one of the many European wars, the western part of the island was ceded to France in 1697, and renamed St. Domingue.

While the Spanish end of the island continued to drowse under the benign neglect of a declining empire, the French end saw a sudden and remarkable transformation during the eighteenth century. French investment and colonial policy, added to the island's natural fecundity, made it one of the most profitable places on earth, creating wealth, trade, and employment for the mother country, but also for its American neighbors on the continent to the north. The new name, however, never stuck with the British and Americans, who called the French colony St. Domingo, only slightly different from their name for the Spanish end of the island, which was called Santo Domingo.[2] The French part of the island would not get its present name of Haiti until a century later, upon gaining its independence.

The French had gained their new colony just in time to ride the cresting wave of the sugar boom. They invested well and found that the rich soil, the proximity to the sea of the major growing areas, and the many small harbors all contributed to a remarkable productivity. The planters at first employed indentured laborers from Europe, but soon found that they were unproductive and sickened too readily. Like planters in the other sugar colonies, they quickly came to depend entirely on the labor of slaves imported from Africa. As a result, as the plantations expanded, so did the slave population of the colony.

St. Domingue became the most productive bit of real estate in the world. In the space of a half century, this colony, with less than one-sixth the land area of Virginia, opened hundreds of sugar plantations and was producing and exporting as much sugar as all the British West

Indies. Its production passed that of the British colonies during the height of the boom, which came after 1780. By 1790, the colony's plantations were producing 40 percent of the world's sugar. Coffee grown in the hills had also become a major plantation crop, and the island produced 50 percent of the Indies' coffee. The production of several hundred cotton, indigo, and other plantations was also funneling back to France, enriching the mother country. In fact, with much of the island's production re-exported to other countries in Europe, St. Domingue came to account for over 40 percent of France's total foreign trade.[3]

The colonial capital and principal port, Cap François,[4] was a town of startling contrasts. With a population of approximately twenty thousand persons, it was a busy and prosperous port, full of activity and with a cosmopolitan and polyglot street life. The center of town was graced with parks and fountains, scores of public buildings, and many two-story houses of stone furnished in the latest fashions of the mother country. French colonial offices, a military garrison, hospitals and churches, even a respected scientific academy, all spoke for the city's importance and wealth, while the arts flourished and a two thousand-seat theater played the latest (well, almost) hits from Paris. Artisans and merchants from all over Europe provided services for the wealthy planters, traders, and officials, as well as for the women who—so very often—were not their wives. A middle class of shopkeepers and crafts-men, some of them freed slaves or mulattos, shared in the prosperity. So, too, and in a more restricted way, did the household slaves of the wealthy planters.

But beyond the parks and theaters, the shops, trading houses, and warehouses, Le Cap (as it was called familiarly) was still a frontier town, full of seedy cafes, gambling houses, brothels, flophouses, and dismal slums. Like any bonanza town, it had attracted a good proportion of drifters and opportunists from around the world, who formed an underclass that was both rootless and restless. And the huge population of plantation field-workers, the slaves on whom the island's economy depended, worked in the background, scarcely sharing in the good times, and with loyalty to no one.

The most productive area of the island was a great fifty-mile by ten-mile, rain-fed plain along the northern coast called the Plaine du Nord, which provided a densely planted backdrop for Cap François. The central region of the colony, called the Western Province, also had a harbor at Port au Prince and good land, but it got less rain and often needed irrigation. The southern peninsula or Southern Province, isolated by its highly mountainous terrain, was well suited for small-scale coffee growing, but remained the least developed region of the colony. The mountains, indeed, were everywhere, and in those days they were still heavily forested, except where cleared for plantations. As a result, the roads, as was the case in the United States, were inadequate for transport of heavy goods. Fortunately, the colony had an exceptionally long seacoast, with the deep Bight of Leogane (now called the Gulf of Gonave) providing numerous harbors that allowed the planters to rely on transport by sea. But the colony, in spite of its dependence on sea transport, had not developed much of a maritime industry; French mercantile policy as well as the planters' concentration on production of valuable export crops had worked against that. Thus the planters were largely obliged to look to others, not only to provide the supplies to keep their plantations going, but also to furnish the transport to bring goods in and to take out their exports. Unfortunately for them, food and supplies from France were expensive, and the French merchant marine was never adequate for the job, in spite of the protection theoretically provided by the mercantilist regime called the *exculsif*.

For American merchants and shippers, the situation in St. Domingo provided an ideal opportunity for profit, and they were eager to seize it. To do so, however, required circumventing the *exclusif*. Smuggling was one way, sometimes by way of false papers issued by complaisant Spanish officials in neighboring Santo Domingo.[5] Another was to work for relaxation of the restrictions in alliance with the planters, most of whom wanted to buy cheap American goods and lessen their dependence on the French trading houses and banks. The Yankees, of course, tried both courses of action.

The first major break had come in 1717, when French authorities allowed their colonies to import cheap salt fish—used to feed the plantation slaves—in exchange for their surplus molasses. Cheap molasses plus competitive shipping made for cheap American rum; the trade mushroomed rapidly, as did the distilling industry in the American colonies. Before long, the British reacted with passage of the Molasses Act, trying to oblige the colonists once again to buy British by taxing away the cost advantage of French molasses. Enterprising American shippers, however, simply became more adept at fooling or avoiding the British revenue cutters, and molasses smuggled in from the French islands continued to be important for the distillers. In 1770, the French West Indies—St. Domingo primarily—provided over 85 percent of the American colonies' molasses imports, and a full 40 percent of that, at least into Pennsylvania and New York, was probably smuggled.[6] By that time, the trade had also broadened to other items, as the French authorities had agreed to let their island planters import American wood products and livestock. Grain imports were still a French monopoly, in theory, but it can be assumed that a great deal of American wheat and flour also found its way to the islands by smuggling or other circumventions.

The trade between America and St. Domingo really took off during and after the American war for independence. With trade to and from Britain and its colonies disrupted, the colonists turned to the French Indies as intermediaries for supplies of gunpowder, arms, and other essentials. The British tried to mount a blockade of Cap François, but it was not fully effective and many goods got through, both legitimate trade and contraband. After the American-French alliance was formed in 1778, the French opened their ports to American goods and cargo, with the result that trade, inasmuch as the wartime conditions permitted, prospered. The most important supplies, though, continued to be munitions for the beleaguered American rebels, and elaborate schemes with irregular papers, phony captures, and false flags were concocted to get the goods past the British fleet.

The most dramatic incident of the revolutionary period was the sending of a large French expedition from St. Domingo in 1779 to join forces with a rebel American army at Savannah. The Americans, who had been trying unsuccessfully to dislodge the British from that city, had sent an appeal for help to Admiral d'Estaing in Cap François. The French agreed to reinforce the Americans, and to send a body of troops reinforced by colonial volunteers, including a militia detachment of over five hundred black and mulatto freemen. Admiral d'Estaing, that summer, landed some twenty-four hundred troops at Savannah to reinforce General Lincoln's force there. Unfortunately, a combined assault on the British defenders failed badly, and the French troops, whose retreat had been covered with distinction by the black volunteers, played no further role in the campaign. The main result of the episode, perhaps, was the exposure gained by some of the Domingan freemen to the ideas of their North American neighbors, including a readiness to fight for political liberty.

The wartime growth of American trade with St. Domingo experienced a short interruption after the U.S.-British peace agreements were signed in 1783. This was because French officialdom instinctively reverted to its mercantilist habits, and once again attempted to close colonial ports to American shippers and to many of their products. They soon learned, however, that a door that had been opened could not so easily be closed. Pressures from the island planters, a lack of French-flagged ships to carry the goods, and harvest shortfalls in France soon led to a relaxing of the lists of permitted commodities, and in due time to the opening of many ports to virtually free trade. With American ships banned from the British West Indies, they soon were the most common ones in St. Domingo, and by 1790 the number regularly employed in the bilateral trade was near five hundred. Trade expanded so rapidly that, by the same year, St. Domingo had become the second trading partner of the United States, with over 10 percent of total trade, and exceeded only by Great Britain.[7] Two-thirds of the coffee and sugar consumed in America was imported from the French West Indies, and molasses from St. Domingo was cheaper in Philadelphia than its equivalent on a British plantation in Jamaica.[8] Going in the other direction were goods from every state: fish from New England, livestock and salt meat, grains and flour from the Mid-Atlantic states, lumber, livestock, and rice from the southern states.

Perhaps the only groups unhappy with this trade boom were the French maritime and diplomatic officials, who still longed for the *exclusif,* and the American makers of maple sugar, who appear to have tried some negative advertising through the newspapers: "West Indian sugar is the product of the unwilling labor of negro slaves, and made in a climate in which insects of all kind abound, so that the best Indian sugar may be looked upon as a composition, consisting of the juice of the cane, and the juices or excretions of ants, pissmires, cockroaches, borers, lizards, mosquitoes, spiders, bugs, grasshoppers, lizards, plus twenty other West Indian insects. To these ingredients is added the sweat of the negroes, and when they are angry, nobody knows what else."[9]

St. Domingo's productivity and wealth, the lucrative trade they created, the prospects for the future—they all were dazzling. Unfortunately, the whole phenomenon was built on unsure foundations. Not that the sugar market was weak; no, it would continue to expand and make new fortunes, elsewhere. The weakness was the colony's social and economic structure. Its prosperity was based on a viciously exploitative plantation regime, and the social system that supported that creation was shallow-rooted, racist, fractured, and inherently unstable.

The sugar boom had created a hothouse society and culture on the island. The dominant mood was one of impermanence, of eagerness to make one's fortune, or to finish a tour of duty (often both), and then move on. There were few permanent civic institutions, and outside of some local courts, no local self-government; everything was directed by the Ministry of Marine and Colonies in Paris. The French officials on the island were transients, and often spent much of their short tours of duty on the island maneuvering against each other: a royal governor controlled the garrison and promulgated the laws, an *intendant* supervised judicial and financial affairs. None of the officials had much real connection with the Creole planters, who in turn generally thought them to be arrogant, clueless, and to be flattered or tolerated largely for the protection that they could offer. Careerism, speculation, and petty corruption were all part of the ambience.

The major planters, the one group among the colonists to have significant investments on the island, also lived in a surprising air of impermanence. A small but dominant minority among the almost forty thousand whites on the island,[10] the resident planters quite often spent most of their time on their plantations, coming to town only for business and occasional shopping or diversion. Perhaps the fact that many of them were in debt to the French merchant houses, slavers, or banks made it more comfortable for them to avoid the traders by simply staying out of town. And yet a disproportionate number of their homes in the countryside were no Edens, but rather sorry, ramshackle things. The poor construction, unrefined nature, and temporary feel of many a planter's villa often contrasted sharply with the indulgence and luxury of the lifestyle enjoyed by its owners—the latter, perhaps, enjoyed as compensation for the boredom and isolation of rural life. Many planters, native-born Creoles as well as recent arrivals, took opportunities for blow-out trips to France whenever possible, in order to escape the heat and the tedium of their plantation lives. These temporary but sometimes protracted absences, added to the very large number of nonresident owners, meant that a good proportion of the plantations were run in practice by hired overseers, men who had even less connection to or investment in the long-term health of the establishments they ruled, or to the colony.

Complementing the officials, the major merchants, and the planters—a grouping known as the *grands blancs*—the white population included a number of professional persons, artisans, and shopkeepers. This group might have, collectively, provided some permanence to the colony's political climate had they had a greater stake in the colony's governance or its future. But they did not, and as a result they played an insignificant role as a group in the drama to come. The balance of the white population, which did come to play an important role, was as amorphous as it was uncontrollable. This was the large population of urban laborers, soldiers, seamen, small traders, draymen, craftsmen, idlers, and criminals, many of whom had come to St. Domingo simply because it was where the money was. Frenchmen, Maltese, Italians, Spaniards, and others, these men were often without families, restless, and resentful. At the bottom of the white social order, these *petits blancs,* or poor whites, shared several sentiments that could unite them—namely resentment of the rich *grands,* added to a racist disdain and hatred for the blacks, whether freemen or slaves.

The white population was, to an abnormal degree, a society of men without their wives. A large proportion of them had been born elsewhere, and many were men who had come in the recent years of the boom. There was a chronic shortage of European women in the colony, explaining the large number of brothels, ladies of easy virtue, and informal households. The sexual imbalance had persisted over the century of the colony's phenomenal economic development, promoting a local custom of keeping black or mulatto mistresses in preference to mixed-race marriages. (The latter did exist, but were relatively few among the planter and merchant groups, where marriage to a black or mulatto woman was considered socially degrading, but having an elegant black mistress was very correct.) Since the children of such unions were generally free persons, the custom had helped create one of the island's more distinguishing demographic features: a significant class of "free persons of color," including mulattos and freed blacks, that numbered over twenty-five thousand by 1790.

The mulattos lived in a strange legal and social world. Often raised in households where they had been respected, educated, and given good opportunities for advancement, they had been given equal legal rights, in theory, by the Black Code of 1685. In fact, they suffered from various forms of official and unofficial discrimination, which had increased as the size and prosperity of the mulatto population grew. The *grands blancs* fiercely resisted assimilation of the free men of color, no matter what their wealth or education. They were subjected to laws that restricted the kinds of European garments they could wear, that required segregated seating in the churches and theaters, that banned them from holding public meetings in the evenings, and that limited their entry into the professions and their ability to serve in public office. But they often found other passages to success. The women often used the bedroom; a census of 1774 estimated that fully five thousand mulattos earned a living as kept women or prostitutes,[11] often in conditions of some luxury.

Mulattos were not banned from ownership of land or businesses, and many men had found this a good way to prosper. They were heavily represented in the retail trade and the crafts. Many other mulattos gained status and wealth through service in the local militias, which were heavily manned by free blacks. The expansion of coffee growing in the south and west of the country during the 1770s also provided a path to wealth and status: coffee plantations were typically smaller and less capital-intensive than sugar ones, so with a modest amount of capital, an enterprising mulatto could set up as a coffee grower. Many did, with the result that by 1790, mulattos owned a quarter of the real estate in St. Domingo, including a third of the plantations. More interestingly, they also owned a quarter of the slaves on the island.[12]

This ascendancy of the mulattos came, in short, to pose a growing threat to the whites, *grands* and *petitis* alike. Their resentment and fear were summed up by the official who wrote, "These men are beginning to fill the colony, and it is of the greatest perversion to see them, their numbers continually increasing, among the white, with fortunes often greater than those of the whites."[13]

The economic success of the mulattos was no help however to the island's slaves. Raised in a brutally exploitative society, the mulattos had no trouble doing the exploiting themselves, when given the opportunity. They did not identify with the small population of freed blacks, estimated at some fifteen hundred,[14] much less with the slaves. Most of the mulattos aspired to social status to match their economic gains, and as a result played up to the landowners—even as the latter discriminated against them—to keep the *petits blancs* in their place. The poor whites, of course, found the mulattos' relative prosperity insufferable, and conspired in their turn with the *grand blancs* to retain the discriminatory regulations.

Whites and mulattos, mutually antagonistic as they were, were still the ruling group, when contrasted to the huge and subservient slave population. Everyone in the ruling group, it goes without saying, feared and distrusted the slaves. And with good reason. Against a white and free mulatto population of approximately sixty thousand, the slaves numbered well over four hundred thousand, with some estimates going as high as a half million.

The majority of the slaves lived on the plantations, but they were ubiquitous in the towns and villages as well, an apparently silent and mute background to everything that took place. They not only had no investment in the success of the plantations or the colony, they did not even have roots there. For the most appalling statistic of St. Domingo—the one which explains both the horror and the prosperity of the sugar business—was the mortality rate of the slave population. From disease, overwork, hunger, punishment, homesickness, or whatever, the slave population died off at a rate of 5 to 6 percent per year.[15] Such a rate assured that the slave population, mostly males to begin with, was not self-sustaining and had to be maintained by constant imports from Africa. During a period of rapid expansion, as the 1780s had been, over thirty thousand new slaves were imported each year.[16] The result was that by 1790 almost two-thirds of the slaves on the plantations were African-born, and the main age group of the workers was fifteen to thirty-five.[17]

The slaves had no personal legal rights. The government had, to its credit, attempted to set some conditions for their employment in promulgating the Black Code of 1685, which regulated the hours of work and the quantities of food, limited punishments, mandated garden plots, and otherwise set formal limits to the arbitrary power of the slaveowners. But it was poorly enforced, and often not at all. In practice, the plantation owner, or in many cases the overseer, was the law for his slaves. And when cases did come before the authorities, they opted for security over justice. Such was the case in the famous LeJeune trial, in which a planter, who had tortured his slaves in connection with a suspected poisoning plot, was acquitted by the highest court in spite of his obvious guilt. The explanation given for the miscarriage of justice was the need to protect the "safety of the colony," but the real reason was that the planters, united on this issue, demanded the whitewash.

And yet, the slaves had proven remarkably tractable over the past century.[18] Perhaps it was a result of the constant renewal of the population, or its ethnic diversity, but there were few plots or uprisings reported. The situation on many plantations, in spite of the inhumanity and injustice of the underlying condition, even represented a kind of normality. Nor were the conditions of slave labor uniformly harsh. Not all masters were brutal, and the revolution, when it came, exposed true cases of affection and loyalty. The house slaves and the craftsmen—the carpenters, coachmen, tally clerks, machinists, etc.—usually had an easier life than the field hands. The latter had to work long hours in the cane fields or mills in insect-filled heat, and under often brutal supervision, even if the drivers (the *commandeurs*) were usually slaves like them.

Over the years, some slaves had fled from this brutal system to live free in the hills. The number of these maroons is unclear, but as they kept apart from the urban population they played very little role in the general life of the colony.[19] They did, however, provide a refuge for Macandal, the leader of the one serious slave disturbance that the island witnessed. The Macandal affair began in 1758 and lasted for a number of years, manifesting itself largely as a campaign of poisoning, directed at whites as well as noncooperating slaves. Poisoning campaigns, indeed, became a significant tool of such slave unrest as did exist—the malcontents could spread fear, and even wreak real damage, by poisoning or threatening to poison a plantation's work force. Such plots, however, were almost always local and small, a consequence of the fact that the slave community was fractured among the hundreds of plantations on the island.

The slaves, however, had begun to develop networks of their own through their peculiar and particular invention—the voodoo practices that had spread widely throughout the island. The authorities had tried to limit the spread of the cult, recognizing only the Catholic faith, but their success was nil. The slaves, in spite of their differing African backgrounds and their isolation on the rural plantations, had formed bonds on the island and were gradually developing their own culture. It was one, moreover, that their white masters could neither understand nor control.

This then was the fragile society that learned, in the summer of 1789, that great events had begun to happen in the mother country. Ships from France brought news that King Louis had been obliged by financial need to call together a parliament called the

Estates General, and that momentous events had been unleashed as a result. The colony buzzed with excitement as news arrived that the commoners in the parliament had asserted power, constituted themselves into a Constituent Assembly with the objective of drawing up a constitution, and passed a Declaration of the Rights of Man based on the latest liberal principles, including that of equality. They also heard that the new climate of liberty had led to outbreaks of popular anger and violence against the royal regime, such as the storming of the Bastille in Paris and risings of peasants in the provinces. They sensed, as did observers in New York, Philadelphia, and Charleston, that nothing would ever again be the same.

As soon as the news began to arrive, Domingan colonists started to look for ways to protect their own interests, or advance their own agendas, in the rapidly changing turmoil of the mother country. The first group to organize was, not surprisingly, the planters. Some of them had been planning for years, as the crisis in France had deepened, to assure that their voice was heard in the Estates General. Now they were determined that they—the key interest group in France's richest colony, as they saw it—would be represented in the king's parliament. Rapidly, they met in conclave and selected a score of their members to travel to Paris. Their objectives were basically economic: to weaken the restraints that the *exculsif* placed on their trade and to weaken the hold that the Paris-based ministries had over the colony. Arriving in June 1789, the Domingan delegation asked that their credentials be approved—only to discover that their request would set off a firestorm of debate, and none of it about their economic agenda.

The planters demanded that their delegation be seated on the basis of the total population of the colony: that is, Frenchmen, free mulattos, and black slaves all together. Their maneuver proved to be costly, however, because it opened up an issue on which they were highly vulnerable—the rights, or lack of them, of the greater part of the populations that they claimed to represent. The times were changing, indeed had already changed, and the planters could no longer assert, confidently and paternalistically, that they would represent all the inhabitants of the island. Debate on the themes that would, later that summer, become codified in the Declaration of the Rights of Man was already in the air, and highly influential men were more than ready to challenge such an assertion. A group of leading liberals called the Friends of the Blacks (the *Amis des Noirs,* whose membership included Lafayette, Jacques Brissot, and Gabriel Mirabeau) had been organized to champion the civil rights of France's black and slave populations. Colonial mulattos, some of whom had established themselves professionally in France, had also begun to speak out for their rights. In short order, the planters' petition was derided and held out to ridicule. In the early July debates, Mirabeau sneered at the planters as follows: "You claim representation proportionate to the number of inhabitants. The free blacks are proprietors and taxpayers, and yet they have not been allowed to vote. And as for the slaves, either they are men or they are not; if the colonists consider them to be men, then let them free them, and make them electors and eligible for seats. If the contrary is the case, have we, in apportioning deputies according to the population of France, taken into consideration the number of our horses and mules?"[20]

The delegation from St. Domingo could only rejoin, lamely but accurately, that the Assembly should be very careful how it dealt with the issues of slavery and the slave trade, because the very security and prosperity of their colony could be threatened by any intemperate actions. More practically, the delegation encouraged those French merchants with major interests in the colony to form a counter lobby, which soon came into being as the Massiac Club. Before long, that group succeeded in blunting the attacks of the *Amis,* and—combined with the Domingans' good record on other issues of interest to the Assembly—assured that they would be allowed to claim seats for the colony. In the end the Domingans obtained a partial success; they were granted six seats on a provisional basis. But it had been in many ways a costly victory. The debate set off by their petition had, indeed, only given ammunition to the radicals in the Assembly, and would eventually lead to actions shaking the very foundations of their colonial home. The Bastille fell in July 1789, marking the beginning of the end of old regime that the planters wanted to reform, not replace. Six weeks later, the Assembly passed the Declaration of the Rights of Man, which presaged the beginning of a new social order that would replace the planters' world.

The American founding fathers had faced the same basic issue at the Constitutional Convention in 1787. Slavery had been as contentious an issue in Philadelphia that summer as it proved to be twelve years later in Paris. There were delegates in both assemblies who despised the institution, delegates who profited from it, and others who sought primarily to mange the differences. What made the result of the American and French constitutional debates on slavery so very different was the fact that the Americans were, above all, political reformers and not social revolutionaries. Their objective was to organize and perpetuate the political liberty that their history and successful rebellion had already granted them. The compromise they reached was therefore a practical one, although in the end a temporary one. They had in fact backed into the formula for compromise, in a way, as early as the 1783 debate over the basis for taxation in the old Confederation. Then, they had agreed on the "federal ratio," which provided that male slaves would be counted for the purposes of taxation, but only in the ratio of three to every five free white men. At the Constitutional Convention years later, the same ratio was agreed to as the basis for determining representation in Congress, as part of the "great compromise" that made the Constitution possible. It did not address the morality of slavery except indirectly, acknowledging that it was a form of property—a right the founding fathers had consistently defended. It rewarded the slaveowning southern states, giving them greater representation than they would have otherwise had, but more importantly, it kept them in the union. It was a pragmatic solution to what they chose to view as a practical, political, problem.

For the French reformers in 1789 and beyond, however, the issue was not just one of political organization; they realized that they were engaged from the beginning in a social as well as a political revolution. Moral issues were important, indeed they were seen as defining the kind of nation the new France would be. Equality was not, for them, merely a slogan or an issue that could be papered over or dealt with in an artful compromise; it had to be addressed directly. Thus the seating of the delegates from St. Domingo had not resolved the problem at all, it had just kicked off the debate.

In St. Domingo, the news of the fall of the Bastille arrived, with the usual forty or so days of trans-Atlantic delay, like a spark in a tinderbox. The pretensions of the delegates in Paris to speak for all the inhabitants of the island were immediately exposed as empty, for the poor whites rapidly took matters into their own hands, in imitation of the Paris mob. They rose in a patriotic fervor—the "leveling spirit" so feared by American conservatives—to riot against the colonial administration, against the mulattos, against order. Tricolor cockades in their hats, they soon controlled the streets and formed impromptu patriotic militias and unsanctioned assemblies. Under such pressure, the colonial administration, still royalist and loyalist but without instructions, began to collapse. Meanwhile, the planters, to protect their own position, sought successfully to keep the patriotic mob on their side, in part by criticizing the colonial officials, in part by firmly squelching mulatto aspirations to political rights. They also began, with a friendly nod from colonial officials, to form provincial assemblies that they could control, and that might also form a nucleus, they hoped, of a more autonomous future regime for the colony. At the end of the year, they had received permission from the governor to form a colonial assembly, to be convened at St. Marc with delegates chosen from the three provincial assemblies. The assembly met in March 1790 and, apparently driven by the planters' longstanding grudges against the colonial administration and the *exclusif,* began immediately to take actions that the French authorities could only see as heading in the dangerous direction of virtual autonomy. Things were gradually slipping toward a confrontation, or multiple confrontations, and there was no national policy to deal with the issues.

In Paris, the colonial issue, and the related issue of the rights of freedmen and slaves, did not reach the front burner again until early 1790. By then, disorders in St. Domingo and Martinique had reached such proportions that the Assembly, under the pressure of the Bordeaux and other merchants whose colonial business had been disrupted, was obliged once again to take up the thorny issue. This time, however, the Massiac Club and its friends had prejudged the issue in their favor—they got it referred to the newly created Colonial Committee, where there would be no inflammatory rhetoric about the Rights of Man because it was to be chaired by a friendly moderate, Antoine Barnave. In early March 1790, the committee, after hurried and secret deliberations, came out with a report that satisfied the planters: reform was mandated, but there would be no template designed in Paris. Each colony's assembly could draw up its own constitution, in the light of its own customs and needs.

The report amounted to a veiled permission to the planter-controlled colonial assemblies to deny political rights to rich mulattos, landless *petits blancs,* and of course the slaves, no matter what happened in mainland France. It was a stinging check to the aspirations of the mulattos and the *Amis des noirs.* They were not defeated, however, and in fact they had been gaining support for abolition—even King Louis was reported to be sympathetic.[21] Less than three weeks later, the *Amis* had succeeded in having the committee amend its report with specific implementing instructions that softened the blow of colonial autonomy. In particular, the colonial assemblies were instructed to grant full civil rights to any owner of real property who was over twenty-five years old. Although this was not the full grant of civic rights that the mulattos had sought, it was an important breakthrough. The *petits* would not be enfranchised, while a small but symbolically significant number of mulattos in St. Domingo would become eligible for full civic rights.

The problem was that Paris could no longer control events on the ground. In St. Domingo, the planters and their temporary allies, the *petits blancs,* chose to implement the parts of the instructions that they liked—that is, to form new assemblies and begin work on a constitution—and to ignore what they did not. By summer, two separate and even rival new assemblies were elected: one in the north, at Cap François, that was still mildly loyal to the old colonial regime, and a second, and much more radical one, at St. Marc. The St. Marc assembly, angered by the fact that the local mulattos had formed an unfriendly alliance with the colonial (and still largely royalist) officials, flatly refused to give mulattos the franchise. It then began to move rapidly in the direction of autonomy, opening its ports to ships carrying American grain, and making moves that seemed to presage a repudiation of the planters' debt to the French merchants. For the governor, who still had some authority if not very clear instructions as to how to use it, this was too much. He worked with the Assembly in Paris to have the St. Marc assembly dissolved. Unwilling however to wait for that process to be completed, he conspired with the northern provincial assembly to have the St. Marc assembly shut down by force. The St. Marc deputies, for their part, insisted that they had adjourned in proper order to take their case to Paris. One way or another, the assembly was suspended, and in October of 1790 its eighty-five delegates found themselves on their way to France on a French warship.

A leader of the Paris mulattos, a businessman named Vincent Ogé, had watched this confusing drama with increasing frustration. The planters of St. Domingo, he foresaw, would not forgive the mulattos' opposition to seating the island's delegation, nor would their new colonial assembly willingly put into effect the enfranchisement instruction from Paris. While the whites on the island might disagree over their responsibility toward or allegiance to Paris, he concluded, or over who would control the new provincial government, they would certainly remain united on one subject: continuing to deny the franchise to free men of color. Only a show of force by the mulattos, he decided, could change the situation, and he would help organize it.

Ogé, unfortunately, was no conspirator. Embarking for St. Domingo, he made a stop at Charleston, where he had an ill-advised conversation with the French consul. What his intentions were in this move is unclear, but the result was that his arrival in October at Cap François was well advertised, and his plans to mobilize the mulattos already marked for doom. He and his co-leader, Jean-Baptiste Chavannes, who had fought with the Americans during their war for independence, did rally some seven hundred men to their cause, and they did set up a sort of headquarters at Grand Riviere outside of the city, where they issued a public appeal to the northern provincial assembly.[22] But the authorities stood firm and the revolt soon collapsed. Pursued by the garrison, the leaders and some of their followers first fled to the hills, and then across the border into Santo Domingo. The Spanish handed them back to the French at the end of the year, and they were tried in March 1791. Both Ogé and Chavannes were executed most brutally—broken slowly on the wheel before being beheaded. Their heads were publicly displayed, and many other members of the unlucky group were hanged or imprisoned in what the authorities hoped was an effective deterrent display of force.

As a revolt, Ogé's effort had been a total failure. But it was nonetheless an important turning point, and precipitated change. The old regime had rallied, but the violence with which it reacted to the rebellion only demonstrated how insecure the governing class of the colony had become. Divided among themselves, it seemed they could unite only to kill uppity mulattos. The colony's governing class had effectively lost what little cohesion it had enjoyed. The red, white, and blue cockade of the revolution no longer had a unifying appeal, and the feuding factions now more frequently sported either the red, revolutionary cockade or the white, royalist one.

WHITE COCKADE, RED COCKADE

What Vincent Ogé had been unable to obtain by his hapless and tragic revolt, his gruesome death achieved. His legacy did not, however, emerge immediately in St. Domingo, where the governing white planters and officials still congratulated themselves for having gotten rid of a troublemaker. The reaction to his death came instead from revolutionary Paris.

The revolution, turbulent as it was, had not yet descended to the level at which political murder was an everyday occurrence. Thus, the news of Ogé's martyrdom, when it reached Paris, truly shocked his old friends and colleagues. More than that, it mobilized them. The mulatto revolt in France's most important colony, particularly its bloody suppression, succeeded in reopening the Assembly debate of the previous spring. Why, the ardent republicans demanded, should not the colonies be governed by the same laws as the mother country, including the principles of the Declaration of the Rights of Man? Those radicals, whose strength had been waxing in the Assembly as well as on the Paris streets, moreover saw the issue as a fine weapon to use against the conservative planters and merchants. The *Amis des Noirs* and the radicals thus joined forces to push for justice—full civic rights for free men of color—in Ogé's name.

When the issue finally came up for debate in May 1791, the government was in crisis. The death in April of Mirabeau, who had led the constitutional monarchists, had weakened the conservatives,

while the republican clubs—Jacobins and Cordeliers—had continued to gain strength. On this issue however, the sides were evenly
matched, and the debate in the Assembly was both long and impassioned. After four days of struggle, the progressives had not gained
their objective, and had to settle for a weak compromise. The
Assembly finally passed a resolution, which became law in a decree
of May 15, enfranchising any mulatto male who had two free parents
and otherwise met the age and property requirements. It was not a
big step—in fact, in St. Domingo there were probably only four hundred or so who would qualify—but it was a first step. A principle had
been established, and the *Amis* had won a token victory.

What was a token step in Paris was, on the other hand, a huge leap in
St. Domingo. When news of the National Assembly's action reached
the island in July, the white colonists were set aflame with indignation. Royalists, republicans, opportunists, whatever, they joined
forces against the common threat represented by this granting of
rights to the mulattos. An already critical situation moved rapidly
toward meltdown. As anger at Paris's action mounted, even those
who called themselves patriots began to entertain talk of secession,
or calling in the English from nearby Jamaica to act as protectors
against the radical current running from Paris. Those who had contacts in the mother country began immediately to work them, seeking a reversal of the decision before, as they feared, this chink in the
armor of their racist regime could prove fatal to what remained of
the colony's social order. As the northern provincial assembly wrote
desperately to the king, "We shall not attempt to paint to your
Majesty the shocking sensations the news of this impolitic decree has
caused this town: and the misfortunes that will follow its promulga-
tion are uncountable; they will be such as will draw after them the
total annihilation of this flourishing colony."[1]

It was, of course, too late. The mulattos would no longer be denied,
and they clenched their teeth for a long struggle. With the island

authorities dead set against implementing the May decree, the mulattos[2] had little choice but to follow the lead set the previous year by Ogé, and take up arms to give weight to their demands. Particularly in the western and southern provinces, where there were a good number of mulatto landowners, they soon achieved critical mass and obliged the whites at Port au Prince to deal with them. Under leaders who included André Rigaud, a Bordeaux-educated goldsmith who had fought at Savannah during the American Revolution, they negotiated a reluctant acceptance in practice of those rights that Paris had granted them in law. Elsewhere on the island, however, whites and mulattos squared off against each other. There was little negotiation, occasional violence, and much mutual hostility.

The explosion, when it came, was from an unexpected quarter. The slaves—omnipresent, taken for granted, patronized, debased—had been watching and weighing the furious debates of the previous two years. Talk of liberty, of the rights of man, of a new dawn, had filled the air of their owners' homes, the marketplaces, the villages, and the ports, and the slaves had listened and absorbed. They had their own networks, too, both voodoo and social, by which to transmit this new information and to promote the numerous clandestine meetings that had sprung up during the turmoil of the past years.[3] They had seen the colonists attack government officials, the mulattos, and each other; they had watched as the social order unraveled, in a colony that required solidarity to maintain its coercive basis. They had their own ideas, and they had leaders. Meeting secretly at night, the slaves of the great plantation-filled plain that formed the hinterland to Cap François began to plan a revolt. In mid-August, at Morne-Rouge, not far from Cap François, their leaders took the decision to act.[4]

A week later, on August 21, the revolt broke out. Slave bands on plantations throughout the region seized their cane cutting tools, or whatever weapons they could, and marched on the plantation houses. There they released their pent-up anger by systematically destroying the plantations: crops, mills, barns, and tools, all too often accompanied by murder and other atrocities against their historical oppressors. Within a few weeks, the rebels' forces had grown from two thousand to perhaps five times that number; they had destroyed over two hundred plantations and occupied most of the plain. With the sky ominous with smoke and those planter families who had been spared fleeing, traumatized, to Le Cap, the inhabitants of the encircled city exhibited grief and panic, but also a burning spirit of revenge. The black prisoners in town were massacred on the Place d'Armes, while militia units made murderous raids into the plantations, killing any blacks they could find (five times as many slaves as white persons were reportedly killed).[5] An exodus of desperate planters and their families soon began, carrying with them to the United States and elsewhere a highly colored version of the momentous events: "Indeed, my friend, I do not know where to stop in this horrible description! And I mention these particulars just to give you an idea of this war of horror and carnage in which we are engaged," one correspondent wrote.[6]

On the plantations, victory at first was paired with disorder. Plunder, drunkenness, and license were the immediate result of the slaves' astounding blow. They had broken their chains, and they exulted in it. And yet, amongst the violence and the terrible atrocities, there were numerous moments of loyalty, of compassion. On the Breda plantation, a manumitted slave, the forty-eight-year-old coachman François Dominique Toussaint, was apparently grateful enough for the treatment and education he had received to ensure that the overseer's wife, Madame Bayon de Libertat, was safely escorted to Cap François.

The conspiracy had been an amazing surprise. Hundreds of slaves had been involved to assure the communications, secrecy, and timing. While the whites and mulattos had been busy savaging each other, the slaves had used their voodoo meetings and tribal networks to build a movement. Several leaders had already emerged: Jean François, Jeannnot Bullet, Georges Biassou, and Dutty Boukman, the latter a voodoo priest. They were unknown quantities and, for the moment, had no political demands; it was enough to have destroyed the symbols, and often the persons, of their old oppression. It was rumored that their revolt had been abetted by mulattos, or even by royalist whites, seeking to channel the slaves' anger against their enemies, but such calculations were now irrelevant. Who would benefit from the slave revolt, and how, was unknown. The scope of the revolt, and of its success, had changed all calculations.

The fury of the rebellion was followed by a period of relative calm. The slaves, free from discipline but with no idea where their revolt would lead them, were happy to settle down on the ravaged but still rich plain. Their leaders began to organize them into informal military bands and to impose discipline. "In possession of the entire plain, they have divided into bands of from three to four hundred, distributed on the various plantations which provide refuge for them," a resident American businessman reported to his home company.[7] Meanwhile in the city, the surrounded whites plotted revenge, and prayed for reinforcements from France. Raid and counterraid kept both sides on edge, but the city was too well guarded for the blacks to attack, and the slaves too numerous to be driven off. An uneasy standoff took shape.

Americans could not ignore such momentous events in a nearby and important trading partner. American business in St. Domingo had remained good in spite of the upheavals of two years of revolution, and at the time of the slave insurrection there were over fifty American-flagged vessels in the port of Cap François alone.

Indeed, the American government had been watching developments on the island with enough concern to prompt Secretary of State Jefferson, in June 1790, to appoint a consul there to protect American trading interests. In those early days of a miniature federal government, American consuls were generally businessmen who served in an unsalaried capacity, receiving what income they could from the sale of official services to other Americans. Jefferson's choice was Sylvanus Bourne, from Massachusetts, who got some strong advice from Jefferson as to the official stance he should assume with respect to the constitutional and political disputes that were wracking the island: "I am to recommend to you in the strongest terms not to intermeddle in the least by word or deed in the internal disputes of the Colony, or those with the Mother country. Consider this as a family affair with which we have neither the right nor the wish to intermeddle."[8]

Unfortunately, the French authorities on St. Domingo did not agree with Jefferson's assertion that he had a right to appoint consuls to French colonies, and they never accepted Bourne's credentials. Bourne, impatient, tried to get Jefferson to press the French on his accreditation, but the secretary of state never saw reason to confront what he knew were traditional French sensitivities on the issue. As late as August 14, 1791—just a week before the slave uprising—he wrote to Bourne advising that he would have to be patient, and told him that he was free to abandon his consular commission if he found it not worth his while.

By the time Bourne got that letter, of course, the black rebellion had changed the whole picture drastically. The French authorities on St. Domingo faced a crisis; France was far away. They urgently needed assistance, and were prepared to let the United States "intermeddle" (to use Jefferson's term) in the island's affairs.

Surrounded in Cap François by thousands of armed and murderous rebels, fearing a shortage of provisions, furious at Paris, and knowing that reinforcements from the mother country would take months to arrive (if at all, given the parlous state of affairs in France), the colonists turned northward. Within days, they had decided to send representatives and letters to the United States to plead for food supplies, arms, even troops. Although most of the American ships in harbor at Le Cap were put under emergency embargo, a few were dispatched urgently with the emissaries and letters. Appeals from the new General Assembly of the island were addressed to the Assembly's supposed counterparts at the U.S. Congress, as well as to the governor of South Carolina. The letters were deliberately alarmist in tone: "The troubles of St. Domingo have reached a peak, and soon this superb country will be but a heap of ashes; already the planters have bathed with blood the land which their sweat made fertile; the fire even now consumes the production which was the splendor of the French Empire."[9]

The American government and public were already favorably inclined to the appeals from St. Domingo. In the weeks since the slave revolt, reports from the island had appeared in the newspapers, almost always expressing sympathy for the colonists and horror at the revolt. Refugees from the looting of the plantations had begun to arrive on the northern continent, and their stories—like this one reported in New York—drew immediate sympathy: "His venerable age was not any protection against the depredations of these outrageous slaves. Neither age nor sex are considered by a brutal flock. . . . What will be the issue of these dreadful disturbances, God only knows."[10]

Sympathy for the white Domingans' plight was reinforced by the fact that most politically active Americans shared important interests with the island's planter class. For the merchants of the North and the Mid-Atlantic states, the rich Domingan sugar kings had provided a good market for American goods, while in the South, feelings of solidarity with fellow planters and slaveholders were most important. Moreover, the steadily increasing spiral of disturbances on the island had come to be seen as the fruit of a French revolution which was itself losing its luster in many Americans' eyes. When the news from St. Domingo arrived in America at the same time as news from France that King Louis had been arrested after an unsuccessful attempt to flee the country, it only added to American apprehensions that the revolutionary current—in France and its colonies—was running out of control.

Given this favorable climate for their appeals, it is ironic that the main obstacle that the emissaries found upon their arrival in the United States was their own countryman, the French minister to the United States. Jean Baptiste Ternant was a cautious diplomat, trained in the ways of the old regime, and careful not to make a misstep in view of the revolution's increasingly fratricidal atmosphere. When the first Domingan envoy, a Monsieur Roustan, arrived in Philadelphia in the second half of September, Ternant wrote to Paris that he intended to be minimally helpful. Ternant had major problems with this initiative of the island authorities. First, he was concerned that the General Assembly might not speak authoritatively; he knew how divided authority had become on the island, and wanted to be sure that the requested assistance would not flow to a group of secessionist, or royalist-minded, planters. Second, he was determined that Roustan have no direct dialogue with U.S. authorities. He feared that direct access would only feed any secessionist ambitions the islanders harbored. (For the same reason, he had opposed Sylvanus Bourne's accreditation as U.S. consul in Cap François.) And third, Ternant was still ready to defend France's mercantile interests; he felt that the Americans should be allowed to sell only those items that could not be supplied from France. He wrote, "The US would probably have been eager to seize this occasion to assure the gratitude of a colony whose trade it desires, and which in its new reorganization begins to have its own sort of political voice, even if subject to the mother country. In view of the proximity of the United States, the business spirit which pervades, and the role which those states are destined to play, it was dangerous to allow a direct negotiating relationship to develop with the richest and most important of our colonies. . . ."[11] In spite of his misgivings, and his lack of instructions, Ternant saw that he could not refuse to act. He insisted that Roustan's appeal be channeled through him, as the official representative of France, but he did send it forward.

With the president and the secretary of state both at their estates in Virginia, Ternant's appeal landed on the desks of Secretary of the Treasury Alexander Hamilton and Secretary of War Henry Knox, who quickly coordinated a positive answer. The basic issue, in the view of Washington and his cabinet members—so often divided on other issues—was simply a matter of helping an old ally maintain control of a colony with which America enjoyed a profitable trade. (America, in fact, was committed by the Treaty of 1778 to help France retain its West Indian colonies, although that clause was not invoked at this time because the threat was internal, not external.) Restoration of order in the colony was deemed to be in the American interest, perhaps all the more so because of the frightening precedent it presented of a major slave revolt. By October, the War Department had agreed to release a shipment of arms and ammunition from the arsenal at West Point, and Ternant had received a letter from Mt. Vernon, in which President Washington expressed his regrets as to "the cause which has given rise to this application," and attesting "how well disposed the United States are to render every aid in their power to our good friends and allies the French to quell 'the alarming insurrection of the Negroes in Hispaniola.' "[12]

The Americans were concerned to some degree at the irregular nature of the request, knowing that neither Ternant nor the colonists had any authority from Paris. What they offered was a credit of $40,000, made available to Ternant so that he (not the Assembly's emissaries) could purchase rifles and ammunition as well as necessary supplies. Given the U.S. government's cash-starved situation, the money was to come as advances on sums that were already owed to the French government, as part of the revolutionary war debt. Ternant however remained cautious; he sent the arms and some supplies, but held back over $30,000 of the credit until he could ascertain more definitively the island's needs or the desires of his home government.

Before Ternant could receive instructions from his ministry, however, he had a new set of colonial emissaries to deal with, and more insistent ones at that. (In fact, poor Ternant never did receive adequate instructions from Paris, where the revolution's unpredictable progress had apparently made bureaucratic caution advisable.) The new representatives of the Assembly were Messrs. Payan and Beauvois, who came in October 1791 armed with a demand for greatly increased shipments of foodstuffs and arms, and insisted that they be put in touch with U.S. officials. Ternant quickly wrote to Paris, to report the envoys' arrival, to debunk the extent of their claims for aid, and to point out that the instruments with which they expected to pay—French government notes—were being honored in the American markets only at a very deep discount. His foot dragging was understandable, both bureaucratically and politically. As he pointed out, "All these means, ostensibly against the blacks, could, if need arose, be used against us. . . ."[13] He may have been relieved somewhat on the latter score several weeks later, when he received a letter from the French governor in St. Domingo assuring him that the Assembly's initiatives had official consent.[14]

Ternant also went to Jefferson to gain some assurance that U.S. officials would not meet with the colonial representatives. Jefferson was the ideal interlocutor for the French minister. Even though Washington and his cabinet members were in full agreement that it was in the U.S. interest to help France keep control over its rebellious colony, each had reached that conclusion by a slightly different path. The secretary of state was the one member of the group who sincerely wished well to France, and believed that the revolution—no matter how confusing and brutal the process—was moving forward toward a better future for mankind.[15] Jefferson agreed that Payan and Beauvois should not have official appointments with senior government figures, though he said that he was prepared to meet with them informally. In response to Ternant's probing, Jefferson said that there was no support in the U.S. administration, or in the Senate, for St. Domingo's independence; such a development, he volunteered, would only benefit England and allow it to control the island and its trade.

Jefferson's meeting with the two representatives, however informal it may have been, was very substantive. Jefferson told them that the United States was willing to help, but with certain understandings. As he reported to the American chargé d'affaires in Paris:

In the course of our conversation, I expressed to them our sincere attachment to France & all it's dominions, & most especially to them who were our neighbors, and whose interests had some common points of union with ours, in matters of commerce; that we wished therefore to render them every service they needed; but that we could not do it in any way disagreeable to France; that they must be sensible that M. de Ternant might apprehend that jealousy would be excited by their addressing themselves directly to foreign powers, & therefore that a concert with him in their applications to us was essential. The subject of independence & their views towards it having been stated in the public papers, this led our conversation to it & I must say they appeared as far from these views as any persons on earth. I expressed to them freely my opinion that such an object was neither desirable on their part nor attainable; that as to ourselves there was one case which would be peculiarly alarming to us, to wit, were there a danger of their falling under any other power; that we conceived it to be strongly our interests that they should retain their connection with the mother country; that we had a common interest with them in furnishing them the necessaries of life in exchange for sugar & coffee for our own consumption, but that I thought we might rely on the justice of the mother country towards them, for their obtaining this privilege; and on the whole let them see that nothing was to be done but with the consent of the minister of France.[16]

With Jefferson's help and the administration's friendly attitude, Ternant had begun to get the diplomatic situation under control. He was momentarily annoyed when Jefferson agreed to forward a letter from the islanders directly to Congress, and again when President

Washington agreed to see them, even if only as "citizens of St. Domingo." But, as he saw it, France's basic interests had been preserved. The Americans would help meet the islanders' needs, but everything would be coordinated with the French government, and he himself would see to it that the flow of goods remained minimal. Even more, any hopes on the part of the emissaries that the United States would support an independence movement had been squelched. Congress seemed disinclined to take any action on the islanders' petition, and other freewheeling initiatives by the planters had also been channeled. Governor Pinkney of South Carolina had sent a sympathetic letter to the St. Domingo Assembly in response to their petition, and had allowed a M. Polony to raise money in that state for the benefit of the islanders, but beyond that had done nothing but refer the matter to President Washington and the federal government—with a helpful warning that the United States had much to fear from the example of the slave revolt. Washington's response to Pinckney was another sign of a positive American attitude: "I feel sincerely those sentiments of sympathy which you so properly express for the distresses of our suffering brethren in that quarter," the president had written, "and [I] deplore their causes."[17]

Ternant's caution, however, did not match the needs of the situation. By the beginning of 1792, fighting had broken out all over St. Domingo, and the various parties were turning to the ever-enterprising American merchants to supply arms as well as foodstuffs and other necessities. The trickle of official aid was soon overtaken by a flood of private arrangements to supply the island. Ternant, anxious as always to maintain the *exclusif,* complained to the American authorities that they were countenancing smuggling of contraband into the island, while at the same time he warned Paris that the American shippers were taking over the sugar trade from the colony to Europe. But no one seemed to be listening. American merchants and the various parties on the island shared an interest in open trade, the French authorities on the island had lost all ability to control it, and the authorities in France were too preoccupied with domestic riots and the threat of invasion from émigré or Austrian armies to send aid, or even effective instructions.

The demands from St. Domingo, moreover, kept increasing, and with them the complexity of the situation. Colonial authorities had begun to order supplies directly from American traders, paying with notes drawn on Ternant in the United States. The harassed diplomat found himself obliged to spend down the original American credits, even though he had no authority to honor the notes. By the spring of 1792, he was reporting to Paris that the island was "in a violent state of revolution," and that he had valid requests from authorities there for $400,000 in new credits.[18] Still without instructions, he had appealed to Jefferson and Hamilton to provide the new credits anyway. They eventually agreed, but only after some serious caviling by the secretary of the treasury.[19] The continued absence of official requests from Paris for these advances, and the irregularity of the of the whole process, also prompted a rather petulant communication from Jefferson to Ternant, including a reminder that the advances were being made only for the purpose of buying goods and services in the United States. Then Ternant complicated the situation still further when he finally refused, in June 1792, to honor any new notes issued in St. Domingo, causing a storm of protests by the American merchants who held this now valueless paper. To deal with their pressure, Hamilton agreed to honor the colonists' notes out of future credits, if the French did not redeem them first. Of course, the French did not pay, and by January of 1793 the total of American advances had grown to over $455,000.

However irregular the procedures for American assistance had been, it had bought time for the colonial authorities in St. Domingo. But that was not enough to bring them success. The rebellion in the north of the island was unbroken, and new revolts had sprung up in other parts of the island. The cautious Ternant felt himself to be dangerously exposed; he had spent French credits without authorization, and with no corresponding political gains to show. As a result, when he received a letter of thanks in mid-summer from the St. Domingo Assembly, his reaction was not one of satisfaction, but of fear. He immediately wrote to his ministry, explaining that the colonists' approbation did not mean disloyalty on his part; his actions had been justified by the urgency of the situation, and he had from the beginning had reservations about the irregular procedures used. At the same time, he wrote the St. Domingo Assembly, scolding them for having exposed him to possible denunciation for having aided them. Knowing that his tour of duty in America was reaching its end, he somewhat pathetically sought to clear his slate before returning to the revolutionary capital: "The executive of the Republic will judge my conduct, and if you explain to it how I have been abandoned or ignored for so long, it will find, as I do, that my public duties can only have suffered, and I would be remiss not to demand either my recall or a suitable communication from the government."[20]

Ternant was right to be worried. While he had been working in Philadelphia to maintain traditional French interests, the revolutions in both France and St. Domingo had been slipping toward the edge of chaos. In Paris, the flight of the king had radicalized the situation. As a result, the National Assembly, already scheduled for dissolution, found itself seized again with the colonial question in an atmosphere of haste and preoccupation with the domestic situation. The problem however was clear: the May 15 decree granting civic rights to mulattos had created such havoc in the colonies, and drawn the ire of so many important merchant and municipal groups, that it could only be sustained at the risk of losing the colonies themselves. The petition of the merchants of Havre de Grace illustrates the passions involved: "At the Cap, the batteries of Fort Picolet have been manned to repulse those who shall be so hardy as to come there with their doctrines of National liberty and philanthropy—doctrines at once productive of blood and cruelty.

The citizens, the government bodies, the regular troops; all have but one mind, one goal: they are ready to curse the connections that ally them to France."[21]

Realism overcame revolutionary idealism. A decree which had risked losing the colonies—either by the secession of the colonists, or to slave revolts along the pattern of St. Domingo—had to be abandoned. The *Amis* fought to keep the May decree, with their ally Jacobin leader Maximilien Robespierre furiously charging backsliders of treason, but they lost. A new decree of September 24 gutted the previous one by remitting back to the colonial assemblies the "situation of persons not free, and the political condition of mulattos and free negroes," notwithstanding the terms of any previous decrees. A group of four commissioners was named to go to St. Domingo, with the tall order of enforcing the new decree and restoring the colony to loyalty. Their mission was probably doomed from the start, designed as it was largely in ignorance of the extent and success of the slave revolt. The situation in the colony had changed, completely beyond the Assembly's calculations.

Five days later, the National Assembly dissolved itself, to make way for a new, more revolutionary and more divisive body called the Legislative Assembly. There, the constitutionalists were outgunned and increasingly irrelevant, and the main debate before long became one between two of the more radical movements: the Girondists and the Jacobins. As the internal debate sharpened, so did the external threat: royalist émigrés and—more importantly—the rulers of Austria and Prussia were on the verge of deciding that the time had come to stamp out the revolution.

When the French commissioners arrived in St. Domingo in the fall, they found that their new decree provided no solution to the colony's disorder. While it may have placated the white colonists to some degree, they were still fatally divided. One American correspondent described the deteriorating situation at the Cap succinctly: "Those everlasting political differences which estrange the colonists from the mother country, and from each other, prevent any important exertion of the public force against the common depredators. Now and then a small detachment of whites makes a sudden excursion into the plantations, expends considerable quantities of ammunition without doing much execution, and gives the insulting rebels convincing proof of weakness. . . ."[22]

Republicans and patriots wore the red cockade and claimed allegiance to the revolution, but they were divided into as many factions as existed in Paris, and many moreover were closet secessionists. A white cockade was worn by the loyalists (or royalists), counterrevolutionaries, and by many open secessionists, but these factions could agree on no more than could their opponents. Disturbances filled the streets, skirmishes and killings were all too common, and the debates in the General Assembly became so heated that swords were actually drawn in the chamber. No one was in charge; the colonial administration had effectively atomized. The military and government officials were also divided, with officers and their troops often on opposing sides. In the prevailing state of disorder, and while the colonists waited in vain for meaningful military reinforcements from France, loyalty to the mother country had begun to erode fatally. In addition, seditious contacts were growing with the British authorities across the water in Jamaica, to whom the Assembly in their extremity had also petitioned successfully for aid.

It would have taken strong leadership on the part of the French commissioners to bring order from this chaos, and they were not the men for it. Three of the four soon absented themselves as political actors, and only the remaining commissioner, Philippe Roume, was left an ambiguous and largely feckless future role to play.

As far as the mulattos were concerned, the September 24 decree was a declaration of war; they saw that they would never get satisfaction from the ruling whites, no matter how divided the latter might be amongst themselves. The fragile truce at Port au Prince soon broke down, and in the ensuing hostilities the town was put to the torch. It burned for two days. By autumn, virtually all the country-side in the western and southern provinces had fallen to a mulatto regime headed by André Rigaud, supported by some royalist ele-ments in the planter community. White planters and officials in the region still controlled the major towns, but they were dependent on outside support and began to look to the British in neighboring Jamaica as potential protectors.

In the north, the French colonials continued to shelter in the cities and towns, while much of the countryside, and particularly the vital Plaine du Nord, was controlled by the rebel slaves. They had begun to organize their territory along military lines, to form the field hands into military units, and to barter plantation goods for arms and ammunition smuggled over from the Spanish part of the island. Boukman, the voodoo priest who had helped organize the revolt, had been captured and killed by the colonists, and the blood-thirsty and dangerous Jeannot had been tried and executed by his co-leaders for his excesses of cruelty. That left Georges Biassou and Jean François as the primary leaders, but the Breda plantation coachman, Toussaint, had joined the leadership and, thanks to his organizational and motivational skills, was rising to a position of importance.

The blacks as yet had no political demands beyond an amnesty; they were focused more on quality of life and workplace issues and moreover were divided among themselves as to whether they could agree to return to the plantations.[23] Fitful negotiations with the French commissioners soon broke down. The basic sympathy of the blacks to the concepts of kingship and loyalty to France, however, made them potential allies of the royalists and the neighboring Spanish, who began supplying them clandestinely with arms. As their military strength was growing, so too was their political poten-tial, and both white and mulatto factions considered how they could win the support of the black army in case of need.

One thing the fractious colonials had been able to agree on was that they needed to keep open a line of communication to the United States. With that in mind, the Assembly had passed a resolution in late September of 1791 setting aside the considerations that had led French officialdom to refuse consul Silas Bourne's credentials the year before. Bourne was invited to stay, but the gesture was too late. He was not tempted; business was not good, and the situation was foreboding. By the end of the year, he had returned home.

St. Domingo was no longer a steady, assured market for Americans. Sales were erratic, and the war had driven up the price of molasses to such a level that American distillers had begun to switch to other raw materials. Some months later, another American businessman also determined to go home, disgusted at the dissension and poor business opportunities in the colony, and voicing his disillusionment in a bit of bad poetry. He called St. Domingo a country

> . . . Where cruel passions the warm heart infest
> And banish pity from the human breast
> Where hostile ruffians draw the vengeful blade
> And slay with infant gore the blushing shade!
> I turn, disgusted, from this horrid scene
> Of tortured captives, slaves, and murdered men. . . .[24]

Sadly, St. Domingo had already become, in the eyes of most Americans, a sort of metaphor for revolutionary excess, rebellion, and disorder.

Jefferson had led the U.S. government's effort to help the French authorities and planters hold on to their colony; indeed, he may well have been frustrated by Ternant's very cautious approach. But the situation on the island had only gone from bad to worse, and Jefferson worried that secession or independence would only help the British. By the middle of 1792, his dissatisfaction with the apparent low priority that the French government placed on its colonial problem prompted him to write to Lafayette with a double plea—both for French action to regain its hold on the Indies, and to permit Americans to trade there freely. He also acknowledged that the blacks would have to be given some sort of political status:

> What are you doing for your colonies? They will be lost if not more effectually succoured. Indeed no future efforts you can make will ever be able to reduce the blacks. All that can be done in my opinion will be to compound with them as has been done formerly in Jamaica. We have been less zealous in aiding them [the colonists], lest your government should feel any jealousy on our account. But in truth we as sincerely wish their restoration, and their connection with you, as you do yourselves. We are satisfied that neither your justice nor their distresses will ever again permit their being forced to seek at dear & distant markets those first necessaries of life which they may have at cheaper markets placed by nature at their door, & formed by her for their support.[25]

Jefferson's appeal to Lafayette was, in any event, stillborn. By the time his letter had reached France, the ci-devant Marquis no longer had a political role.

By the spring of 1792, it was evident in Paris that the September decree had not improved the situation in the colonies. Leadership of the new and more radical Legislative Assembly was in the hands of the Girondists, a group of provincial reformers who were challenged by the still more radical Jacobins. Neither group, however, was prepared to let the colonies be lost. Both strongly supported the principles of the Rights of Man, and saw the colonial planters as part of the problem, rather than the chief interest to be defended. Concluding that the dangerous slave insurrection could best be neutralized by gaining the support of the mulattos, the legislators drafted a new decree. Passed on March 24 and signed by the king

on April 4, the new decree gave full political rights to all mulattos
and free blacks. The new decree, the Assembly realized, would
be resisted by the white colonists, so it put the teeth of coercion
behind it. Three new commissioners were named to enforce its terms,
and they were to be supported by six thousand fresh troops.

The commissioners had a problem from the beginning. All three
were good Jacobin revolutionaries, but the troops that accompanied
them were not. In fact, four thousand of the troops were in units with
strong royalist leanings, and could not necessarily be counted on in
case of a confrontation with the planters. Nevertheless, when the commissioners arrived in St. Domingo in the fall, they found the planters
outwardly accommodating. Happy finally to see reinforcements and
the hope of reestablishing order, including the return of the blacks to
their plantations, the planters put on a good face and professed their
readiness to cooperate, even to accept the mulattos as equals.

It was the commissioners who overplayed their hand. The dominant figure among them was the ascetic, uncompromising Leger-
Felicité Sonthonax, scion of a well-to-do provincial family who had
turned radical, joined the *Amis des Noirs,* and despised the old establishment. Perhaps taking the planters' expressions of accommodation
as a sign of their weakness, he and his fellow commissioners began an
abrupt and thorough shakeup. The General Assembly was dissolved,
numerous officials purged and some deported as counterrevolutionary plotters, the planters freely insulted, and taxes raised. For a
moment, his efforts seemed to succeed. The black insurgency was contained by the new alliance between the mulattos and loyal troops, and
negotiations were progressing toward an amnesty for its leaders and a
return to the plantations. Rigaud in his mulatto territory in the south
had been, more or less, enlisted as an ally. But the success was shaky
and temporary; the army's loyalty was uncertain, and the alliance with
the mulattos caused the planters' original welcome to evaporate.

By winter, the kaleidoscope of political groups had been
rearranged but the situation had not basically changed. The island's

governance had fractured beyond repair; the white power structure was all but shattered. The French authorities and the colonists, divided into factions that scarcely coexisted with each other, held on in the major towns, but most of the countryside was controlled by insurgent slaves in the north and mulattos in the west and much of the south, while a confederation of white planters had established their own zone of control in the western reaches of the southern peninsula. Violence was widespread, racial hatreds inflamed, atrocities frequent, and even though no major armies fought, there was no peace.

In France, too, there was little peace, either at home or on the borders. The Girondists had finally led the country into a war with Austria and Prussia, while the domestic situation had become increasingly radicalized. Over a tumultuous summer, the Gironde government fell, the increasingly dominant Paris mob stormed the royal Tuilleries palace, the king was suspended from his functions, and the mob then returned to storm the prisons and massacre many political detainees. What was left of the old order quickly fell apart. Lafayette was impeached and fled the country, the king was deposed and a republic installed, and at the end of the year the king was put on trial.

On January 21, 1793, King Louis was executed. Two weeks later, the French Republic widened the crisis by declaring war on Great Britain, Holland, and Spain.

THE COST OF NEUTRALITY

President Washington was troubled by the outbreak of war in Europe. He and his cabinet colleagues knew that their country would inevitably be drawn into the dispute, if not the actual war. Previous wars between Britain, Spain, and France had been fought in the Americas as well as on the old continent, and the United States' new independence was not enough to isolate it from the coming hostilities. Although many Americans asked nothing more than to be left out of the Europeans' wars so they could develop their country's western territories, there was no way the United States could remain unaffected. America's position along the major sea-lanes, and its resources, were sure to make it a significant factor in the coming struggle. The Europeans would carry the war across the seas into their Canadian, Louisiana, and Caribbean possessions, and each of the warring nations was likely to try to draw the Americans to its side, or, failing that, to destabilize their new union or even provoke them into hostilities against the other powers.

War would put great pressures, both external and internal, on the fledgling U.S. government. The national union was still new and fragile, its institutions tiny and untested, and the extent of its authority still being defined. The country was effectively disarmed; it had no national army or navy to speak of, and the local militias could neither protect the long coastline from incursions nor prevent foreign powers from inciting the Indians in the interior. Moreover, there was no national consensus with respect to the European powers, beyond a generally shared disdain for Spain's remaining pretensions as a major power. Pro- and anti-British, as well as pro- and anti-French sentiments from the revolutionary period still smoldered, and were susceptible to manipulation by ambitious politicians and foreign agents alike. The president, in short, had a weak hand, but had to find some policy that would minimize America's risks in the coming hostilities.

And yet, for some Americans a European war promised great rewards. Not only would American goods be in great demand, but also American shipping. The Europeans would almost surely need to buy large quantities of American grain, lumber, livestock, and maritime products to pursue their war and, at the same time, keep their hungry West Indies colonies supplied. American exporters were likely to prosper. America's merchant marine was also ready to seize advantage of the situation. In peacetime, only the mercantilist policies of the European powers had kept the highly competitive American seamen from dominating the West Indies trade, among others. Hostilities would increase the need for their services, since as soon as the belligerent powers began to prey on each others' merchant fleets, neutral flag ships like those of the United States would be in great demand. There would, of course, be risks. International law (then called "the law of nations") allowed belligerents an absolute right to stop and search neutral flag ships, and to confiscate them or their cargoes as prizes if they were found to be carrying contraband to the enemy. American ships would thus be subject to constant harassment from the belligerents, but were likely to do well as long as they did not carry contraband. The problem was that the definition of contraband was not universally agreed, and could—indeed, probably would—be changed unilaterally by the belligerents under the pressures of war. That, however, was a risk the merchants could accept and insure against. Profits would be excellent from successful voyages, and they could always petition the government for redress if their ships got arrested under debatable circumstances.

The merchants and seamen of the Atlantic ports, then, saw opportunities. The more enterprising of them were even tempted to take sides on a personal basis by accepting commissions (or letters of marque) from one or another of the belligerent powers, and then arming and outfitting privateers to prey legally (and profitably) on the shipping of that power's enemies. The mercantile interests generally believed that they would prosper from a war in Europe, as long as American neutral rights were observed by the belligerents and the trade routes—particularly with the major trading partner, Britain, but also to the West Indies—were open to American ships. In this, they had important support in the government from the group that rallied around Alexander Hamilton. The treasury secretary and his friends were firm in their belief that regularizing the new republic's finances depended on a healthy financial community, and that particularly important in that respect was a healthy trade with England, which generated the customs revenues that were essential to the government's financial future. For this important group, therefore, it was essential that any American policy toward the European war not compromise American-British relations.

Many other Americans were apprehensive. The war, they feared, would only embroil the United States in the quarrels of Europe, to the detriment of its own development, particularly its opening up of the West. A loose alliance of small farmers, city workers, planters, and frontiersmen was forming that distrusted the merchant interests and any expansion of government power. (Some of its members were already resisting the new federal government's efforts to tax distilled spirits.) Many in this movement, which called itself "democratic," worried that the demands of a war would increase government intervention, require the raising of national defense forces, and generally favor the expansion of executive and oligarchic power. Firmly republican, they had welcomed the revolution in France, in spite of its increasing radicalism. Their spokesmen in government were the two Virginians, Jefferson and Madison, whose philosophy abhorred all measures that could increase the "tyranny" of government over the individual.

Nobody, as yet, wanted the United States to take sides in the war. There were, indeed, sympathizers to both of the European sides, but no open proponents for American partiality between them. President Washington, in his message to Congress in March 1793, just as his first term was expiring, had expressed his concern that the United States could be drawn into the European conflict against its will. He suggested that the country needed a stronger national defense, and asked Congress to agree to a declaration designed to "adopt general rules which should conform to the treaties, and assert the privileges, of the United States."[1]

Congress was amenable to the president's suggestion, but the devil of drafting such a declaration was, as always, in the details. The major issue became how to shape an evenhanded policy that at the same time "conformed" to the fact that the United States had different treaty relations with the two major belligerents. With Britain, there was a peace treaty but no treaty of commerce and friendship. Britain's active assertion of economic nationalism since the American colonies had become independent had precluded such a treaty, in spite of efforts to reach one during the old Confederation. With France, on the other hand, the United States had both a treaty of alliance dating from the revolutionary days of 1778 and a consular convention negotiated by Jefferson during his time as U.S. minister to the court in Paris. Those agreements gave the French, in times of war, rights that the British could not claim, such as the right to outfit ships and land prizes in the United States. The treaty of alliance even committed the United States to help protect French possessions in the West Indies. Technically, then, the country could not remain neutral in the war; its treaty required it to favor France.

To get around this inconvenient fact, Hamilton's group argued that the 1778 treaty was no longer valid, that the French Revolution and abolishment of the monarchy had fundamentally changed the situation. Jefferson and his colleagues rejected that argument, insisted that the treaty be honored, and even that any declaration avoid use of the term "neutral," as it implied a setting aside of French rights. Ironically, a policy discussion over how best to stay out of the European war was impacting on American politics by sharpening the differences, and the public debate, between the American friends of England and the friends of France.

American public opinion appears, in early 1793, still to have been largely favorable to the French revolution. France's traditional friends had been joined by democratic politicians, who used the powerful symbolism of French revolutionary progress to promote their populist ideals. Pro-French, pro-republican rallies dominated the popular politics of the cities, as the new republic's successes against the despotic continental monarchies were celebrated at every possible occasion. The turn of the year had seen a particularly heady series of popular rallies in Boston, Providence, New York, Princeton, Savannah, Charleston, and other cities. Militia parades, ox-roasts, public illuminations, fireworks, speeches, banquets, and full punchbowls punctuated these major civic events. Even the merchant and financial elites (who, in private, may have voiced unfavorable opinions on the French revolution and its lack of respect for private property and contract) were often constrained to join the ubiquitous toasts against Tyranny, and in favor of Liberty, Equality, and the Rights of Man.

Washington and his cabinet, officially ignoring this clamor, were in agreement on at least the basic principle: that American interests would be best preserved by avoiding acts—public or private—that would make America a party to the war. A compromise was reached. As Jefferson described it,

It was therefore agreed that a proclamation should issue, declaring that we were in a state of peace with all the parties, admonishing the people to do nothing contravening it, & putting them on their guard as to contraband. On this ground it was accepted or acquiesced in by all, and Edmund Randolph, who drew it, brought to me the draught, to let me see there was no such word as *neutrality* in it. . . . The public, however, soon took it up as a declaration of neutrality, & it came to be considered at length as such. . . . In our consultation, it was agreed we were by treaty *bound* to prohibit the enemies of France from arming in our ports, & were *free* to prohibit France also, and that by the laws of neutrality we are bound to permit or forbid the same things to both, as far as our treaties would permit. All, therefore, were forbidden to arm within our ports, & the vessels armed before the prohibition were on the advice of a majority ordered to leave our ports.[2]

The president's proclamation, issued on April 22, made no specific mention of U.S. treaty obligations, but had the result of leaving those with France in place, even if limited by the new interpretation of neutrality. It enjoined American citizens from engaging in, or abetting, any hostile act, including the carrying of contraband. Hamilton's customs department was made responsible for enforcing the U.S. restrictions that this implied, and American citizens who acted in spite of the warning were advised that they would get no protection from the belligerent powers if the latter punished them for violating their interpretations of international law.

The proclamation had set the general objective and framework for a policy, but its lack of detail meant that it would be challenged and tested many times in practice.

In Paris, the Girondists were, for the moment, triumphant. French successes at Valmy and Jemappes the previous autumn had turned the tide of war against the Prussians and Austrians. The revolution in early 1793 was no longer under attack, indeed it had moved onto the offensive by offering assistance to all peoples who wished to throw out their monarchs. But domestically, the Girondists were still in a fierce competition with their more extreme rivals, the Jacobins.

Hoping that further military successes abroad could help silence this opposition, they had taken a great risk, and broadened the war.

War with Britain and Spain, unlike one with Austria and Prussia, would mean war at sea. England's powerful navy would attack French shipping, interdict neutral shipping carrying war materials, and—most importantly for our story—disrupt French trade with St. Domingo and the other West Indian possessions. France's navy was not up to the task of fully protecting the country's trans-Atlantic interests. The revolution needed friends.

The Girondists were determined to forge an alliance with the new regional power, the United States. To win the Americans to their side, they selected a bright, highly active and dedicated republican, Edmond Charles Genêt,[3] to be the next French minister in Philadelphia. Genêt, indeed, had a record of almost overenthusiastic republicanism; he had already been expelled from Catherine the Great's Russia for an excess of zeal. But he was capable, and dedicated, and the Gironde entrusted to him the task of revitalizing the somewhat moribund special relationship that had existed with the Americans since the 1778 treaty. Indeed, his objective was to get the United States to sign a new treaty—this time a full treaty of alliance.

Genêt's December 1792 instructions gave him a shopping list of specific projects to achieve, one of which was to get a renewed American guarantee of the French West Indian colonies, in return for which the Americans would get free trading access to those colonies. "It is important to the prosperity and peace of France that a people whose resources are growing rapidly, and whom nature has placed so close to our rich colonies, be committed by their own actions to the protection of those islands," his instructions read. In more general, hortatory language, his instructions sought to inspire the new envoy, noting that "As large as this project may be, it will be easy to carry out if the Americans want it, and convincing them that this is so should be Citizen Genêt's priority. . . . Their fate depends on ours, and if we were to succumb they [too] would fall, sooner or later, under the iron yoke of Great Britain."[4]

To help the Americans realize the advantages of a French alliance, the Girondists offered a significant incentive. In February 1793, after the declaration of war, and again in March and May, the government issued decrees suspending the old restrictions on American ships trading with its colonies. American ships would be able enter the colonial ports freely, pay the same fees and duties on foodstuffs and supplies as French ships, and export limited amounts of sugar and molasses directly. Admittedly, these concessions were the product of France's need as much as generosity toward the Americans. Everyone knew that the colonies would desperately need supplies, and that the British Navy was fully capable of blockading the French West Indian ports and interdicting supplies from Europe. But Yankee traders did not worry about motivation where they saw opportunity. They quickly got busy selling American goods in the islands, and the U.S. flag was soon the dominant presence in the St. Domingo trade.

St. Domingo was severely shaken by the expansion of France's revolutionary war. The situation in the mother country had slipped further into chaos. News of the abolition of the monarchy, and then the execution of King Louis, had affected the colonists strongly—and not just the white colonists; many slaves also felt unease at the loss of this symbol of order and stability. Most French army units were boiling with unrest and could not be counted on to deal with the expanding disorder. Commissioner Sonthonax's alliance with the mulattos had not allowed him to prevail over either the royalist whites or the rebel slaves, and the political situation remained on edge. Even André Rigaud in the southern region had accepted to be under Sonthonax's command more out of convenience than conviction. Moreover, the plantation economy in many parts of the island, already damaged by the civil war, threatened to come to a full stop as trade was cut off by a British blockade of the colony's ports.

The declaration of war with Spain and Britain had brought new external dangers in addition to the blockade. The Spanish presence at the other end of Hispaniola, feeble as it had been, suddenly had to be reckoned a real threat. The Spanish officials there, who had a notoriously liberal attitude toward slavery, were busy trying to win over the insurgent ex-slaves of the North, whom they had been supplying all along. Before long, Jean François, Biassou, and Toussaint had taken Spanish commissions and, more comfortable under a ruling king, were directing their insurgent bands against the regicide French. Moreover, the important British garrison on nearby Jamaica also posed a serious threat, both militarily and politically.

With the outbreak of war, many planters, already infuriated by the revolutionary blows to their racist regime, began to question their loyalty to Paris. Secessionist as well as royalist sentiment flowered, as the fear of a long British blockade and loss of their trade frayed the colonists' ties with the mother country. Some even began to look to the British on Jamaica as more friendly to their interests than the National Convention in Paris. Informal contacts with Jamaica expanded, allowing the British authorities there to cheerfully feed the secessionist sentiment. Early in the year, they had already offered the French planters a deal, which they called the Propositions: they would provide a sort of British protectorate for St. Domingo, for the duration of the European war, if the planters invited them in. The protectorate would both insulate the island from the dangerous revolutionary currents in Paris and guarantee for the planters the free trade that they had always sought, even if under the less-than-benign protection of the British Navy. For many of the planters, it was an attractive offer.

The tide was evident. The progress of France's revolution was slowly eroding the ties that had held this precious colony to its mother country.

The arrival of Citizen Genêt in the United States seemed, at first glance, to be a triumph for French diplomacy. On his arrival in

Charleston in early April, he was bathed in a sea of pro-French sentiment. He was feted by the leading merchant families and officials, whose strong ties to France and St. Domingo had prompted them to support a magnificent pro-French rally just two months before. The Democratic-Republicans from the back country, not to be outdone, praised and honored him as spokesman for the republican cause. It was heady stuff for the young and already hypermotivated envoy. Surrounded by so many well-wishers, all of whom were as yet unaware of the impending issuance of the Neutrality Proclamation in faraway Washington, Genêt felt empowered to move forward rapidly on the tasks that had been given him by Paris.

His instructions, indeed, went well beyond that of seeking a new treaty of friendship. One of his first tasks was to arrange for supplies to be sent to the French West Indies, a task that the American merchant interests were more than ready to help him achieve. But other parts of his mission would be more contentious. He was also instructed to take maximum advantage of the privileges that France saw itself entitled to by the 1778 treaty. The French interpreted that treaty as offering them a monopoly among the belligerent states in fitting out warships and privateers in the United States, as well as in landing and disposing of the prizes they seized.

Genêt was quick in executing the tasks assigned to him. He had, it turned out, hundreds of presigned letters of marque in his kit, and within ten days he had issued commissions to four American citizens authorizing them to fit out, in American ports, privateers that would fly the French flag and prey on British and Spanish shipping. He also authorized his consul in Charleston to set up an admiralty court, with authority to confiscate legal prizes and dispose of the seized ships and their goods. Genêt, at the same time, began to make contacts for another effort against France's enemies—inciting the frontiersmen and Indians of the West to take action against the Spanish authorities in Louisiana. With instructions that envisaged liberating the colony from Spanish rule, he had been supplied with a large number of presigned commissions for anyone wishing to take up arms against the despised Dons. His preparations to start another front in the war, from American soil, began to gather momentum.

Genêt was elated. His first reports to Paris were full of his successes, and indeed he had moved very fast and effectively. Leaving Charleston, he began a measured and triumphant progress toward the capital in Philadelphia. Greeted and feted with political rallies in virtually every town and city on his route, Genêt flaunted the banner of French republicanism and basked in the admiration of the many politicians and ordinary citizens who welcomed and flattered him. Having learned along the way that the U.S. government had adopted a position of neutrality, he began to paint a picture in his own mind of a divide between official America and the real people, whose sympathies he felt were with France. On arrival in Philadelphia in mid-May, he sent a self-congratulatory dispatch to his superiors in Paris: "My trip was a succession of uninterrupted civic festivals, and my entry into Philadelphia a triumph for liberty. The true Americans are full of joy. The good farmers took me into their arms and into their modest homes, and have offered much grain and flour. I have proposals for 600,000 barrels, but vessels are short even though being built. Our frigates and privateers take new prizes daily, the merchant ships of our enemy no longer dare to leave port, and their sailors are inactive. . . ."[5]

Genêt's enthusiasm for his mission and the warmth of his popular reception had, unfortunately, blinded him to the political realities of his diplomatic role. His progress through the southern states had been watched warily, and with increasing consternation, by the very officials in Philadelphia to whom he would have to make France's case for the new treaty. And they had been deeply troubled and offended by his actions, beginning with his unexpected arrival at a distant port, proceeding through his injudicious steps infringing their concept of America's sovereignty and the new neutrality policy, and ending with the climax of his tumultuous popular reception in Philadelphia.

Washington's cabinet, alerted to Genêt's activities in South Carolina and his attempted provocations directed at the Spanish, had been considering countermeasures. Hamilton, undoubtedly pleased to have been handed such an opportunity, was pushing for an official disclosure of Genêt's activities that would serve as a sort of reprimand. Jefferson, his sympathy for France severely strained by Genêt's antics, argued for a more cautious and diplomatic approach. He had already sent a sharp note to Ternant, protesting the reported arming of vessels in Charleston, and what he saw as the illegal exercise of jurisdiction by the French consul's admiralty court. All the same, his frustration with Genêt's behavior is evident from the account he made several months later to his confidant James Madison:

> Very soon afterwards we learnt that he [Genêt] was undertaking to authorize the fitting & arming vessels in that port, enlisting men, foreigners & citizens, & giving them commissions to cruise and commit hostilities against nations at peace with us, that these vessels were taking & bringing prizes into our ports, that the Consuls of France were assuming to hold courts of Admiralty on them to try, condemn & authorize their sale as legal prizes, & all this before Mr.[Genêt]—had presented himself or his credentials to the President, before he was received by him, without his consent or consultation, & directly in contravention of the state of peace existing & declared to exist in the President's proclamation, & which it was incumbent on him to preserve till the Constitutional authority should otherwise declare.[6]

Genêt was received, somewhat frostily, by the president on May 18. The coolness of his official reception in Philadelphia, unfortunately, only confirmed the impression he had gained in his six weeks in the United States—that he could manipulate the division between the "real people" and the government so as to "neutralize the declaration of neutrality of President Washington."[7] Washington's administration, he came to believe, was dominated by pro-English businessmen, exiled

French aristocrats, and agents of Great Britain, and the way to counter it would be to get Congress to direct a more pro-French policy. He began to lobby for an early session of Congress. At the same time, he reported to Paris, he continued to pursue his activist course by "exciting" the Canadians against England, arming various Kentuckians against Spain, and readying a fleet to help them attack New Orleans.[8]

By mid-summer, Genêt's aggressive public diplomacy and frenetic activities had created a significant disturbance in U.S.-French relations. They would be shaken still further over the coming months by the collapse of French authority in St. Domingo.

The island's new crisis began in May with the arrival of General Thomas François Galbaud as the new governor general. An absentee plantation owner of strongly conservative views, Galbaud may have been considered a compromise choice by the Paris authorities, but he was totally unacceptable to the radical commissioners, who by the time of his arrival were at swords' points with the planters on the island. A showdown ensued, which the commissioners won. Galbaud was blocked from assuming his powers, and sent back on board the fleet units that had brought him. But before the commissioners could decide their next steps, the initiative passed from their hands. The soldiers who had come with Galbaud mutinied (whether or not the general had a hand in instigating the mutiny is unclear). Cap François soon became the scene of disorganized fighting between the mutinous troops and such forces as the commissioners could muster, with the commissioners' troops getting the worst of it. Near defeat, Commissioner Sonthonax called on his last card; he invited the insurgent slaves of the Plaine du Nord to help save the revolution. He offered them freedom in return. They soon agreed, but with their agreement Sonthonax lost what little control of the situation he had enjoyed.

At the commissioners' invitation, the ex-slaves poured into Cap François. By their numbers alone, they soon overwhelmed the mutinous troops and whatever other defenses the planters could muster. What ensued was chaos. During four days of pillage and arson, the panicked white colonists deserted their capital, taking with them what few belongings they could salvage. Often, the most portable possession they could take were their slaves, who swelled the number of refugees. The immediate refuge of the fleeing colonists was on the hundreds of ships, military and merchant, French and American, that lay in the harbor. On land, the city was destroyed before their eyes; smoke and ashes rose over the once bustling, opulent, and sinful capital of the now disintegrating colony. Sonthonax and the insurgent ex-slaves were for the moment victorious, but for the former the victory did not signal success, and the latter had many more trials to go through before their victory was complete.

Ten thousand colonists, of all classes and colors, had embarked on the ships at the Cap. At the end of June they set sail, a fleet of disaster in over a hundred miscellaneous merchant vessels, escorted by eight French warships. Many of the destitute and distressed refugees crammed into the ships would never see the island again. They headed north, toward the nearest friendly state, one which was at the same time the home of revolutionary ideas about the rights of man, and the seat of a racist plantation society, the United States.

The flood of refugees from St. Domingo would affect America strongly. It was, at the most basic level, a humanitarian crisis of the kind to which Americans have traditionally responded generously. But it was much more. At the political level it enlivened the American scene, contributed to the furor of our relations with France, sharpened the domestic political debate, and encouraged a growing sense of insecurity among American slaveowners. The revolution in St. Domingo had suddenly and unexpectedly become an important issue in American politics, and it would remain so for a crucial generation.

The French fleet arrived in the Chesapeake Bay in mid-July. Some vessels had headed off earlier for southern ports; others, separated from the main fleet, had been stopped by British cruisers, who confiscated any French property. But their escort of French warships had assured a safe arrival for the majority of the refugees in the heartland of their new home. Norfolk was the first stop because, some said, Virginia law allowed the planters to land their slaves there without problem. St. Domingo's refugees soon began to disperse to other cities along the coast as well: Baltimore, New York, Wilmington, Charleston, and New York all took in sizeable groups of the often destitute ex-colonists. But the most sizeable community took root in Philadelphia, home already to thousands of refugees from revolutionary France, and the site of many merchant houses familiar with St. Domingo, as well as vibrant French cultural institutions.

The plight of the refugees was quickly recognized, and assistance marshaled—sometimes on the basis of alarmist and exaggerated stories, such as this from a senior government official, writing to his father:

> It is said that this town [Cap François] was as large as New York, and more populous. All the whites who did not escape on aboard the vessels are supposed to have been exterminated, and the destruction will probably extend to Port au Prince and the other towns of the French part of St. Domingo. American property to a great amount has been lost, besides the loss of a valuable market. The wretched remains of the whites are daily falling in here, and in the Chesapeake, many of whom are in a deplorable state of poverty, and for whose subsistence immediate provision will be necessary.[9]

Thomas Jefferson also urged aid for the refugees, but his reaction was typically more principled, and yet highly political. Writing to Virginia senator James Monroe, he invoked both domestic and foreign issues in his analysis of the situation: "The situation of the St. Domingo fugitives (aristocrats as they are) calls aloud for pity & charity. Never was so deep a tragedy presented to the feelings of man. I deny the power of the general government to apply money to such a purpose, but I deny it with a bleeding heart. It belongs to the State governments. Pray urge ours to be liberal. The Executive should hazard themselves more on such an occasion, & the Legislative when it meets ought to approve & extend it. It will have a great effect in doing away the impression of other disobligations towards France."[10]

Assistance for the most needy refugees was quickly raised by civic organizations. The French expatriate community in America had already set up two years earlier, with the assistance of Minister Ternant, its own charitable organization. American organizations quickly joined in the effort, and private charitable collections were made and distributed in Baltimore, Norfolk, Philadelphia, New York, Massachusetts, and elsewhere. State governments were also approached to contribute, and before long the legislatures of Maryland, Pennsylvania, Virginia, New York, Massachusetts, and both Carolinas had approved limited assistance. The federal government was much slower to take action, however, prompted in part by Jefferson's constitutional hesitations on the score. But President Washington and other officials were regularly petitioned by deserving refugees, such as Auguste de Grasse in Charleston, a descendant of the French admiral who had bottled up the British army at Yorktown during the American Revolution. The president's secretary responded to an appeal from de Grasse to assure him that "No man feels more for your distresses than the President, nor is any one more willing to contribute to the alleviation [of your countrymen], than he is."[11] In early 1794, the federal government finally authorized assistance for "such of the inhabitants of St. Domingo, resident in the United States, as may be in need of support."

The refugees quickly became active members in the communities of their exile. Those without means but some skills took up crafts or professions, others traded or set up shop, and still others lived by renting out their slaves for labor, where such a practice was countenanced.

(In Philadelphia, local law allowed a slave to be held for only six months before being freed, which resulted in many slaves being nominally freed but then indentured on seven-year contracts.) A few of the refugees lived on charity, but most became active and productive residents. They did not necessarily assimilate; many aspired above all to return home or to France, and the French communities in most of the receiving cities were large and lively enough to allow them to remain separate if they wished.

Political assimilation however was even more complicated, and the newcomers did not meld easily with the already large French émigré population in the U.S. cities. Many, indeed most, of the émigrés were of the old aristocracy, or disappointed constitutional reformers. The new refugees on the other hand, even though a large proportion of them were extremely bitter over what they saw as the French government's mishandling of its St. Domingo policy, were of all political colors, and generally more radical in their emotions. The result was that the political battles of France were fought in all their ferocity, once again, on American soil. Royalists, constitutional republicans, Girondists, Jacobins, counterrevolutionaries, all had their groups; each faction, it seemed, had its own French language newspaper, rallies, and meetings. Rumors and misinformation flew, passions were heated, competition for attention fierce. Most of the passion of the debate, however, remained within the francophone community. Americans, while amused by or even participating in the occasional rallies sponsored by the French, generally chose to keep their politics separate—but by no means uninfluenced—from the ferment of the French community.

The influx of disgruntled colonials from St. Domingo was a major headache for Citizen Genêt. As a good revolutionary activist, he thought that most of the planters among the refugees had brought their problems down upon themselves. Nonetheless, he had to do the right thing for the destitute among them, and on this aspect of his mission, at least, he was generally quite useful and his efforts were appreciated.

Genêt estimated that only half of the refugees supported the revolution, and that even many of those opposed the Girondist policies of his sponsors. He did not want his own countrymen to undercut his mission, and grew anxious about potential counterrevolutionary conspiracies within the French community. Fearful that such conspiracies might fatally influence an American administration that he considered to be already antirepublican and mortgaged to British interests, he intervened actively in French community politics. There, as usual, controversy swirled around him.

Genêt also worried about the loyalty of the French naval and military units that had accompanied the refugees from St. Domingo. He believed, apparently not without cause, that General Galbaud and other officers were plotting to return to the island to restore the situation there, and eventually claimed in his dispatches that he alone had nipped the plot in the bud. He himself had different plans for the fleet; he wanted to use it for his planned expedition against the Spaniards in New Orleans, or even to attack the British West Indies. But in this he had clearly gone beyond his assigned diplomatic role. The French military quite properly declined to take orders from him, and the fleet eventually sailed for France.

The Washington administration's patience with Genêt's activities by this time had all but worn out. He had attempted to arm still more privateers, in blatant and public defiance of the government's policy, while his conspiracy against Spanish Louisiana, involving the Revolutionary hero and western champion George Rogers Clark, was gathering momentum. Exasperated, Washington called together his cabinet in early August 1793 to discuss what they should do. Jefferson could no longer defend the Frenchman, nor in fact did he want to. He had concluded that Genêt's behavior was not only an embarrassment for him personally, it was a liability for all France's friends in the United States. Almost a month earlier, he had written privately,

"Never in my opinion was so calamitous an appointment made as that of the present Minister of France here. Hot headed, all imagination, no judgement, passionate, disrespectful and even indecent toward the President. . . . He renders my position immensely difficult." As he noted in another private letter in July, he wanted to give no more ammunition to Hamilton and his anti-French colleagues: "I fear the disgust of France is inevitable. We shall be to blame in part. But the new minister much more so. His conduct is indefensible by the most furious Jacobin. I only wish our countrymen may distinguish between him & his nation, & if the case should ever be laid before them, may not suffer their affection to the nation to be diminished."[12]

The cabinet came to a unanimous decision. They would ask the French government to recall their envoy. The French, in fact, might welcome the American move for a simple reason: Genêt's political backers had lost power. The French armies had done poorly over the recent months, fatally weakening the Gironde government that had pushed for the war. The Jacobins and the Paris Commune had seized the opportunity to strike, had suspended the National Convention, and had established the powerful Committee of Public Safety. Many Girondist deputies had been thrown in jail. With these dramatic changes in the situation in Paris, the Americans foresaw that a new foreign policy might also be expected. But diplomacy then took time. It would take two transatlantic voyages, plus a period for negotiation and drafting of instructions, before the American decision to ask for Genêt's recall could be translated into action.

By autumn, Genêt's suspicions about possible counterrevolutionary activities among the refugees had reached a crescendo, and was focussed on St. Domingo. He advised Paris that there was a plot to recapture the island and make it independent, and that the plot had the support of many American plantation owners, although not that of the government. France should not resent it that the Americans had effectively taken over the trade with the island, he advised Paris; American goods were preventing starvation there. Moreover, France could still retain the island, he argued, if only it dealt fairly with the mulattos: "St. Domingue, squeezed by the Spaniards, threatened by the English, excited by the royalists and independents, torn by the opposition of all parties to the 4 April law, is held together only by the energy and courage of those men who, before that law, were regarded as scarcely human. They are defending, not only the authority of the Republic against its external and internal enemies, but fight successfully as well to defend the rights that have been granted them. . . . The colored, provided that they have Delegates at their head who respect their rights, will defend the territory. . . ." Even more, he insisted, it would be necessary to enfranchise the slaves: "We have only one means to preserve our colonies and keep them out of the hands of our enemies (or our friends), and that is to let the Revolution of Color run its course. It is too far advanced for us to stop, and all the forces which we may send to St. Domingue to support a mixed and impracticable system will be consumed by this volcano, just as all those we have sent."[13]

Genêt's concerns about the purported plot led him to make some rather bizarre demands of the American government, ones which only succeeded in convincing Jefferson that the Frenchman little understood the concept of or limits to sovereign jurisdiction. First, Genêt asked—in excited language that must have tried Jefferson's patience in itself—that the Americans arrest General Galbaud for plotting against France:

I have just discovered the most horrible conspiracy which has been formed against the arms of the French republic; I have just discovered the whole clue and all the proofs of the infernal plot which, for these two months, detained the whole French fleet in your ports in a state of nullity, of that plot which threatened, not only the safety of our vessels, but also of our colonial possessions. The traitors Galbaud and Tanguy, and several other villains, not satisfied with having caused, at St. Domingue, the spilling of the blood of an immense number of people . . . concerted here, at Baltimore and at Philadelphia, the project of bringing our forces to concur with them in the execrable project meditated by these men, whose crimes have forced them to flee their country, to return to St. Domingue for the purpose of renewing there the horrors and misfortunes which they have already committed in that place.[14]

Genêt had already warned Jefferson of this supposed plot, on the basis of which the cabinet had decided, back in August, to request the governor of Maryland to block any military expedition. But, as the secretary of state patiently explained to the hyperactive Frenchman, the U.S. government would not, and indeed could not, arrest a Frenchman for plotting against his own government.

Undaunted, Genêt called on Jefferson again, proposing this time that the United States allow him to effectively control American shipping to St. Domingo. He demanded that the Americans ban all voyages to the island that did not have his written permission. Jefferson, in his reply, admitted the possibility that American ships might have carried arms to rebels in St. Domingo, but insisted that the obligation of stopping trade in contraband lay on the belligerent power, not the neutral one. In an exasperated tone, he concluded that "it would be unnecessary to enumerate the objections to which [the proposal] would be liable."[15]

Genêt, as autumn rolled around, knew that he was likely to be recalled. Moreover, he had finally realized that he could no longer count on Jefferson to help defend his version of French interests in the cabinet. He recognized he had lost Jefferson's confidence, but typically he took none of the blame. His analysis, for all that, was not too far off. He saw in Jefferson a political ambition that had made him passive in pushing the losing cause of Jacobin France, and observed as well that Jefferson and his Virginians had been shaken by the fact that "the St. Domingue revolution has spread fear among all slaveholders."[16]

France, Genêt believed, could no longer hope for any favorable action from the administration. President Washington, he felt, was a closet royalist, and overly influenced by the anti-French faction headed by Hamilton. Genêt's reaction to this situation was typical: he became still more active. In an effort to influence the upcoming session of Congress into a more pro-French line, he began to place articles in the newspapers, seeking to reach over the administration's head directly to the American people, whom he still considered to be more pro-French than their government.

It no longer mattered. The new French government had already decided to replace Genêt. The Ministry of Foreign Affairs had taken him severely to task back in July, accusing him of trying to exercise proconsular powers and acting with "indiscrete enthusiasm." But now, faced with the American request for the envoy's recall, the ministry pulled its punch in its recommendation to the Committee of Public Safety. In a half-hearted defense of the envoy, it suggested that "some opponents, more familiar with the true nature of the American people than Citizen Genêt, purposely surrounded him with a false popularity in order to make him appear disagreeable to the United States Government. This Minister was too enthusiastic, badly advised, and carried away by his reception. . . ."[17] The Committee of Public Safety, however, was not so lenient. Robespierre called Genêt a traitor, and in November named a commission of four, headed by Jean Antoine Joseph Fauchet, to replace him in function— and arrest him in person—upon their arrival in the United States.

At the beginning of 1794, President Washington informed Congress that Genêt's conduct had been "unequivocally disapproved,"[18] and that his recall was expected shortly. To add to Genêt's woes, the Congress, in which he had placed so much hope, had turned out to be no more pro-French than the administration. Moreover, Jefferson, worn out by his often losing battles with the Hamilton faction, had resigned and returned to an ostensibly private life at Monticello.

Genêt's brief mission was effectively over, although he continued to defend himself to Paris and insist that he would "fight to the death."[19] Finally replaced in February, he would marry Cornelia Clinton, daughter of the governor of New York, be defended against his successors' attempt to arrest him by the very U.S. government that he had so vexed, and finish his days in America. But the legacy of his mission, conjoined as it was with the exodus of the refugees from St. Domingo, would affect U.S.-French and U.S.-Haitian relations for years.

TROUBLE WITH BRITAIN

The stormy march of Citizen Genêt across the American political scene had blown the Gironde government's hopes for a treaty of alliance well off the diplomatic highway. Genêt's aspiration of mobilizing broad American sympathy for French policy had fared no better. His enthusiasm, most certainly, had energized the pro-French groups, provided them with a mission, and expanded their rolls. But that was not success. The very activism of France's friends, and the outrageousness of Genêt's defiance of the administration had, instead, spurred on those whose interests or sympathies lay with Great Britain. People were taking sides. The arrival of the unfortunate refugees from St. Domingo had simply fed the fires of controversy. Bringing with them all the furor of the French revolutionary struggle, along with a shadowy menace of slave revolts, the refugees posed a daily reminder of the dangers of involvement in Europe's quarrels.

But official neutrality could not stop the growth of partisanship, and Europe's divisions had come to roost in America.

The European war, and Genêt's antics, had only added a new set of issues to the increasingly nasty struggle between the Hamilton and Jefferson groups, the nascent Federalist and Democratic-Republican parties. Already divided fundamentally over the nature and role of their new government, the founding fathers now had to cope as well with the passions and issues raised by the European war. President

Washington's effort to avoid compromising the country's official neutrality had been designed to keep Americans from getting implicated in the actual hostilities. But few Americans could remain neutral in thought or argument. Public debate sharpened, and pointed toward a polarization of party politics.

Surprisingly, considering the furor over the Genêt mission, American public opinion took a decidedly anti-British turn at the beginning of 1794. The French could take little credit for this change in direction, however. True, the sharp edges had been taken off American-French relations by the arrival of Genêt's successor in February. Joseph Fauchet had much more modest instructions that those of his predecessor. His goal was still to seek a new a treaty, but his specific objectives were limited: to obtain supplies and aid for the French in the West Indies and to seek France's rights under the 1778 treaty. Received by the new Secretary of State Edmund Randolph and then by President Washington, Fauchet virtually disowned much of what Genêt had done, disclosing that he would disarm the controversial French privateers and stop the filibustering expedition against Spanish New Orleans. Within days, he had placed announcements in the papers that made the new, less assertive French policy clear to all. The announcements warned that "Every Frenchman is forbidden to violate the Neutrality of the United States. All commissions or authorizations tending to infringe that Neutrality are revoked, and are to be returned to the agent of the French Republic."[1]

Moreover, Fauchet wanted to buy $1 million worth of American supplies for the French forces that still held on in St. Domingo. With this businesslike kind of proposal and his fresh new approach, Fauchet was assured a cordial reception. Relations would have been on the mend even had there been no crisis with the British.

Britain's problems were of her own making. Her war plan had been to seek naval supremacy in the West Indies, both to retain her valuable position there and to squeeze France hard where she was highly vulnerable. However, by opening her ports in St. Domingo and elsewhere to American ships—neutral ships that could carry the French trade without limit as long as they carried no contraband—France had so far managed to sidestep Britain's effort to throttle the French colonies. But by late autumn, the government of William Pitt had decided to retaliate, and to close off this American end-run. Orders in Council were issued in November that would allow the seizure of all neutral ships carrying goods to or from the French West Indies, and confiscation of the cargoes. The Orders were highly controversial. Not only were they contrary to international practice in that they rejected neutral rights to carry peaceful cargo, but they were also put into effect without warning. Hundreds of American ships were already at sea when the orders were suddenly issued.

Within weeks, the British Navy had pounced on over 250 unsuspecting American vessels and sailed them off as prizes—all for contravening a rule that their unlucky captains had never heard of. To boot, the short-handed Royal Navy had begun impressing seamen from American ships, claiming (sometimes accurately, admittedly) that they were British deserters. When the news of these high-handed British actions reached American ports, a wave of public indignation and anti-British feeling arose that soon erased all of France's remaining embarrassment over the Genêt affair.

By the turn of the year, the British had backtracked somewhat, applying their interdiction only to ships carrying contraband. But the damage had already been done. The circumstances of the earlier seizures had convinced American merchants that Britain wanted to bend America to its will, and that Royal Navy officers were simply hungry for the prize money that sailors of the day won by successful confiscations, and thus were ready to define and seize contraband as it pleased themselves. As anger in the maritime cities increased, it combined with other, more longstanding American grievances about British practices on the western border. There, the British were still refusing to evacuate their military posts in the Northwest Territories, in spite of a commitment to do so in the 1783 peace treaty. The British, of course, had reason to complain that the United States had not lived up to all its commitments either, and in a normal, peacetime atmosphere the resulting stalemate might have been allowed to continue. But the war had lent new urgency to the situation. Americans feared that the British might be hanging on in the territories in order to destabilize the West, which was already plagued by suspicious Indian troubles. An anti-British consensus soon developed. With westerners and easterners, settlers and merchants, all equally angry at Albion, and the papers whipping up war fever, the administration found itself obliged to act.

A military response was out of the question, yet diplomacy alone was seen as insufficient. Trade policy seemed to be the only way to influence Britain. Congress had long clamored for a debate on U.S. trade policy, but Jefferson, who long before had been tasked to prepare a report on the subject, had put off releasing it because, presumably, he knew that the debate would line up the proponents of Britain and France on opposite sides. Now the administration was obliged to present the report, even though Jefferson was no longer in office to defend it. The report, when it emerged, was roundly attacked. Jefferson had tried to belittle the importance of the trade with Great Britain by inflating the importance of American trade with St. Domingo and the other French colonies. In the House of Representatives, debate was heated, yet it remained inconclusive.

Eventually, congressional sentiment moved toward the idea of an embargo against England. The idea behind the embargo was to demonstrate to the British, by depriving them and the British West Indies of vital American goods, that they needed to take the American grievances seriously. Yet the requirements of neutrality, not to mention domestic politics, dictated that Britain not be singled out—after all, the French were seizing and confiscating American ships as well. In the end, Congress passed a largely toothless thirty-day general embargo in late March, designed as a demonstration to the warring parties of the importance of America's trade and traders. It lingered on until late May, without any evident effect on America's trading partners, or on their policies.

The congressional debate on trade, and the weakness of the embargo action, had at least shown to the lawmakers the weakness of America's options for meaningful action. Satisfaction, if any, would have to be gained from the British by negotiation. Hamilton and the Federalists had been urging this course all along; they were horrified that trade sanctions or a serious embargo against Britain might do long-term harm to the bilateral trade, on which the collection of duties and the whole federal financial structure depended. By April, the Senate had agreed to negotiations and confirmed Washington's nominee for negotiator, John Jay, Chief Justice of the U.S. Supreme Court.

The embargo, and the decision to negotiate, had been successful in calming the anti-British agitation. And in buying some time. With trans-Atlantic negotiations in the days of sail being as slow as they were, it would be months before there would be results. In the meantime British—and French—harassment of American shipping had subsided to routine levels.

Jay traveled to London with a long list of American demands concerning maritime and trade issues, as well as the removal of British troops from the West. He was also under one major negotiating constraint: he was instructed to do nothing that deprived France of its rights under the 1778 treaty. Jay however suffered from a political handicap: his intentions were suspected in the South and West, where his readiness to sell out the interests of "the inhabitants of the western waters" in 1786 was remembered with anger.[2] So, in order to balance the Jay mission somewhat (both in terms of domestic and international politics), Washington also nominated a new envoy to France: James Monroe from Virginia, a political confidant of Jefferson's who was favorably known in the South and West, and also a friend of France.

Minister Fauchet, all in all, was pleased with the way things were developing, and reported reassuringly to Paris that the Jay mission was designed just to resolve some routine problems. He would be proven very wrong.

Paris, in any event, had other problems to deal with. By the end of 1793, French armies had suffered defeat after defeat, and the loss of nationalist momentum had allowed revolts to spring up throughout the provinces. The country was torn by bloody faction and revolt. Commissioners sent to the provinces by the National Convention quite often spread as much terror and death as the counterrevolutionaries and rebels whom they had been sent to rein in. In Paris, the Committee of Public Safety itself was divided, nobody's position was secure, and politics had become a game of extremes.

As the Reign of Terror gripped the country and paralyzed normal policy debate, political measures became more and more radical. God was legally abolished, the Gregorian calendar scrapped, everything smacking of the old order made suspect, if not banned. The leading Girondists were let out of jail only to be executed, and other prominent revolutionaries would follow them to the guillotine, or be assassinated in the daily turmoil of politics. Jacobin revolutionary fervor, personified by the coldly rational yet horrifying Robespierre, had come to shape the country's image, as an increasingly uneasy external world watched the revolution go out of control.

While Minister Fauchet, in Philadelphia, was deliberately downplaying the revolutionary component of French policy so as not to alarm his socially conservative American interlocutors, Commissioner Sonthonax in St. Domingo had continued to play the Jacobin firebrand.

Sonthonax's victory over General Galbaud had turned out to be largely hollow. Cap François was in ruins. Unleashing the black insurgents had driven out Galbaud and the supposed counterrevolutionaries, but also many solid citizens, as well as most of the French troops whose muscle had allowed the commissioners to exercise such authority as they had. Moreover, Sonthonax's rash step of promising freedom to those blacks who fought with him in June had severely damaged his alliance with the mulatto leaders. As racist in their way as the white planters, they had been horrified by the unleashing of the blacks, and were determined not to share power with them. Sonthonax desperately needed to find a new power base, and characteristically he took a still more radical step. He turned for support to the ex-slaves.

In late August, Sonthonax—without instructions from Paris—declared slavery abolished in St. Domingo. The immediate effect of his decree, however, was less than electrifying on the local scene. Over much of the island, the commissioners had no real authority, and the decree was ignored in practice. Even in the north the decree brought relatively few insurgents to the commissioners' banner. The major groups under Jean François, Biassou, and the rising commander Toussaint (who was a devout Catholic) looked with suspicion at what they saw as a revolutionary, regicide commissioner and his efforts to recruit them. Cautiously, they continued to occupy most of the Plaine and the surrounding areas, in the name of the Spanish monarchy that was paying and supplying them. As a result Sonthonax was, for the moment, little more than mayor of the burnt-out ruin of Cap François.

In much of the southern and western provinces, André Rigaud continued to govern in the name of France, and as a nominal ally of the commissioners. Actual French control over the area, however, was virtually nonexistent, and Rigaud's appetite for autonomy and more territory was growing.

But the real threat to French rule came from the French planters themselves. Determined at all costs to stop the contagion of a revolution that had led to the slave revolt in the north, mulatto rule in the south, and now emancipation of the slaves, many of them were ready to seek the security offered by a British protectorate. The collapse of French colonial rule in the north, it seemed, made it all but imperative. What was not overtly mentioned, but a powerful motivator to the planters, was the fact that the British government (which had been flirting with an abolitionist policy just a year earlier) had veered back in wartime to defending the rights of slaveholders.

First to actually sign the Propositions were the coffee planters of the Grande Anse, an area at the far end of the southern peninsula that had always had close contacts with neighboring Jamaica. British troops landed there in the fall of 1793, and before long planters throughout St. Domingo were offering to sign the Propositions. British rule seemed preferable to them over that of their mother country, particularly after news reached the island of a new, and earthshaking, decree passed in France. There, in February 1794, having been upstaged to some degree by Sonthonax's sending of black and mulatto delegates to Paris to personify his daring abolition decree, and impelled even more by the revolutionary rhetoric of equality and universal rights, the National Convention abolished slavery in all French territory. For most of the colonial planters, this emancipation decree broke the last thread that tied them to revolutionary France.

Aided by the disarray in French ranks, the English occupation of St. Domingo expanded opportunistically. The occupation, however, was a patchwork thing. To begin with, Rigaud was not to be pushed aside, and he defended his southern territory tenaciously. But by late spring the British had bypassed Rigaud's area to occupy Port au Prince and much of the coastal areas of the Western Province, where the planters preferred to sign the Propositions rather than face a Spanish takeover and a more liberal policy toward slavery. The British also occupied the bastion of Môle St. Nicolas, at the end of the northern peninsula, a strong point from which they could control the straits to Cuba. And then the British advance slowed to a stop.

The causes were several. For one, the British were not at all gracious occupiers, and there was backlash against their rule, one that would eventually culminate in a series of revolts. Rigaud held fast in his territory, a hard nut to crack and a barrier to expansion. But more importantly, the French military commander at Cap François, the capable and energetic General Etienne Laveaux, had begun to mount a counteroffensive. While his hastily assembled troops had some success against the British and Spanish occupiers, his major coup was political. He simply recruited the most effective of the insurgent generals away from the Spanish.

In May, the dynamic and successful Toussaint, along with almost five thousand disciplined fighters, rallied to the tricolor. Toussaint had come to see that service with the Spaniards was a dead end, both professionally (he did not lack ambition) and politically, since the Spaniards and their British allies did not favor large-scale emancipation. News of the French government's abolition decree, it seems, convinced Toussaint that he could best serve his fellow blacks by serving revolutionary France. Finally succumbing to Laveaux's repeated blandishments, he came over with two of his colleagues, Dessalines and Christophe, and a ferocious energy. Quick strikes against both Spanish and British occupying forces soon gave him control of the vital Artibonite valley in the Western Province. From then on, he would be a constant thorn in the occupiers' side.

The British occupiers were, in addition, being let down by their own superiors. The war cabinet had been obliged to rearrange priorities for forces in the area, and the St. Domingo expedition was downgraded. It was decided that Guadeloupe and Martinique, where the fight against the French was most intense, would absorb the major share of any new resources. In addition, the overtaxed Royal Navy was finding it harder to support the troops occupying St. Domingo. Supplies began to arrive erratically if at all. The main problem, however, was replacements, since disease had already begun to lower the effectiveness, indeed the numbers, of the occupying troops. It seemed that one of Citizen Genêt's predictions about St. Domingo, at least, was coming true: that foreign troops sent to the island risked being "consumed by this volcano."

American merchants were making good money from the four-sided war in St. Domingo. Each of the warring parties badly needed food, ammunition, uniforms, guns, and other supplies, all of which America had to sell. The war had caused a drop in the volume of trade, but prices had risen to compensate. In addition, the island's products had become so valuable that a small return cargo could create fabulous profits. The risks were large, since each warring party would try to stop American trade with its enemies, but the potential gains were too attractive to ignore. American skippers, in any event, were most enterprising at avoiding or confounding blockades or trade restrictions. The safest trade, of course, was with the British-controlled ports, since it was protected to a good degree by the Royal Navy; American newspapers carried frequent reports of which ports were under British control, and what the local market conditions were. But American skippers took their goods to whichever port they could, or wherever the market was most needy. Many ships were lost to the warring navies or privateers (146 confiscated American ships were for sale in Martinique alone[3]), but that did not deter. The civil war and occupation of the island was, for Americans, good for business.

Many other Americans, on the other hand, viewed the war and the dizzying progression of events in France and St. Domingo with anxiety and fear. The French revolution, they felt, had spilled entirely out of control. Genêt's mission had already sensitized many Americans to the possible disruptive effects of French radicalism; "Jacobin" had become a virtual epithet as a result. Now, the Terror had greatly inflated those anxieties. Regicide, violent social upheaval, official atheism, political murder, export of revolutionary subversion, all of those were practices so alien to the American political consensus as to be abhorred. The Whiskey Rebellion in Pennsylvania, which seemed for a short time in 1794 to threaten social order, property rights, and government authority, had only added to the anxieties about the revolutionary ideas coming from France and its colonies. The situation in St. Domingo, so close and such an active trading partner, began to be a source of apprehension. Looking at the island's civil war, its slave revolt, the continuous atrocities, and now abolition, many Americans began to fear that it might become a springboard for radical activities in the United States.

"Friends of Order," the growing Federalist party members had begun to call themselves, as a sort of shorthand for an antirevolutionary, anti-French position. It was a clever title; it made their Democratic-Republican opponents seem to be friends of disorder. Events, indeed, had thrown the republican friends of France somewhat on the defensive. They could scarcely justify the bloody and fratricidal course that the French revolution had recently taken, and championing the basic ideals and values of the revolution was no longer convincing, given the dangerous chaos that had been unleashed in France and St. Domingo. As a result the republicans, deprived to some degree of the progressive rhetoric that formed part of their traditional platform, had to fall back into open Anglophobia, or attacking the Federalists as incipient oligarchs and pseudo-monarchists.

On one element of the debate, however, the two sides' positions were curiously reversed. When it came to looking at what the French revolution had produced in St. Domingo, it was the Republicans who were more worried than the Federalists. More heavily represented in the southern states and numbering many plantation owners in their leadership, the Republicans were highly vulnerable to any spillover of revolutionary French egalitarianism into the large slave population of their home states. The Federalists, on the other hand, more heavily centered in the North and with many abolitionists in their ranks, could look at the potential threat from St. Domingo with a greater sense of detachment.

Concern about possible effects of the St. Domingo situation had been growing since the slave revolt in 1791. South Carolina governor Thomas Pinckney's answer to the appeal for aid from the

St. Domingo assembly at that time had been explicit: "when we recollect how nearly similar the situation of the Southern States and St. Domingo are in the possession of slaves, and that a day may arrive when they may be exposed to the same insurrections, we cannot but sensibly feel for your situation. . . ." Pinckney, a Federalist, had also been clear that he saw the threat as a law and order issue. In informing the House of Representatives of his correspondence with the St. Domingo representatives, he noted that "while we sympathize with our Friends and lament their sufferings, they very thoroughly prove the Policy of having our Militia always in a situation to act with promptness and Effect as Circumstances may require. . . ."[4]

Fear that the St. Domingo example would prove contagious spread throughout the American South during the following summers. Rumors of slave plots spread in Virginia and other states; alleged conspiracies were unearthed in Norfolk, Petersburg, and Northampton, York, and Powhattan counties. And even though the actual number of violent master-slave incidents turned out to be normal, and none of them had any apparent French or West Indies inspiration,[5] the fear was firmly planted and rumors persisted of "frenchness" among the slaves. South Carolina, with its tropical-product plantations and heavy dependence on slave labor, was the first state to try to insulate itself from the contagion, banning the importation of French slaves in 1792. Virginia, with a less oppressive slaveholding system and an actual surplus of slaves, had already banned any imports. The other southern states moved over the course of the next decade to ban the import of any slaves from the dangerous West Indies, hoping to stop the infiltration of provocateurs or agitators among their slave populations.

It was the arrival of the 1793 refugees from Cap François, however, that most dramatically broadened the fear of Jacobin contagion. Americans were aghast at the destruction of lives, property, and commerce that had taken place in the quondam Pearl of the Antilles; the American people's respect for property and industry had been deeply offended. And even though Federalists and Republicans differed in ascribing causes for the disaster, they were united in their determination that no such collapse of public order should ever occur in the United States. (It is no surprise, in this light, that the outbreak of the Whiskey Rebellion in western Pennsylvania, just a year later, caused so much anxiety.)

The refugees, constant reminders of the excesses of the French revolution, posed a political problem as well as a humanitarian one. Their raucous internecine feuds influenced the general political debate—law and order versus liberty—and contributed to the widening split between Federalists and Republicans. But it was the presence of the thousands of French blacks, slaves and freemen, that gave the greatest cause for anxiety. None could be presumed to be free of contagious ideas about emancipation and liberty; each one was, in the eyes of Americans, a potential conspirator.

In Virginia that summer, reports began to flow in to the governor's office concerning alleged subversive contacts of the black refugees with the local slave population, and a French hand was suspected in any disturbance, whether or not a connection to France or St. Domingo could be shown.[6] Virginia's lieutenant governor warned his counterpart in South Carolina about possible repercussions of an alleged slave conspiracy discovered in the Old Dominion.[7] In Charleston, the arrival of a new shipload of refugees, white and black, led to demands that they be denied admittance as security risks, while the press reported that "the negroes have become very insolent, in so much that the citizens are alarmed and the militia kept a constant guard. It is said that the St. Domingo negroes have sown those seeds of revolt."[8]

Throughout the South, St. Domingo had become more than a political metaphor; it was a vivid symbol of anarchy, destruction, and revolutionary subversion.

French policy fed the fear of contagion from St. Domingo. The dynamic of the revolution, and the incessant power struggle in Paris, had led to the declaration of abolition. That, itself, was cause for the most grave concern among America's southern planters. Now, the dynamic of the war was pushing the French government to use its abolition decree as a weapon against the country's enemies. Emancipation, proponents of the action had argued in the National Convention, would enable France to raise a powerful Caribbean force against Britain. The idea was to destabilize the British in their sugar colonies by promoting unrest among the slaves. "The plan is to enfranchise all the negroes in the French colonies. Then, with these first freedmen, to bring about the enfranchisement of all the foreign colonies, and thus to carry revolt and independence throughout the new World—a thing which, according to its authors, will give them supremacy over all the Powers of Europe."[9]

While the plan never became official French policy, there was enough truth in it to implant it firmly in the American popular imagination. The Dominican planter-refugees, happy to heighten American loathing of the revolution, most likely helped feed the rumors that the French government was following a policy of Jacobin subversion in the Western Hemisphere. The rumor inevitably prompted political action. The governor of South Carolina, for example, received this rather ambiguous, but nonetheless rumor-reinforcing warning from the U.S. secretary of state in Philadelphia: "It is my duty to communicate to you a piece of information, though I cannot say I have confidence in it myself. A French gentleman, one of the refugees from St. Domingo, informs me that two Frenchmen, from St. Domingo also . . . are about setting out from this place for Charleston with a design to incite an insurrection among the negroes. He says that this is a part of a general plan formed by the Brissotin [Girondist] party at Paris, the first branch of which has been carried into execution at St. Domingo."[10]

America's fear and revulsion, however, did not constitute a policy. St. Domingo was, in the eyes of the Washington administration, still a part of France in revolt; its revolution was dangerous to American interests, and its effects were to be contained as much as possible. But no specific measures were taken to control trade with any part of the island, and the British occupation was officially ignored. The government's inaction extended to a hands-off attitude toward Fauchet's efforts to stop the return of those refugees (traitors, he considered them) who wanted to regain their properties in the British-controlled areas of the island. Fauchet and his fellow commissioners continued to buy supplies and send them to the French authorities at Cap François, and to push for an American advance of funds (which Hamilton was resisting).

Fauchet, in fact, remained steadfastly upbeat in reporting to Paris on events in St. Domingo, predicting in September that "the colonies, the conquest of which made the British and the émigrés who accompanied them so proud, will soon become their tombs. . . ." He had also written to General Laveaux at Cap François, whom he urged on with appropriate revolutionary zeal, as follows: "May all the miserable quarrels of pride and passion and humanity that have devoured St. Domingue not trouble you; as friends of liberty nothing should disunite us: prejudices of color, rank and distinction, none of that exists any more; we are all free, children of the same country, with the same enemies to fight and the same causes to defend. . . ."[11]

Fauchet would eventually be proven right on one count: the British occupation would not fare well. Laveaux and Toussaint had formed a good working relationship, and had made strides in pushing back the occupiers. Rigaud, too, continued to harass the British and foment rebellions behind their lines. Moreover, Commissioner Sonthonax had been recalled to France in apparent disgrace; he would no longer keep St. Domingo in an uproar. The French position on the island was indeed stabilizing. As, in fact, was the situation in the mother country.

In Paris, the Terror was subsiding. Robespierre himself was caught in the fratricidal whirlpool, and executed at the end of July.

(Monroe, reporting from the French capital, commented that he had "merited his fate.") The Paris Commune and the Jacobin clubs, those engines of revolution, were finished politically. And French armies, once again, had begun to win victories in Europe. By spring of 1795, both Prussia and Spain had withdrawn from the war, and moreover Spain had ceded its half of Hispaniola to the French through the Treaty of Basle. Although it remained for the French still to actually wrest that new possession from the Spanish colonial authorities in Santo Domingo and their insurgent black allies, the strategic situation on the island had drastically changed. It appeared as if the French might be in a position to seize the initiative and regain their troubled colony.

Jefferson did not share Fauchet's optimism about the long-term prospects for France's colony. Ever since the French collapse at Cap François, he had feared that French rule on the island would end, indeed that European rule of all the West Indies was doomed. Writing to Monroe shortly after hearing news of the disaster, he had confided, "I become daily more & more convinced that all the West India Islands will remain in the hands of the people of colour, & a total expulsion of the whites sooner or later take place. It is high time we should foresee the bloody scenes which our children certainly, and possibly ourselves (south of Potommac,) have to wade through, & try to avert them." In another private letter of the same day, he was slightly less gloomy as to the domestic consequences: "it cannot be doubted but that sooner or later all the whites will be expelled from all the West Indian Islands. What is to take place in our southern states will depend on the timely wisdom and liberality of their legislatures."[12]

Jefferson's concern about the viability of slavery in the United States, after its apparent overthrow in St. Domingo, was much more than an idle thought born of fear. He recognized that slavery was a moral as well as a political issue, one that required resolution. He had even conceived a possible remedy to the South's slavery dilemma: education, emancipation, and deportation of the potentially unruly slave population to the West or even (an idea he toyed with later) to St. Domingo. But he knew it was an explosive issue and very dangerous politically; he hated confrontation, and as a result he never tested these ideas in action. Now, he was out of government and prepared, in effect, to simply react to what he saw as the inevitable spread of radical ideas—of emancipation and personal, rather than political, liberty—from St. Domingo.

By late 1794, in any event, St. Domingo was no longer at, or even near, the center of the public stage. After some six months of anxious waiting, the results of Justice Jay's negotiations were beginning to be known in Philadelphia, and had rekindled the fires of controversy. Jay, it seemed, had not been very successful. The vain and Anglophile emissary had allowed himself to be flattered, dined, and gradually won over by Foreign Minister William Grenville and London society, abandoning large parts of his instructions in the ensuing formal talks. News and innuendo from London, however, preceded Jay's official report, so that the American political scene was wracked for months by debates over partial or inaccurate news. The issues at stake were huge: whether the United States would favor one side or another in the war.

The treaty was signed in London in late November, but its text was not carried to Washington until March 1795. Even then the administration held back, releasing it neither to the expectant public nor even to the Senate, which was required to ratify. The administration's delay, in truth, was due to nothing more than indecision, but in the supercharged atmosphere it only heightened tendentious speculation and sharpened the already shrill partisan debate. The proposed treaty, which had been designed to lay to rest the war fever over British actions, had itself become a highly divisive issue in American politics even before its terms were known, and the president's policy of neutrality was as a result under attack from all sides.

TROUBLE WITH FRANCE

The ship slipped quietly out of Philadelphia's port on a cold day in December 1794, before the customs collector knew it was gone, and headed downriver toward the sea. The collector was not fooled for long, however; he had been keeping an eye on the vessel, called *Les Jumeaux,* as it was being fitted up. His suspicions had been raised when the ship's agent, a Mr. Guenet, had installed four cannon on board and loaded small arms, in addition to the usual equipment of an innocent merchantman. Now, the ship's surreptitious departure heightened the customs official's suspicion that the vessel was headed out on a voyage that would violate the nation's neutrality regulations. He quickly alerted the militia.

That evening, off Bombay Hook, the ship was intercepted by the revenue cutter *General Green,* commanded by James Montgomery, who had forty militiamen on board to enforce the government's orders. The *Jumeaux* was ordered to heave to, where it was boarded by Captain Dale of the militia, Deputy Customs Inspector Robinett, and Deputy Marshall Rothwell. They ordered the *Jumeaux's* skipper to take his vessel back to port for inspection, and he made pretense of agreeing. But as soon as the government officials were seen off, he commanded his men to put on sail, and once again headed out toward the sea. When the cutter approached to cut him off, the *Jumeaux's* skipper mustered his full ninety-five-man crew, ran out the cannons, and gave every sign of readiness to fight. An uneasy standoff developed, with the government officials unwilling to chance their lightly armed and manned cutter against the apparent determination and firepower of the *Jumeaux*. They did, however, obtain the skipper's agreement to remain at anchor overnight. Their plan, naive in retrospect, was to return in the morning with a larger force.

It was a mistake. In the night the *Jumeaux* once again slipped away, and this time the ship reached the sea unnoticed, disappearing from American jurisdiction. The customs officials had to satisfy themselves, for the moment, with prosecuting Mr. Guenet, who was fined and sent to jail. But they would not forget the incident.

Eight months later, a French privateer called the *Cassius* turned up in Philadelphia, commanded by an American, Samuel Davis. The ship was easily recognized as the old *Les Jumeaux,* and Davis as one of the passengers who had been on the ship during its questionable outgoing voyage. It turned out that the customs collector's suspicions had been justified, since the ship had sailed directly to St. Domingo. There, General Laveaux had commissioned it as a French vessel under the new name, with Davis as captain, and sent it out to harry enemy shipping. One of the ships it had captured had been an American schooner, the *William Lindsay,* which had then been condemned and sold as a prize by the St. Domingo admiralty courts.

The *Cassius* was quickly put under a court order, while the owners of the confiscated schooner sued Davis for damages. To their chagrin, the suit was dismissed when the judge ruled that only French courts had jurisdiction over a case that involved a ship caught on the high seas and taken into a French port.

The schooner's owners were not to be turned away. They then initiated action against the impounded ship in Circuit Court, on the grounds that it was a vessel illegally armed as a privateer, in violation of neutrality laws. This of course threw the case into the diplomatic arena, where it became part of a running debate over the acceptability of France's maritime seizures under America's new legislation. As the case dragged its way through the court, it was also the subject of numerous angry exchanges between the French legation and the State Department. In the end, the court issued a ruling that pleased no one. The French won the legal argument when the court decided that it had no jurisdiction over what the legation claimed to be a French government ship. But the American authorities, in effect, won the day, because the ship had been kept out of action for over a year, and was no longer fit for sea.[1]

The *Cassius* case was one of many, many cases—French, British, and Spanish—that would clog the courts and the diplomatic exchanges during the European war. American mariners were, above all, enterprising. The profits that they could make during the hostilities were too good to pass up; the risk of capture by one of the belligerents became manageable. American shipping grew immensely, and successful ship owners grew prosperous. Few owners went so far as to fit out privateers in violation of the neutrality laws, but the temptation was there and the risks acceptable—Captain Davis had simply been stupid to bring the *Cassius* back to its original home port. Others were ready to take the risk of carrying contraband to one or another of the parties at war in the Indies and St. Domingo. Still others, in perfectly innocent trade, were seized under one pretext or another by the prize-hungry British or French navies, or by the swarms of privateers and even unlicensed pirates that infested the Caribbean from bases in St. Domingo and elsewhere. Their only recourse, in most cases, was to appeal to the government to add their case to the list of complaints for which reparations would eventually be sought.

Neutrality, in short, was a headache for the Washington administration to maintain and implement. Still, and in spite of the clamor from the political parties to take sides, President Washington doggedly stuck by a policy which kept the nation both out of the war and prosperous. French minister Fauchet summed it up neatly when he said, "It is easier to understand the patience with which the United States puts up with the violations of their neutrality, when one sees the extent of the trade which it allows her to carry."[2]

Justice Jay had been sent to London to damp down a superheated political debate that had threatened to lead to war with England, and his mission had mercifully bought almost a year's time for tempers to cool on that score. But, with the European war raging and American neutrality regularly put to the test by one or another of the belligerents, the respite could only be temporary. Both political parties were poised to exploit the results of the negotiation for their own benefit, and—long before the results of the negotiation were officially known—had begun to put their particular spin on the news.

French minister Fauchet, in spite of his initial optimism concerning the Jay mission, had soon become concerned that the deck was stacked against French interests. Even before Jay left for London, Fauchet reported to Paris that Washington's cabinet, with the possible exception of Edmund Randolph, were apprehensive about the spread of French revolutionary principles and were leaning toward Britain.[3] On the other hand, the people, he said (here he followed Genêt's line of thought), favored France in its struggle against the monarchies, and he hoped to be able broaden support for France among the electorate. Moreover, he advised, the newly appointed American minister in Paris, James Monroe, would be a friendly intermediary and should be cultivated.

What Fauchet did not know was that infighting within the administration had become brutal, and that the pro-British party among the Federalists had tried to undercut Monroe from the beginning of his mission. The enthusiastically republican Monroe, sad to say, made their task all the easier by his ill-considered flattery of the French regime. Reported selectively back to Washington by his opponents, his effusions raised enough questions so that Secretary of State Randolph was required to call him to order for "the extreme glow of some parts of your address." Monroe, he said, should "cultivate the French Republic with zeal, but without any unnecessary eclat. . . ."[4]

By the time the Jay mission reached its climax, the damage had already been done. Monroe had been compromised by his opponents, and he was given very little information about the London negotiation that he could pass on to the French, in spite of his repeated complaints that he needed to brief them. At the same time, Fauchet was also being offered little more than bromides by Randolph. The administration was determined to keep the French in the dark on the progress of negotiation with the British, so as to minimize the chances that they might play a spoiler role. In fact, the administration kept most Americans uninformed as well. But the French resented the treatment, and waited to get back.

The administration's hesitancy in releasing the details of the treaty, even after the text finally arrived in Philadelphia in early 1795, was not entirely due to political machinations. The fact was that Washington and his colleagues did not know exactly what to do with the misbegotten text that Justice Jay had brought home. Jay, in short, had achieved only a few of his negotiating objectives. He had, it is true, gained peace with Britain, and with it a British promise to withdraw from the northwestern forts, the establishment of joint commissions to settle border claims and pre-revolutionary debts, and some trade concessions. But he had obtained no satisfaction on American shipping rights as neutrals, on impressments, on claims for slaves removed by the British, or on other demands dear to both the maritime and farming interests. Many Americans were unhappy with the terms, and thought the treaty a sellout. The treaty had another serious flaw, since ratification would in practice—even if not in explicit language—deprive France of the relative privileges it had enjoyed under its 1778 treaty.

The treaty created a firestorm of controversy and invective. The Republicans attacked it as a sellout of American interests, a capitulation to the British, and an insult to the French alliance, while Hamilton led the Federalists in an equally spirited defense. President Washington, trying to remain above all this partisan fury, had serious problems with the treaty, which he saw as generally unsatisfactory. He delayed advising the Senate on ratification because, quite simply, he was unsure what to do. Balanced against the text's lack of merit, however, was the certainty that failure to ratify would expose the country once again to instability and war fever.

The Senate finally convened in June. A long and stormy debate ensued, punctuated with insinuations that the French minister had attempted to bribe some of the lawmakers to block ratification. If he had tried, he was unsuccessful. The votes were there to ratify the treaty, but only after certain changes were made in the articles on trade with the British West Indies. The Republicans refused to admit defeat, even after ratification was approved in the Senate, and tried (unsuccessfully) to block the treaty in the House of Representatives by withholding funds for its execution. In July, almost a year after it was signed, the president had not yet moved to exchange the articles of ratification, and the treaty was still not in force.

It would take a bit of skullduggery to assure ratification. The British obligingly supplied the mechanism, in the form of intercepted copies of correspondence between Fauchet and Secretary of State Randolph. As Randolph was the lone holdout in the president's cabinet arguing against immediate ratification, the British envoy in Washington knew what to do with his windfall. He passed the purloined file to the leading Federalist in the cabinet, Secretary of the Treasury Oliver Wolcott. Although much of the correspondence was dated, and all of it was ambiguous, there was still enough in it to make a case—however weak—that Randolph had conspired with Fauchet, and perhaps had even solicited a bribe. Wolcott seized the opportunity with relish, writing dramatically to his mentor, Hamilton, that "one month will determine the future of our country. . . . I shall take immediate measures with two of my colleagues, this very day—they are firm and honest men. We will, if possible, to use a French phrase, save our country."[5]

Walcott consulted with his even more pro-treaty colleague Timothy Pickering, the new secretary of war. They decided to show the intercepted communications to the president, hoping thereby to undercut Randolph and discredit his reservations about the treaty. Washington reacted exactly as Wolcott and Pickering wished; he began to question Randolph's previous advice, and even his probity. When Washington confronted his secretary of state with the evidence, Randolph—protesting his innocence but unable to refute the charges in the rush of events and without further evidence— resigned. The Federalists had won; there were no Republicans left in the cabinet. Soon after, the trick played out: Washington agreed to ratify the treaty.

The treaty debate had been wrenching and polarizing, in an already highly partisan atmosphere. Few were fully happy with the result. But a bad treaty, and peace with Great Britain, was seen as preferable to war. Inevitably, it was recognized, France would find fault with this American move toward its English enemy. But Paris had been struggling with the aftermath of the Terror and seemed, at the time, to be less of a threat. How strongly it would react, and what it would demand in return, remained to be seen.

Toussaint's victories over the Spanish and British occupiers had made him the colony's most successful general, and defender of the mother country's interests in St. Domingo. Toussaint, a small, wiry, and seemingly unimposing figure, had nonetheless begun to dominate the political as well as the military scene by his determination, sleepless energy, and skill at out thinking his opponents. General Laveaux, who had recognized his talents early, encouraged him to operate independently and build up the black army. Indeed, as news of the Spanish cession of Santo Domingo began to percolate through the island, more and more of the insurgents who had originally sided with the Spanish came over to Toussaint, who had adopted the highly symbolic surname of Louverture,[6] reputedly because of his ability to seize every available opening for success. Even though Biassou and Jean François continued to fight for another year, their relevance to the situation disappeared, and their eventual exile was an anticlimax.

Toussaint and Laveaux, in the meantime, kept up such pressure on the British that, by late summer of 1795, they were left holding little more than a string of coastal towns: Port au Prince, St. Marc, Jérémie, and Môle St. Nicolas. And even in their reduced enclaves, they were threatened by disease as well as by periodic plots hatched by the blacks, unhappy as they were at the reinstitution of slavery. The black army, as Sonthonax had foreseen in abolishing slavery, had become the fist of the revolution in France's prize colony.

Toussaint's position was solidified as the result of a serious miscalculation by the mulattos. Joseph Villate, the leader of the mulattos in Cap François, had come to feel that his supporters' position was threatened by the growing accord between Toussaint and Laveaux. Apparently egged on by André Rigaud from his redoubt in the south, Villate attempted a coup. In March of 1796, he and his followers rose to arms and arrested General Laveaux. But the crisis blew over as quickly as it had arisen, thanks to the forceful action of Toussaint, who issued an ultimatum. Either Laveaux would be released, he threatened, or the black armies would be unleashed once again upon the city. Villate's rebellion rapidly collapsed, and in fact backfired; the mulattos were finished as a political force outside of Rigaud's enclave. A grateful General Laveaux returned to his office a free man, and soon after formalized what was already evident: he appointed Toussaint lieutenant governor of the island.

A few months later, Commissioner Sonthonax reappeared on the island with still another group of commissioners from France. Somewhat surprisingly, he had been fully exonerated by the new and more conservative rulers in Paris, who had been convinced by his vigorous attacks on his accusers. The planters, he had charged, were reactionary "aristocrats of the skin," and his radical measure had been necessary to save the revolution on the island. Sonthonax's return was a joyous affair for the ex-slaves who, two years earlier, had been freed by his abolition decree. Riding this tide of popular acclaim, he tried to regain his leadership position by launching an investigation into the Villate rebellion, using it to turn sentiment against the mulattos. The effort was botched, however, and only succeeded in sparking more massacres in the south and strengthening Rigaud in his mulatto-governed area. The audacious young commissioner was frustrated. He no longer had any good cards to play. The military campaign against the British had taken the spotlight away from his political maneuverings, and Toussaint had come to rival him in the affection of the black islanders. The two leaders were bound to clash.

In this awkward situation, Toussaint proved to be a better politician than Sonthonax. One of the pieces of news that Sonthonax had brought back from France was that the new national legislature, the Council of Five Hundred, wanted to have two representatives from St. Domingue on its rolls. Toussaint, in short order, manipulated the elections that were held to fill those two posts, and saw to it that Laveaux and Sonthonax—neither of whom had actually requested the honor—were chosen. Laveaux, it turned out, was ready to go. He saw, correctly, that the military situation had improved markedly and that Toussaint was fully capable of prosecuting the remaining campaigns against the British successfully. He was happy at the opportunity to go home, and did so. Sonthonax, however, did not.

Sonthonax and Toussaint, beyond their rivalry for power, differed on many of the issues facing the colony. Both were adept at manipulation, but Sonthonax was much more ready to espouse dramatic and confrontational actions. Both wished to establish a system of contractual labor to replace the slave system, for example, but Toussaint was prepared to allow the return of some of the colony's old plantation managers and even owners, in the interests of productivity. Sonthonax opposed, arguing that anybody who had owned slaves could not be trusted, and should be driven away or eliminated. Similarly, Toussaint was prepared to make use of the American traders who supplied the colony, both for the goods they brought and for the external political support they might muster.

Sonthonax, to the contrary, considered the Americans—who were, of course, also supplying the British—to be opportunists who had no claim to protection and could be taken advantage of wherever possible. In consequence, he commissioned privateers freely, and in late 1796 authorized them to seize any American ships trading with British ports and to confiscate the cargoes. Soon, a rash of near-piratical attacks on American ships began to discourage the flow of vital American supplies to the colony. Eventually, this reckless policy would lead to a serious problem with the United States.

Over time, Toussaint wore Sonthonax down. Sonthonax and his fellow commissioners had only a short, eighteen-month mandate. He had achieved very little, and had seen his field of maneuver on the island, as well as his popularity, dwindle. After the departure of General Laveaux, Toussaint controlled most of the levers of power. Moreover, the increasingly conservative government in Paris was beginning to criticize Sonthonax, and his political back was no longer secure. In the summer of 1797, he finally agreed to return to France and take up his seat in the Council of Five Hundred.

Sonthonax's departure left Toussaint, for the moment, as the leading French official on the island. Rigaud, Sonthonax's choice as deputy in the south, was nominally Toussaint's co-equal, but his actual writ only ran to the borders of his enclave. The remaining commissioners were nonentities, their mandate about to expire. The British were frozen in their coastal towns, the Spanish driven back into Santo Domingo (and in power there only until someone chose to take it over in the name of France). Throughout the rest of the island, Toussaint was the de facto ruler. The little coachman from Breda plantation had come a long way.

Unfortunately for St. Domingo, it was out of step with the mother country. The colony's bloody history since 1790 had provided it at least with one distinction: it had come to exemplify the victory of revolutionary ideals, the Rights of Man, and abolition. But in mainland

France, the times had changed, and the government had begun to turn away from revolution.

The end of the Terror had ushered in the Thermidorian response, a period of reconsolidation and even reaction. The surviving Girondists were readmitted to the assembly, the Jacobin clubs and the Paris Commune were stripped of power, and the business interests that had been silenced during the Terror began to regain their voice as the government struggled to resolve its financial crisis. A new constitution (the revolution's third) produced not only the new legislature or Council of Five Hundred, but a new hydra-headed executive called the Directory.

By autumn of 1795, all internal insurrections had been put down, the domestic situation was stable, and the Directory, brimming with confidence, decided to take the offensive in the European war. Armies were sent into the Rhineland, and the young and ambitious general who had restored order in Paris with his "whiff of grapeshot," Napoleon Bonaparte, was sent to drive the Austrians out of Italy.

It was not long before the Directory's new and more assertive stance had an impact on its relations with the United States, as well as with the troubled St. Domingo colony.

The French had been watching the debate over the Jay treaty with great interest and no little exasperation, fueled by Fauchet's bitter reporting from Philadelphia. Fauchet had voiced numerous complaints about America's neutrality policy, which, he claimed, violated France's treaty rights in a number of ways: not allowing French privateers to bring prizes in for adjudication, refusing to give French consuls jurisdiction over the French community in the United States, preventing French consuls from arresting French deserters, and more. But most of all Fauchet accused the administration of insincerity toward France in its handling of the Jay treaty negotiations. As he saw it, both he and Monroe in Paris were being deliberately kept in the dark, and President Washington and the pro-treaty, pro-British group had in effect decided not to listen to France's views: "Everything proves, in fact, that hatred as much as the consciousness of weakness guided the American administration's conduct toward us. General Washington ceased to view our republic with a fair eye as soon as he saw Lafayette and the King struck. . . . All the individuals who composed his council, excepting Mr. Jefferson, all who had the right by their reputations and former services to influence his conduct through their correspondence, all were united against us and strengthened him in his hostile intentions. . . . Mr. Hamilton was the soul of this enmity."[7]

The Directory had, as a first step, decided to replace Fauchet with a still more assertive envoy, Pierre-Auguste Adet. Adet arrived in June 1795, just as the Senate was getting into the treaty ratification debate, and immediately tried to block approval though some energetic, controversial, and ultimately unsuccessful lobbying. His introduction to America was further embittered by a controversy surrounding Fauchet's departure. One of the British warships that constantly patrolled the American coasts had intercepted a packet boat, in American waters, on which the departing French minister had been traveling a few days earlier. Since the British had clearly acted with good intelligence, and with the obvious intent of seizing Fauchet and his official papers, Adet angrily accused the administration of virtual complicity in this infringement of American neutrality.

It was not, all in all, a good beginning to Adet's mission.

In Paris, Monroe, who sincerely wanted to stop the decline in Franco-American relations, was facing increasing difficulties. The French told Monroe that they considered ratification of the Jay Treaty in late 1795 to have effectively annulled the 1778 Franco-American treaty of alliance, and that they intended to send a special mission to Philadelphia to remonstrate with the U.S. government. Monroe, realizing that such a mission would most likely simply add to the anti-French sentiment at home, was able to convince the French to drop the idea. However, he had no arguments to quiet

French anger over the treaty, and could only offer bland assurances that the treaty would not harm their interests.[8]

Monroe, in fact, was being set up to fail by his own superiors in the cabinet, now solidly Federalist. The arch-Federalist Pickering, after having contributed to the downfall of Randolph, had surprisingly replaced him as secretary of state. Knowing he had been Washington's seventh choice, he had at first shown appropriate humility by questioning his qualifications for the job.[9] But the ambitious Pickering did not hold out for long. A man of Manichean views and strong partisanship, he would use the powers of his new job for political purposes, and one of his first objectives was to destroy the influence of the Republican and pro-French Monroe. It was not hard to prejudice Washington against Monroe; after all, even Randolph had been obliged to curb the envoy's republican zeal. Pickering, once in office, was able to get the president's approval for additional criticisms of Monroe's job performance, including a blistering attack in mid-June.[10]

The ammunition with which to finish off Monroe came, interestingly enough, from St. Domingo. Hamilton wrote to President Washington in late June 1796 with a report that Sonthonax had authorized the confiscation of any American cargoes that could be intercepted by the privateers which swarmed around the island. Although the report turned out to be inaccurate, it nonetheless gave Hamilton grounds to suggest that the fault lay in Paris, where, as he archly put it, "the United States should have some faithful organ near the French Government to explain their real views and to ascertain those of the French."[11] The president, his mind already poisoned against Monroe, took the bait. He immediately asked Pickering for his advice, and the secretary—whether in collusion with Hamilton on this or not—had no trouble in recommending that Monroe be replaced. Completing the transaction took weeks more, but by September Pickering had the satisfaction of writing the following brutal notification to Monroe: "General Pinckney will be the bearer of this letter. He is to succeed you as the Minister Plenipotentiary of the United States with the French republic."[12]

Monroe left Paris in late 1796, in a rage at what he saw as the betrayal of his mission by the Federalists. With Minister Adet in Philadelphia also reproaching the Federalist administration to his own government, there were no more buffers in the way of a breakdown of Franco-American relations.

The Directory, in any case, was not that interested in smoothing over the situation. With a growing sense of confidence and assertiveness, inspired in part by Napoleon's stunning victories in Italy, it had determined to take a new look at its relations with the United States, and to counter British successes across the Atlantic. Strengthening the American alliance had proven to be beyond France's reach, and the United States had instead made its peace with Britain. Since the Jay treaty had effectively removed those few wartime advantages that France had enjoyed in America, the French concluded, it was time to punish the Americans for their abandonment of the 1778 alliance, and to pressure them into a more pro-French, or at least less pro-British, policy.

The Directory decided early in 1797 to strike back by hitting at American shipping, allied as that activity was with Federalist interests. American ships were, it was true, carrying much of France's trade—a situation that rankled national pride but was a necessary evil in wartime. But they were also helping Britain's war effort, and on an even larger scale. The Directory's objective, then, was to make American trade with Britain and its colonies more expensive. It issued a decree to the effect that all American ships trading with the British West Indies, whether carrying contraband or not, would be subject to seizure.

By the middle of the year, hundreds of American ships had been taken in, trade with the West Indies was disrupted, and insurance rates were skyrocketing. When Sonthonax published still more punitive rules in November, the situation reached crisis proportions. The waters of St. Domingo, particularly in the Bight of Leogane, swarmed with armed gunboats, closer to pirates than privateers. They took shelter in the many creeks and inlets of the coast, coming out to overpower merchantmen with their large cannons and crew, and few ships once seized were not considered fair prizes.

A few merchants, even those who had been in the trade for years, found it too dangerous: "The risks to which our flag is exposed in navigating your waters, and the insults etc. we receive daily from the pirates (a more suitable term than that of armed vessels) leaves me to give up for a time shipments to the islands," wrote one longtime trader to his agent in Cap François.[13] However, most American skippers wanted to continue the trade in spite of its risks. Demand for imported foodstuffs and war material remained high, while highly remunerative return cargoes were still available in spite of the damage caused by years of war and the partial collapse of the plantation system. Both groups, of course, demanded that their government find some way to ease the French "depredations." In St. Domingo and other parts of the West Indies, then, the Directory's pressure seemed to be working.

The Directory had also decided to send the Americans another strong message of displeasure by refusing to receive the new American minister, Charles C. Pinckney of South Carolina, when he arrived in late 1796. It was not a smart move. Pinckney, a cordial and moderate Federalist who had declined the post of secretary of state, was well respected in Philadelphia and would have been a fine envoy. The French may have made their point, but at a high cost: the action was taken as an insult in America.

Another source of potential leverage for the Directory was the 1796 American presidential elections. But however much the French may have preferred to see Republican candidate Thomas Jefferson, or even Aaron Burr, replace the departing President Washington, they steered clear of overt interference. The active and pugnacious Adet was nonetheless widely accused of doing so, as when, for example, shortly before the elections, he issued a public letter to Secretary Pickering in which he scathingly listed French complaints against United States policy. He also "suspended" the functions of the French mission, as if preparing for war. But even if he had had the intent of scaring the electors into a more pro-French policy, it did not work. John Adams emerged as the narrow but clear winner for the presidency, and the Federalists were still in power.

Adet was scornful about the new president. At the same time, he was hopeful, reporting that Adams's "inflexible vanity, absolute self-confidence, and headstrong character will never permit him to listen to or follow the advice of anyone, much less that of Alexander Hamilton, whom he detests." Adams, he commented accurately, was not necessarily pro-British. Nor, he continued, could Jefferson be truly considered pro-French, being, "I repeat, an American, and as such cannot sincerely be our friend. An American is the enemy of all Europeans."[14]

The Directory decided that it would be useful, tactically at least, to extend a small olive branch to the new administration. Early in 1797 it backed off a bit from its hurtful shipping policy. A new decree limited seizures somewhat by giving French vessels the right to confiscate only enemy cargo on neutral ships. Stringent new documentation requirements, and a tendency to interpret "enemy cargo" liberally, meant however that the new rule made little real change in French harassment of American shipping.

The Directory's long-range worry was that the Jay treaty, and continuation of the Federalists in power, might mean eventual alliance with Britain. They needed some point of strategic pressure. As a way of both neutralizing America's growing importance and thwarting possible British expansion, the idea of regaining possession of the Louisiana colony began to look attractive. Fauchet, Adet, and others had been arguing for some time that France should look to Louisiana to cement its place in the Americas, hem in the United States, and feed its West Indies colonies. Fauchet had contended strongly that

France could, by possessing Louisiana, supply its West Indies colonies itself and break the American trade "monopoly." He was especially motivated to make this argument after Jefferson had pointed out, cynically but accurately, that the war "hands over the French colonies to us; France enjoys the sovereignty and we the profit."[15]

The French government was indeed interested in regaining Louisiana from Spain, but it was not a priority. They had, in fact, tried to get it back in the negotiations leading up to the Treaty of Basle, but had had to settle for Spanish Santo Domingo. In the following year, the Spanish had even offered to sell Louisiana, but the Directory had considered the price too high. But in 1797 the arguments for regaining the colony found an influential new spokesman.

Charles Maurice de Talleyrand Perigord, ci-devant bishop of Autun, had just been made minister of foreign affairs. Obliged to leave France during the Terror because of his aristocratic background, the brilliant but slippery Talleyrand had found exile in England and then the United States. During his two years as a luminary of the French colony in Philadelphia, Talleyrand had tried to recoup his fortunes through trading in commodities and speculating in land, and had become friendly with leading politicians, including Hamilton. He also developed during his stay some lasting and not necessarily friendly attitudes toward America. First of these was his conviction that Americans had a natural affinity for the British, and that they could never be counted on as friends of France. Second was his belief, shared by Fauchet and Adet, that France should regain Louisiana as a counterweight to the United States. Permitted to return to France after the end of the Terror, Talleyrand had published a long article on that subject, successfully drawing attention both to himself and to the project. Now, as minister, he was in a position to push the idea forward.

France's tough new line had not won it friends in America, but it had drawn attention. The number of American ships lost to French cruisers, and particularly the privateers operating out of St. Domingo and Guadeloupe, continued to mount, and with it the need for some government response. America's leaders, however, were not of one mind as to how to deal with this nominally friendly nation, which had such important strategic and commercial ties to the United States.

The first response was noncontroversial. Concerned over the plight of the many American seamen who had been stranded in St. Domingo after confiscation of their ships, Washington appointed consular officials to the island to protect American interests, headed by Jacob Mayer for Cap François. Minister Adet at first objected to this American presence in France's troubled colony, but in the end acquiesced, recognizing the need for someone to help sort out the complications of the war being waged on neutral commerce.

President Washington, typically, had continued a cautious path, and in his last message to Congress before retiring he had limited himself to urging that consideration be given to strengthening the country's defenses by rebuilding the neglected navy.

It took French rejection of Pinckney's credentials to light the tinder. Yet, even as popular indignation grew over this French insult to American pride, President Adams—new on the job, but not to public controversy—remained cautious. He did not want bad relations with France and was aware that, for all the clamor about French depredations, the British had seized as many American ships, if not more.[16]

Adams however had made the unfortunate mistake of keeping Washington's old cabinet (which now included still another henchman of Hamilton, Secretary of War James McHenry). As a result, he was getting uniformly anti-French views. His cabinet colleagues all represented the moneyed and commercial interests of the port cities, and were "men of order," while Pickering was, from the beginning, the leader of a faction that was willing to go to war. The secretary of state, self-righteous and intolerant, was in fact so outspoken that Hamilton not only preferred to do his backstage work with the calmer Wolcott but found it necessary on occasion to advise that Pickering show "steady resolution rather than feeling."[17]

Adams was—as Adet had predicted—a man who would follow his own inclination, not his cabinet's fulminations. He favored a measured response to the Directory's insult. The United States, he proposed, should send a mission to replace Pinckney, with instructions to secure a renewal of the 1778 treaty. He suggested that Madison be the leader. His cabinet, however, balked at the nomination of a Republican, and one who had opposed the Jay treaty at that. In the end, they would agree only on a delegation of Federalists: Pinckney once again, John Marshall from Virginia, and Elbridge Gerry of Massachusetts, whom Pickering tried to oppose as an inconsistent loyalist, but who was chosen anyway because he was an old friend of the president's. The president got Congress's approval in May, balancing this peaceful gesture toward France with the recommendation that the country begin at the same time to strengthen its defenses, just in case hostilities became necessary.

The president's overture failed. In Paris, the American commissioners were received that autumn by a government brimming with confidence after its recent victories in the Rhineland and Italy. The commissioners were ignored, slighted, and, in the end, told that they could only begin the negotiations with Minister Talleyrand if they agreed to finance a war loan, including a substantial bribe to the minister himself. In what became known as the XYZ Affair, the commissioners reported home their anger, their defiance in face of the French demands, and their failure. Marshall and Pinckney returned home in a huff, but not before leaking their bad news to prepare public opinion. Gerry, on the other hand, stayed on in Europe under a very liberal interpretation of his instructions, to see if there was any way he could pick up the pieces from the fiasco.

News of the new French insult to young America's pride gave the war hawks the opportunity they had been seeking. When President Adams laid the full accounts of the humiliating non-negotiation before Congress in April of 1798, public opinion swung sharply in favor of war. Jefferson and the remaining friends of France were thrown on the defensive, and even though they suspected that the news was being deliberately manipulated, they recognized that public opinion had taken a major turn. As Jefferson later wrote to Gerry, "The people, in many places, gave loose to the expressions of their warm indignation, & of their honest preference of war to dishonor. The fever was long & successfully kept up, and in the meantime, war measures as ardently crowded."[18]

War with France, it seemed, was inevitable.

TOUSSAINT'S CLAUSE

The XYZ Affair was like a torch put to a haystack. Americans had become increasingly frustrated by the demands of neutrality during a war that seemed to allow the belligerent powers to push around the less powerful. Many wanted the government to take sides. Certainly, the two political parties already had done so, despite the warning that President Washington had given in his farewell address that "foreign influence is one of the most baneful foes of representative government."

Three years earlier, indignation and war fever had been focused on Britain and its naval seizures. Jay's mission and treaty had damped down that fire, but the embers of discontent smoldered on, and partisans on both sides were eager to fan them into flame. The Directory's hectoring and punitive reaction to the Jay treaty, combined with its naval seizures, had simply shifted popular indignation toward France.

Over the past few years, the excesses of the Terror and Jacobin radicalism, the Directorate's bullying posture, French maritime policy, and the possibility of security threats from the unrest in St. Domingo and the other sugar islands had all eroded public support for France. Republican politicians rarely spoke out in favor of French policy or ideals anymore, and even Minister Adet had decided to ease back on official support for pro-republican rallies, because he found that they irritated, rather than inspired, the average American. So when the

American commissioners' reports on the XYZ Affair began to filter back to the United States in the later part of 1797, they found a ready audience. Anger at France's perceived arrogance grew with the new year, augmented by judiciously timed leaks of new, damaging information on the part of Pickering and the other war hawks. War with France, the arch-Federalist hawks expected, would bring about an alliance with England and set the course of U.S. foreign policy for generations.

In April 1798, Adams was obliged by the public outcry to publish a full record of the XYZ discussions in Paris. The revelations in the correspondence, and the slogan "millions for defense, not one cent for tribute," produced an irresistible pressure for dramatic action. Anti-French demonstrations were held around the country; Liberty caps were banned; some French privateers unlucky enough to be caught in port were burned. Even Adams, much more cautious now as president than he had been as a firebrand Continental Congressman, saw that a vigorous response to the Directory's insult was necessary. But he was unwilling to fall into the hands of the hawks, and determined to explore diplomatic avenues, even while agreeing to strong defensive measures that might convince the French of American seriousness.

Between April and July, Congress debated a string of groundbreaking defensive measures. While they were warmly contested and the votes were often close, in the prevailing mood of anti-French indignation they all passed, even though the Democratic-Republicans had a narrow majority in the House (the Senate was strongly Federalist). The 1778 treaty of friendship with France was formally repealed. Authorization was passed for the arming of privateers against France, and the landing of their prizes in the United States. In a move toward the kind of large government that the Republicans normally opposed, a Department of the Navy was established, and money voted for building ships and fortifying harbors. In an even more bitter pill for Republican purists to swallow, a standing army of ten thousand soldiers was approved. Direct taxes on homes and other property (including slaves) were also approved to pay for this huge increase in public spending.

Jefferson, elected as vice president under the voting system then prevailing, was obliged as president of the Senate to preside, powerless, over this wholesale defeat of his concept of governance. It would get worse. Toward the end of the congressional session, the odious Alien and Sedition Acts were passed. The first was an extension of the climate of anti-French, anti-Jacobin suspicion that had been building since the execution of King Louis years before. Not surprisingly, suspicion was directed with particular intensity toward anybody with a St. Domingo connection. A climate of paranoia was encouraged by Pickering, Wolcott, and others who worried about French intelligence and sabotage operations from among the some thirty thousand French citizens resident in the United States. Authorizing as it did the deportation of aliens considered dangerous, or even suspected of "treasonable or secret" inclinations, the act caused a good number of French refugees in the United States to depart, even though it was never rigorously enforced. The Sedition Act, on the other hand, was directed at intimidating the Republican press, and was famously enforced by Federalist judges.

A fierce and impassioned party struggle continued well after passage of the new laws. The normal political dialogue between liberty on the one hand, and law and order on the other, became exaggerated for the next few years into an invective more raucous, more vituperative, and more impassioned than at almost any other time in America's history. The Republicans, beaten in the congressional votes, fought back through the press and public opinion against laws and practices that they considered despotic, unconstitutional, and leading to a military oligarchy, if not a monarchy. Jefferson, in not so secret opposition to his president, joined with Madison to encourage development of a divisive and dangerous theory by which individual states might nullify federal acts they found distasteful.

The lines were equally sharp on matters of foreign policy, with Hamilton and the Federalists arguing that it was necessary for Americans to stand with Britain against France's efforts at world domination. The Republicans riposted that national security requirements should not be allowed to compromise hard-gained republican and constitutional principles. The debate raged in the press, in the government, and in private—accusation and counter-accusation, slander and counterslander—and while the sides were fairly evenly matched, the Federalists and the war party definitely had the popular momentum.

A final law passed that spring, and which most directly concerned St. Domingo, was designed as economic retaliation against France's maritime seizure policy. The act suspended all trade with France, "or elsewhere under the acknowledged authority of France," for a period of nine months. Pickering gloated, in a letter to Jacob Mayer informing him of the bill, that open war with France was now all but inevitable.[1] The law was sold in Congress as a means of applying pressure on France, revocable if they changed their maritime policy; it would squeeze Paris by depriving the French West Indies colonies of their vital American supplies. The law was supported by most maritime interests, presumably in the expectation that it would bring the French to relax their policy of seizure and confiscation. The Federalist John Rutledge of South Carolina indicated another reason why the shipping interests could support the bill: they were having great difficulties anyway in getting paid for goods sold or confiscated in St. Domingo.[2]

But Pickering did not want to starve St. Domingo; his objective in fact was to use trade as a way to weaken Paris's grip on its colony. The part of the act quoted above was, in fact, a deliberate effort on the part of the administration to keep open the trade with St. Domingo. Pickering instructed the consul in Cap François, Jacob Mayer, that the act was "limited to places under the acknowledged power of France. Consequently, if the inhabitants of St. Domingo have ceased to acknowledge that power, there will not, as I conceive, be any bar to the prompt and extensive renewal of trade between the United States and the ports of that island. . . ."[3]

This amounted to a virtual invitation to the French commander at the Cap, Toussaint, to declare that the colony was officially free of

France. Pickering, it would appear, was far ahead of Congress, or even perhaps his president, in pursuing a policy aimed at separating St. Domingo from its mother country.

While the United States and France had been drifting toward crisis or actual war, the fighting in St. Domingo had continued its bloody course. One outcome at least had become clear: the British occupation was doomed. The pressure from Toussaint and Rigaud was relentless. The few British replacement troops that could be scraped up were unseasoned, that is, accustomed neither to the climate nor the guerrilla warfare they had to face; they died in skirmishes and in hospitals with alarming regularity. Port au Prince fell in early 1797, causing still another exodus of French planters and their slaves to an increasingly suspicious and unwelcoming North America. After that, the British War Ministry all but wrote off the occupation as too costly, and agreed to the recommendations of the second in command, Colonel Thomas Maitland. Going behind his superior officer's back, Maitland urged that remaining forces be withdrawn to a few key strong points. When the commanding general returned to England in exasperation over Britain's losing effort on the island, Maitland then began negotiations with Toussaint on his own authority. By spring, the two commanders had agreed to an evacuation of all the west, and concentration of the remaining British troops at Môle St. Nicolas and Jérémie.

France's two native generals, Toussaint and Rigaud, now controlled the vast majority of the colony.

The Directory had watched events on the island with concern, distrustful of Toussaint's growing power and autonomy but lacking the force to bring him into line. In an effort to control Toussaint by political means until an adequate detachment of loyal troops could be sent to reestablish full French governmental authority, they assigned a new special agent, General Marie Joseph Hedouville. His instructions were, starkly put, to divide and rule.

When he arrived in early 1798, Hedouville saw however that he had only two instruments to use against Toussaint: one was Rigaud, the other was the last remaining commissioner, Philippe Roume, who had been placed in charge in Santo Domingo. Hedouville soon realized that the cautious and ineffective Roume would be no help. His strategy, therefore, for lack of better, had to be to drive wedges between Toussaint and Rigaud. He was, by and large, successful. The two leaders had cooperated in a coordinated push against the British forces at the beginning of the year, but were natural rivals, and as a result Hedouville's constant intrigues succeeded in increasing the tension between them. But Hedouville's machinations never succeeded in producing a clean break, and in the meantime Toussaint's power continued to grow.

Toussaint and Maitland had maintained contact since the first negotiated withdrawal, with the latter more and more convinced that British occupation of even the remaining towns was pointless. Eventually Maitland convinced his superiors to allow him to negotiate a complete withdrawal as long as two strategic objectives could be assured: the continuation of British trading rights with the island and a guarantee that the freed slaves on St. Domingo would not export revolution to neighboring Jamaica. The latter point had become particularly important in view of Hedouville's repeated attempts to incite Toussaint into just such foreign adventures. (While the incitement appears to have reflected provocation by Hedouville as much as it was formal Directorate policy, the threat was taken seriously by both British plantation owners and American southerners.) Maitland found Toussaint ready to negotiate on both points. And Hedouville had no choice but to agree to the negotiation: it was the power of Toussaint's army, after all, that was obliging the British to depart.

In August 1798, General Toussaint was received with full military honors by the British garrison of the Môle, and a withdrawal agreement was signed. The amicable nature of the withdrawal, after years of bloody warfare, caused no little speculation in the American press: "Gen. Maitland, on evacuating St. Domingo, sent all the black corps raised by the British to Gen. Toussaint, allowing each man his musquet and fifty rounds of ammunition. A few days before he left the Môle, he had many private conferences with Toussaint which, added to a great many corresponding circumstances, renders it probable that an agreement has taken place between Generals Maitland and Toussaint; that the latter is to drive away Hedouville, declare the island independent, and offer a free trade to the British and Americans."[4]

The reporter had it mostly right. Toussaint had accepted the British conditions; they would have the right to trade, and had his promise not to interfere in Jamaica. In return, the last British troops would leave. But there was no agreement on independence. Maitland had, it seems, offered British protection to Toussaint if he broke his ties with Paris. But Toussaint was not ready, even had he trusted the British, to take such a drastic step. He refused.[5]

The five-year occupation was over; St. Domingo was once again entirely French. At least in form. Real power on the island was in the hands of Toussaint and Rigaud. But Toussaint, controlling the capital at Cap François as well as the richest areas of the country, was clearly the emerging leader.

General Hedouville could only exercise France's diminished authority indirectly, when at all. And finally he made a fatal mistake, interfering in the army's affairs to a degree that obliged Toussaint to raise the Cap François troops against him. Surrounded and with no support, Hedouville was forced to flee in October. As a parting shot, he tried to pass what remained of his authority to André Rigaud, whom he considered to be more loyal to France than Toussaint. But Toussaint ignored the measure and invited the feckless Commissioner Philippe Roume, from his post in Santo Domingo, to assume authority as France's agent in St. Domingo. Roume, Toussaint knew, would be compliant and was no threat.

Toussaint was now unquestionably the leading figure on the island. A French general, he ruled ably, and by most accounts justly, in the name of France. And yet clearly, after defeating Spanish and then British armies, and after sending two French generals and a commissioner home like scolded schoolboys, he had ideas of his own. Exactly what those ideas were was unclear, certainly to the very interested observers in North America, perhaps even to Toussaint himself. Independence for St. Domingo had been in the air ever since the planters had tried to separate themselves from French domination back in 1790. But a half dozen years later, the possibility was now the amazing one of an independent state ruled by black ex-slaves and freemen. An account by a New York journal illustrates the perplexity: "General Toussaint, at the head of his dark host— beloved and respected for his talent, mild manners and good faith— is director in chief of that extensive, fertile, populous and wealthy island. General Rigaud, indeed, has been in possession of Port au Prince and the Southern department, but the authority of Toussaint appears, as yet, to have met with no resistance. . . . What is Toussaint's plan? To be permanently independent and neutral, or only to the close of the war? . . . These questions, which are considerably interesting to this country, in the present portentous and incalculable situation of the world, time will answer."[6]

Secretary of State Pickering had his own answer. He wanted the man he had referred to in his letter to Consul Mayer as the "amiable and respectable Toussaint" to become an instrument of an American policy, aimed at France.

The French were somewhat taken aback by the vehemence and emotional nature of the American reaction to the XYZ Affair. Forced loans, extortion against weaker countries, and a certain amount of corruption in public affairs had become a staple of France's war against its neighbors in Europe; that the American reaction could be so different was unexpected. Talleyrand, in particular, was embarrassed by the failure of his diplomacy. Now, with no American minister in Paris and Adet having been given his papers in Philadelphia, Talleyrand scrambled to keep open informal lines of communication with the Americans through Eldridge Gerry and, later, the American minister in the Hague, William Vans Murray.

As the American Congress passed act after act hostile to French interests, it became necessary for the Directory to make preparations for a serious breach of relations. The American embargo gave cause for anxiety, because if it were to be rigorously maintained and long-lasting, it would be very costly to the French islands. In view of the tenor of American opinion, with the American press already boasting that "Citizen sansculotte is about receiving a fraternal hug from citizen starvation, [as] a just reward for his perfidy,"[7] the French quickly sought ways to soften the impact of the embargo. The Ministry of Marine rushed to line up supplies from other sources, and the minister, whistling past the graveyard, even tried to take some solace from the flight of white settlers and soldiers from St. Domingo and other islands, suggesting that "the freedom of our negroes guarantees that we can keep our colonies, as the blacks, even the soldiers, will if necessary support and defend themselves on local produce."[8] The French also tried to find ways around the embargo. Consul Phillipe-Andre Letombe, the senior French officer in the United States after Adet's departure, reported at the end of the year that he was trying to buy supplies for St. Domingo using Spanish intermediaries to hide his transactions. (The effort ultimately failed when the Spanish minister refused to go along with the maneuver.)

An outbreak of hostilities with the United States would, in spite of these precautions, be damaging to the French West Indies. Worse yet, a war would raise the even more dangerous prospect that the Americans would, as the arch-Federalists wanted, enter into an alliance with Britain. Talleyrand, who was more alive to these dangers than the members of the Directory, began to look for ways to back off from the confrontation.

Talleyrand had learned from Victor Dupont (the French consul in Charleston, whom he had queried on the subject after the departure of Adet) that French naval seizures in the West Indies had indeed been extravagant and often illegal. Dupont's full report, describing the widespread and improper commissioning of privateers and adjudication of prizes, concluded that the Americans had good cause, indeed, to complain of "rampant acts of violence, brigandage and piratry" by French-flagged corsairs. Talleyrand quickly took the information to the Directory, recommending that France needed to remove and disavow the abuses in its system that had helped fuel the crisis.[9]

The Directory took the minister's advice, and in early August— only some six weeks after the embargo had been approved on the other side of the Atlantic—a decree was issued, tightening up the conditions on which French letters of marque could be issued, and instructing French agents in St. Domingo and Guadeloupe to rigorously respect the interests of neutral and allied shipowners. It was definitely a step in the right direction, but it could not stop the momentum. An undeclared war between the two countries' navies had already broken out.

Given the scope and importance of the war raging between France and Britain, the naval battles with the United States were mere pinpricks, but Talleyrand was anxious that they not expand into something more dangerous. His contacts with Gerry and Murray were, as summer turned into fall, beginning to make progress. Gerry had returned home, where, fiercely attacked by his fellow Federalists, he nonetheless succeeded in convincing his old friend Adams that his contacts with Talleyrand had shown that the French were seriously interested in reopening negotiations. Murray, for his part, made it clear to the French that President Adams could not, after the XYZ insult, countenance a renewal of formal negotiations without a guarantee that the Directory would receive his envoys with the dignity and consideration due a serious power. Both Talleyrand and Adams were proceeding cautiously. Each had his hawks to contend with, but both wanted to keep the hostilities from blowing up into a major war with unpredictable consequences.

Hostilities and diplomacy were proceeding on parallel tracks in the Caribbean as well. St. Domingo's successive colonial governments had been inching toward a kind of autonomy in foreign relations for years, ever since the planters had sent their missions to Philadelphia in 1791. Now that he was the paramount ruler, Toussaint, too, needed to look to the colony's foreign support. That would mean, in effect, a steady source of supplies and some sort of protection from the possible anger of his parent government. The British had offered to protect him, but he could not really trust them, and he was unsure if Maitland's suggestion had been officially sanctioned or not. On the other hand, the Americans could— and were eager to—provide the necessary supplies, while a regular commerce between the island and the mainland would probably invest the Americans in the island's future.

There were two problems, however, facing such a course of action. One was that Sonthonax and Hedouville (as well as French officials in Guadeloupe) had sanctioned the plague of privateers that threatened to cut off the American trade entirely. The Directory had moved, by their decree of August, to cut back on the abuses, but Toussaint would have to go a step further if he was to attract the Americans; he would need to close the colony's ports to the privateers. The second problem was that the Americans had themselves closed off the trade, with their Non-Intercourse Act. It was due to expire in early 1799, but was likely to be renewed as long as the crisis with France continued.

Toussaint took the initiative, less than a month after General Hedouville had been sent packing. In early November 1798, at about the same time that Pickering was writing to Consul Mayer suggesting that the colony might wiggle through the loophole in the present act, Toussaint wrote to President Adams asking for an exemption. To carry the message, he deputized a Cap François businessman, Joseph Bunel, to go to Philadelphia. Jacob Mayer, the American consul, would also accompany. Toussaint's letter to Adams, after bemoaning the absence of American ships in the ports, proposed that American trade with St. Domingo be permitted, and promised in return: "You can be assured, Mr. President, that Americans will find protection and security in the ports of the Republic and St. Domingue, that the flag of the United States will be respected there, as that of a friendly power and ally of France; that orders will be given to our privateers on cruise to act in that manner; and that I will facilitate by all means available to me, their prompt return to their country, and that they will be paid promptly for cargoes that have been brought to us."[10]

As soon as Bunel and Mayer arrived in Philadelphia, the French consul Letombe wrote to Paris about their doings. By Christmas, both Mayer and Bunel had called on Pickering, and were hoping to see the president. Bunel had not yet called on him, Letombe complained, but his immediate objectives were well known: to promote trade and offer to control the corsairs. All this was being done, Letombe reported, in collusion with Britain's agent, Maitland. But Toussaint, Letombe added, was preparing for a long-range goal, which was "to declare the independence of the colony, but he did not dare do it before knowing the opinion of the federal government on the subject."[11]

Letombe, lacking full diplomatic credentials, could not lobby effectively to block Toussaint's envoys. It would have been an uphill battle in any event, as Pickering and others, wanting to harm France by helping St. Domingo, supported Bunel's mission strongly. By the time that Bunel dined with the president in early January, the administration had already advanced a bill in Congress that would make possible a deal with Toussaint. Bunel, perhaps savoring his victory, did not communicate with Letombe until mid-February—and then only to inform him of his impending return to St. Domingo. By that time, he already had what he had come for.

The bill advanced by the administration proposed to extend the embargo against France for the duration of the new Congress, with one major change: it would allow the president to suspend its effect to selected French territories, and under certain conditions. The language eventually negotiated was vague; it simply authorized the president to discontinue the restrictions of the act "either with respect to the French republic, or to any island, port, or place, belonging to the said republic, with which a commercial intercourse may safely be renewed." The intent of this clause, however, was very clear to Congress; it was intended to reopen the trade with St. Domingo. It quickly was named the Toussaint Clause.

The title of the clause was helpful to its chances of passage. Bad as the image of St. Domingo had become after years of bloody civil war, massacres, atrocities, Jacobinism, and abolition, Toussaint himself had come to enjoy a much more positive reputation. His piety, the honesty of his dealings, his competence, and his moderation had all been noted favorably since his rise to prominence, in correspondence and in the press. The fact that he had encouraged some of the old planters to return to the island, so as to raise productivity under the new labor contract system, was also noted to his favor. Toussaint cultivated this good opinion; he kept up a steady correspondence with French officials in America, the press, and American merchants, all with the aim of improving the colony's image, as well, presumably, as his own.[12]

It also helped that the patriotic clamor of the XYZ Affair had given the Federalists comfortable majorities in both houses of the new Congress. They were likely to get the clause through, no matter what the opponents chose to say against it.

Still, initiating a debate over St. Domingo was not without risks. The situation on the island had been brought up in Congress over the last half dozen years only in a pejorative sense, and most often as an example of republicanism gone wild, or as a threat to the internal security of the United States. Such had been the case during debate on the naturalization act, some four years previously, when an amendment was proposed to bar the naturalization of any foreigners holding slaves. The proposal, clearly aimed at the French refugees, was voted down after it was attacked as too inflammatory in a time "when the West Indies are transformed into a immense scene of slaughter, when thousands of people have been massacred, and thousands had fled for refuge in this country, when the proprietors of slaves in this country could only keep them in peace with utmost difficulty."[13]

The St. Domingo bugaboo had surfaced in Congress again in 1798, when the governor of Pennsylvania created a scare about the security risk that might be posed by persons arriving from the island. He had proposed a bill restricting the entry of French citizens, alleging that some of the Frenchmen who had fled the fall of Port au Prince, with "their armed slaves," were a potential fifth column in America. The bill actually passed the Senate before wiser counsel prevailed. Frivolous as it was, the incident showed once again how easily the lawmakers identified St. Domingo with revolution, subversion, or the menace of slave rebellion.

The House of Representatives debate over the Toussaint Clause took place over several days in late January 1799. It, more clearly than any other record of the time, exposed the depths of feeling, the differences of opinion, and the substantial ambiguities entertained by informed citizens about the stance that the United States should be taking toward the rebel colony, and particularly toward its burgeoning aspirations for independence.

One of the early speakers was the influential Samuel Smith of Baltimore, a stalwart Republican but also a prosperous merchant with much business in the West Indies. His pocketbook had evidently outweighed his heart on the issue, as he came out in support of the clause, claiming that it was a necessary step to reduce the problem of piracy in the St. Domingo trade. His Republican colleague, John Nicholas of Virginia, immediately raised the first objection to Smith's rather oversimplified argument. Nicholas argued that the measure would have important diplomatic connotations, putting the United States in a position of favoring "usurpers," and that it "holds out an invitation to agents to abandon their country and set up Governments of their own."

The basic case for the clause was then made by Harrison Otis of Massachusetts, a good Federalist and one of the sponsors of the legislation. "The interests of this country, and of our mercantile citizens in particular," he said, demanded the protection the clause would offer. Toussaint, he insisted, was not a usurper, he was the legitimate replacement of Hedouville. If he had sent off Hedouville, so what? He had also sent off Sonthonax, but the commissioner had returned. He would not argue, Otis said, that the independence of St. Domingo, should it happen, would be in the American interest, but it was in the American interest to be on good terms with the half million inhabitants of this richest West Indian island, thirty to forty thousand of whom were armed and disciplined. If "driven to despair" by American policy, they could easily "inflict deep wounds on our commerce."

Robert Goodloe Harper of South Carolina, a usually voluble debater and militant convert to Federalist causes, then rose to make a surprisingly weak argument for the clause. In fact, he damaged his case somewhat by admitting that the St. Domingo trade had become, in the wartime conditions, not entirely correct, but rather a "species of gambling, by which some made large fortunes and others sustained heavy losses."

Albert Gallatin, the brilliant Swiss immigrant from Pennsylvania who had emerged as the Republicans' leader in the House, immediately took the floor against the amendment, and to undo the damage of the two previous interventions. He pointed out that the United States should not encourage rebellion, after having accused the French of attempting the same thing. Then, in a highly intemperate moment, he went too far, voicing the deep fears which his

Republican colleagues, many of them slaveholding planters, held about St. Domingo and its possible independence:

> Suppose that island, with its present population, under present circumstances, should become an independent State. What is this population? It is known to consist, almost altogether, of slaves just emancipated, of men who received their first education under the lash of the whip, and who have been initiated to liberty only by that series of rapine, pillage, and massacre that have laid waste and deluged that island in blood. Of men, who, if left to themselves, if altogether independent, are by no means likely to apply themselves to peaceable cultivation of the country, but will try to continue to live, as heretofore, by plunder and depredations. No man wishes more than I do to see an abolition of slavery, when it can be properly effected, but no man would be more unwilling than I to constitute a whole nation of freed slaves, who had arrived to the age of thirty years, and thus to throw so many wild tigers on society. If the population of St. Domingo can remain free in that island, I have no objection, but, however free, I do not wish to have them independent, and would rather see them under a government that would be likely to keep them where they are, and prevent them from committing depredations out of the island. But if they were left to themselves, they might become more troublesome to us in our commerce with the West Indies than the Algerians ever were in the Mediterranean; they might also become dangerous neighbors for the Southern States, and an asylum for renegadoes from those parts.

Shortly after this outburst, Samuel Smith regained the floor to give a long discourse on the history of St. Domingo, in which he attempted to show that all the senior French officials there had been obliged to work somewhat independently of Paris. Then, returning to Gallatin's description of a dangerous independent St. Domingo, Smith painted a diametrically opposed picture: "But suppose this independence were to take place, would all the dangers to this country actually take place, which has been stated? No, the reverse would be true. Refuse to these people our commerce, and the provisions of which they stand in need, and you compel them to become pirates and dangerous neighbors to the Southern States. But, so long as you supply them, they will turn their attention to the cultivation of their plantations."

The same point was made shortly afterward by the respected Thomas Pinckney, former governor and member of a prominent Charleston, South Carolina, merchant family. As a southern Federalist, his refutation of Gallatin's argument, while not original, was particularly telling. He said that he did not believe

> that this bill will have the tendency to promote the independence of St. Domingo . . . but should the independence of that island take place, the event would be more advantageous to the Southern States than if it remained under the domain of France, . . . unreasonable and arbitrary as we have found it. . . . If our dispute with France should not be accommodated, and they keep possession of St. Domingo, they could invade this country only from that quarter. . . . If these people in St. Domingo find that we withhold from them supplies which are necessary to their subsistence, though they are friendly disposed toward to us, they will look elsewhere for support; they must either turn their attention to cultivating their land, look to Great Britain, or become freebooters.[14]

The Federalists had succeeded in speaking with one voice. The Republicans, on the other hand, continued to show their differences on the issue. Nicholas attacked his colleague Smith, saying that his commercial interests had allowed him to "disregard the evils" that would flow from passage of the clause. And the plain-spoken Nathaniel Macon, representing the small farmer Republicans from the western areas of North Carolina, raised another problem that might arise from an independent St. Domingo: that the great powers could manipulate it against American interests, just as they had traditionally used the Indians on the frontier.

But the debate, effectively, was over. The Federalists had the votes; they had had them all along. With Pickering and others actively pushing the Toussaint Clause, the bill passed easily in both houses, and was signed into law by President Adams on February 9, 1799. Toussaint's Clause, ostensibly intended simply to open trade with a lucrative American market, would however have more extensive ramifications than its sponsors openly acknowledged. It would, in practice, allow the United States to take sides in a foreign civil war and encourage the colony's leaders to reach for independence.

CREATING A QUARANTINE

O n the very day that President Adams signed the new ban on trade with France, the first significant American victory in the now open but undeclared war took place. Off St. Nevis in the West Indies, the *Constellation* defeated and captured the French frigate *L'Insurgente,* reputed to be the fastest ship in the French Navy. This new "quasi-war," as historians have called it, was nonetheless real enough at the time, and its action was centered in the strategically important West Indies, where the fate of St. Domingo was crucial both in the context of American-French hostilities and in the longer-term struggle between France and Great Britain.

The Adams administration had made the reopening of trade with St. Domingo an exemption to the trade ban for a number of short-term reasons. Primary was a desire to get back at the French. Attacking French interests in the West Indies was the most direct method to do this, and helping the insurgents in St. Domingo was a way to deprive France of the benefit of what had been its most profitable colony.

A second rationale for the Toussaint Clause had to do with the logic of the embargo itself. If the general cutoff of trade was intended to hurt France, after all, then why should it apply to a colony that France scarcely controlled, and which might actually separate itself from the mother country if it could find supplies and political support in the United States? Moreover, supporters of the legislation had argued, weakening the island's ties with France would limit the ability of radicals in Paris to use as it a springboard for the export of their revolutionary schemes. And if the island prospered under a free trade regime, it would bring about an ideal political result: a St. Domingo shorn from France, yet dependent on American mercantile interests and the British and American navies.

That this logic coincided neatly with the business interests of the merchants and shipowners who supported the Federalist party was not, of course, coincidental. The maritime interests were looking forward eagerly to a satisfactory pocketbook result from the new policy. If only Toussaint could control the privateers, they could make profits from trade with St. Domingo that would allow them to recoup some of their earlier losses. "Commerce offers the sole prospect of indemnity for the immense injuries done us by France," Pickering had advised the president.[1]

And yet the administration was almost as uncertain as the members of Congress were over the long term implications of their action. It was still open to argument whether the United States should help promote the colony's independence, or what such an event might mean to American interests over time.

President Adams was torn. He was, to begin with, not convinced that the trade with the colony would be all that important over the long run.[2] And while he and others could foresee that the independence of St. Domingo (indeed, of all the European colonies in the Caribbean) might be inevitable, he did not think it would be in the United States' best interest. He most certainly did not want the United States to take the lead in bringing about such a result, and he was prepared to leave the matter to the British if, as he suspected, they opposed independence for St. Domingo. It was not until April however that he tried—and not entirely successfully, at that—to clarify his thinking to his secretary of state, who he knew had been pushing forward on the issue:

> The whole affair leads to the independence of the West Indies Islands. Although I may be mistaken, it appears to me that independence is

the worst and most dangerous condition they can be in, for the United States. They would be less dangerous under the government [of the European powers]. . . . The independence of St. Domingo, and consequently all the other islands, in the West Indies, may be brought about without our interference, and indeed in opposition to all we can do to prevent it. . . . My own ides are these: 1) it would be most prudent for us to have nothing to do in the business, 2) that if we should meddle, we had better leave the independence of the island complete, in commerce as well as legislation, to the people who assert it, the inhabitants of the island.[3]

Adams, in addition, had another reason for a cautious policy toward St. Domingo. He had begun to distrust his colleagues' all-out rush to war, and was prepared to reopen a negotiating track with the French. But, for the moment, he was not going to tip his hand on that issue.

Pickering, indeed, was well ahead of his president in promoting St. Domingo's independence. His father had been an abolitionist minister, he himself had proposed the abolition of slavery in the Northwest Territories, and the prospect of a black-run state in the neighborhood was not as frightening to him as it was to the largely Republican southerners. Pickering's enthusiasm for Toussaint's rebellion in fact was such that he had given the British minister in Washington reason to worry, as early as 1797, that he favored "a regime of blacks in St. Domingo."[4]

What Pickering did fear from St. Domingo was its use as a platform for French revolutionary action against the United States, either subversive or military. Independence would diminish that risk, he contended. "Nothing is more clear than, if left to themselves, than the Blacks of St. Domingo will be incomparably less dangerous than if they remain the subjects of France," he wrote just after the embargo bill had been signed into law. Indeed, Pickering had been lobbying Congress on this very point, and successfully.

"Of this, the Southern members of Congress were convinced, and therefore cordially concurred in the independence of St. Domingo, if Toussaint and his followers should will it," he wrote in the same letter.[5] For Pickering, the bill's passage meant more than just trade, or the de facto recognition of St. Domingo as a political entity that the trade would entail; he saw it leading to an independence that the United States should welcome. He wrote to his mentor, Hamilton, about the Toussaint Clause, on the day that it was signed into law: "I suppose everybody understands the main object of this provision is to open the commercial intercourse with St. Domingo. . . . The President sees the immense advantages of the commerce of that island, and will undoubtedly give the act as liberal a construction as will be politically expedient. Toussaint, if certain of our commerce, will, Mr. Mayer assures me, declare the whole island of St. Domingo independent; confident in his power to defend it, provided we will allow a free commercial intercourse. . . . This act of independence I fully expect, and I persuade myself that Great Britain will consent to share in it. . . . "[6]

Hamilton, it appears, was taken aback by his colleague's zeal. He was not averse to the idea of helping the French colonies gain their independence; as a matter of fact he had written to Wolcott almost a year earlier that the subject should be considered carefully.[7] But Pickering, he saw, risked moving too fast and too blatantly. Hamilton hurriedly wrote Pickering a return note in which he tried to rein in his intemperate colleague. "The United States," Hamilton advised, "must not be committed on the independence of St. Domingo. No Guarantee, no formal treaty, nothing that can rise up in judgement. It will be enough to let Toussaint be assured verbally, but explicitly, that upon his declaration of independence, a commercial intercourse will be opened and maintained. . . . "[8]

If the Federalist members of the administration welcomed the possibility of renewed trade with St. Domingo but worried about the possible implications of encouraging the colony's secession, Vice President Jefferson opposed both. As the bill and its amendment moved through Congress, he had kept his correspondents aware of its progress and his forebodings. The bill, he informed James Madison, was openly designed to "facilitate the separation of the island from France." Unhappy already at Congress's rush to war, he did not want to add another aggravation to U.S.-French relations. "This circumstance, with the stationing of our armed vessels round the French islands, will probably be more than the Directory will bear," he complained. He was depressed that the South Carolinians had deserted their slaveholding colleagues to vote for the act, but more importantly he was worried about the security implications for the South of trade with the black-ruled colony. After the act was signed into law, he wrote that "We may expect therefore black crews, & supercargoes & missionaries thence into the southern states. . . . If this combustion can be introduced among us under any veil whatever, we have to fear it."[9]

Jefferson chose not to speculate on the possibility of an independent, black St. Domingo. For the moment, he was prepared to consider a sort of British protectorate over the island, as a way to protect the American South from the probable spillover from black rule there. But he knew, as he wrote to his confidant Madison, that there would be difficult political and social consequences for the United States from the island's revolution, and that only domestic reforms in the South could provide, in the long term, a "remedy" for the problem:

> The treaty made with them by Maitland is (if they are to be separated from France) the best thing for us. They must get their provisions from us. It will indeed be in English bottoms, so that we shall lose the carriage. But the English will probably forbid them the ocean, confine them to their island, & thus prevent their becoming an American Algiers. It must be admitted too, that they may play them off on us when they please. Against this there is no remedy but timely measures on our part, to clear ourselves, by degrees, of the matter on which that lever can work.[10]

Missing from all this speculation, however, was firm knowledge of a key factor: what Toussaint's intentions were. Toussaint's overt pose at the time was still that of a loyal servant of France. He signed his letters as General in Chief of the Army of St. Domingue; he wrote fraternally to French officials in Paris and the United States. Letombe had even intercepted and read some of the general's correspondence, but he was obliged to admit to Paris that he had found it all to be entirely loyal.

And yet. The Directory, as well as American observers, could not but notice that Toussaint's actions were increasingly those of an autonomous governor, to say the least. Correspondence with a neighboring head of state was not, for example, the usual job of a general, even a general in chief. That Toussaint was determined to defend the freedom of his fellow ex-slaves was clear; his correspondence with the Directory had been adamant on the point for over a year. But did he want to make St. Domingo independent? He himself, it seems, was ambivalent on the issue. While strengthening his hold over the island, he was carefully taking no steps that would irretrievably cut its ties with France—or that would make him overly dependent on the British Navy for survival. Pickering and others were in reality acting on an unproven assumption about Toussaint's desire to declare his country independent. That did not, of course, mean that they were wrong.

Pickering had been wrong, though, on another very important issue, which was the intentions of his boss the president toward France. He can to some degree be excused, as Adams had been corresponding with William Vans Murray for some time behind his secretary of state's back. Murray had finally gotten a written assurance from Talleyrand that if the United States were to nominate new envoys to Paris, they would be met with the "respect due to the representatives of a free, independent and powerful nation."[11] No more snubs, condescension, or hints of bribes. Adams had won his point with the French. He would now use it to curb the bellicosity of his warlike colleagues. Their enthusiasm for service in the expensive new standing army and waging war with France had, he thought, passed all levels of prudence.

Writing to George Washington to inform him that he intended to take the dramatic step of appointing a new envoy to Paris, Adams took the opportunity to comment acerbically on the motives of his colleagues in government, in words which still ring true. "In elective government," he wrote, "peace or war are alike embraced by parties, when they think they can employ either for electioneering purposes."[12]

Adams dropped his bombshell on an unsuspecting cabinet and Congress. On February 18, less than two weeks after renewing the trade embargo on France with its Toussaint Clause, the president nominated Murray to be his envoy to Paris, to resume talks with a view to resolving the crisis. He had bypassed the hawks in his cabinet, infuriating them but leaving them to fight a rearguard action over the composition of the delegation. Pickering, especially, was livid. Adams's coup put the Hamilton group in a corner; the president had already won George Washington over to his view, as well as John Marshall and Hamilton's well-respected friend Attorney General Charles Lee.

The president's bold move had spiked the guns of the arch-Federalist group. A diplomatic resolution of the crisis was by no means foreordained, but at least it was no longer ruled out. The diplomacy would take months, and in the meantime the naval quasi-war would continue, as would the opening to Toussaint. The president's courageous act had given the country options other than war. It would, in time, also cost him the presidency.

Congress's debate on the Toussaint Clause had aired many aspects of the issue, but had resolved none. The clause had passed because the Federalists and the major merchant interests wanted it, but it was clear that it could have much further-reaching ramifications. This was no longer business as usual. The law opened up a period of unparalleled cooperation between the U.S. government and a rebel regime, amounting to de facto recognition. It would help, in time, to turn a colonial revolt into a revolution. True, the debate about the colony's possible independence had shown that the policy makers were not unaware of the possible implications of their action. They simply did not know how the scenario would play out.

Pickering, it appears, had begun to realize that his open enthusiasm for independence might have to be tempered, in view of the president's moves toward a rapprochement with France, and—probably more importantly—Hamilton's admonition. At the end of the month, he assured the latter that "the President will certainly do no act to encourage Toussaint to declare the island independent."[13] But Pickering, while backtracking in describing the official policy, had by no means abandoned his desire to promote independence by indirect means.

Curiously missing from the debate, however, had been any serious discussion of the revolutionary aspects of the situation in St. Domingo itself. Rarely were the concepts of liberty or freedom, those moving symbols of the American Revolution, applied to the emerging reality of black rule in the colony. Possible parallels with the American revolutionary experience were generally ignored; American public opinion simply could not accept that the free mulattos and blacks of St. Domingo might be seen as counterparts to the propertied gentlemen who had led the American rebellion. Admittedly, the situation in St. Domingo smacked little of republicanism. Personal freedom may have been gained for the people of the colony, but there was precious little in the way of democracy, or institutions on which to base a representative government.

Toussaint's rule, indeed, was authoritarian, even if largely benevolent. Given the demographics and bloody history of the island, even the most ardent champions of liberty could expect little else for the moment. The colony needed law and order, and Toussaint and his army supplied it. The "cultivators"—the new euphemism for ex-slaves—were urged (even forced) to go back to work under production-sharing contracts, and the plantations were run either by the army or by the old managers, who had been trickling back with Toussaint's encouragement. The return of order in the areas governed by Toussaint had begun to revive the economy, in spite of the prevailing political uncertainty and the threat of continued war. Burned cities were being rebuilt. But, other than a rubber-stamp assembly, there was no effort at republican government. Few, in fact, argued for it. Certainly not the Federalists in the United States. Hamilton had even advised Pickering that the best form of government for St. Domingo might be all but medieval. "No regular system of Liberty will at present suit St. Domingo," he wrote, "The government if independent must be military—partaking of the feudal system." He suggested a president for life, with military rule and compulsory military service.[14]

President Adams had gotten his way; he had checked the move to war. But the arch-Federalists would not forgive him, and the cost of his victory was a serious split within his own party. The timing could not have been worse. The fierce struggle between the Federalist and Republican parties had already divided the country, and now Hamilton's group was threatening to divide the Federalists, with presidential elections less than a year away.

French consul Letombe misread the situation entirely, reporting home that Adams's nomination of the peace delegation to Paris had been simply an election maneuver. Adams, he said darkly, "seeks to execute other projects useful to his ambitions and the greed of his party. I suspect he is mounting an intrigue with St. Domingo."[15] Perhaps Letombe's judgement had been warped by annoyance over the unfriendly reception given to General Hedouville when he transited the United States after his expulsion from Cap François. Anyway, he was wrong. Adams's position had been weakened, not bolstered, by his initiative toward peace, and he contemplated no hidden "intrigue" with Toussaint—the project was largely in the public record.

But, quite possibly, there was another connection between the two measures. On the surface, it seemed inconsistent to make peace feelers toward France while at the same time undermining its hold on its prize colony, a fact that Hamilton had pointed out to Pickering.[16] But Adams could have no expectation of an early settlement with France, and meanwhile the leverage provided by the St. Domingo action might help in negotiating such a settlement. Moreover, on the domestic front, the two measures provided an expedient political tradeoff. The arch-Federalists were fighting a bitter rearguard action against the president's project of sending a delegation to Paris, insisting on prior written guarantees from the French government and otherwise hindering a rapprochement. In the circumstance, it might be useful to mollify their anger somewhat by speedily putting the Toussaint Clause into effect and allowing a trade to resume from which they would be the prime beneficiaries.

According to the new law, the president could open trade with St. Domingo once he was in a position to declare that it was safe to do so. That would require an agreement with Toussaint to curb the privateers, as the general in chief had promised to do. A second agreement with Britain would also be prudent, given that the Royal Navy was the predominant power in the Caribbean and could disrupt the American trade with St. Domingo if it chose to. What was needed was a trusted emissary, one who could both negotiate an agreement with Toussaint and mange the emerging interface with the British and, eventually, the U.S. Navy over trade with the island.

As the American representative to Toussaint, the president nominated a respected physician, Dr. Edward Stevens. Stevens was by origin a West Indian, a lifetime friend of Alexander Hamilton (and, some suspected, the illegitimate Hamilton's half brother). In addition to his impeccable contacts, Stevens was a person who both knew the West Indies and spoke French well. His nomination to the new post of consul general "in the Island of St. Domingo" (thus carefully sidestepping the issue of what government Stevens might be accredited to) passed the Senate with only token opposition from the Republicans. Stevens quickly went to work.

Much of the ground for Stevens's mission had been well prepared by Toussaint's envoy Joseph Bunel, accompanied by Consul Mayer. In a series of meetings with Pickering and leading political and merchant figures in Philadelphia, they had sought to gain support for the opening of trade, and to line up supplies. In return, they led their eager listeners to believe that Toussaint might eventually break free from France.[17] Now that the act had been passed, they could look forward to a relatively rapid resumption of trade.

In early March, Stevens received his official instructions. Whatever the sponsors of the Toussaint Clause may have wished privately, the official position was that the aim of Stevens's mission was to be limited to opening the trade. His first priority was to get Toussaint to take measures that would stop the privateer attacks on American shipping. French warships and privateers were to be barred from the island, and if possible French merchantmen as well, while American warships and merchantmen were to be admitted freely. The instructions made no mention of independence, and yet were eloquent in what they allowed Stevens to imply: that a prosperous St. Domingo, under the tutelage of the United States, would be in a position to throw off its ties to France. "The colony of St. Domingo is so far abandoned by the Mother country as to be under the necessity of providing for its own wants," the instruction drafted by Pickering read. "It is worse than abandoned, for without supplying its wants, the measures authorized by the French Republic have operated to cut off the supplies which the colony would otherwise have derived from neutral nations, & above all from the United

States." Renewal of trade would bring about prosperity, and "by the abundance of imports and exports, the revenues of the island may be rendered adequate to all the exigencies of the administration."[18]

The instructions may have been silent on independence, but when Senator Smith of Maryland asked whether or not the law amounted to de facto recognition, Secretary Wolcott expressed the war hawks' real desires by trying to have it both ways:

> Dr. Stevens is not to treat with any British agent; his object is to persuade Toussaint to renounce privateering, and to agree to other arrangements which will justify opening the trade, and there is good reason to think he will succeed. Nothing appears to have been proposed, discussed or settled between the British and Toussaint, respecting the independence of the island, and with this question the United States will not interfere. Our object is to gain a trade on safe principles; questions of interior policy and government are to be settled by the people of the island, and others concerned, in their own way. As, however, I will not be insincere or conceal an opinion on a subject respecting which I profess to give information, I must add, that I believe the island will assert and maintain its independence.[19]

In mid-April Stevens, Mayer, and Bunel embarked for Cap François on the USS *Kingston*. The ship carried, in addition to its important passengers, a shipment of flour, uniforms, and other provisions designed to "favorably dispose the mind of Toussaint" and to meet some of the pressing needs in St. Domingo. Its sale was also designed, in the absence of congressional funding, to contribute to the expenses of Stevens's mission. The irregular method of financing the mission, and Stevens's potential role in selling the supplies, had been controversial; Attorney General Lee had opposed it strongly. But, like everything else in this venture, it had been pushed through the cabinet by Hamilton's allies Pickering, McHenry, and Wolcott.[20] They were determined to have the mission succeed.

Success would require the cooperation of the British. The Maitland-Toussaint agreement of the summer before had appeared to give Britain preferential trading rights, but now Toussaint had also invited the United States to supply his needs. In London, American minister Rufus King had been badgering His Majesty's Government, ever since he had heard of the Maitland-Toussaint agreement toward the end of the previous year, to respect traditional American trading rights with the island. The British had agreed in principle. Both governments, after all, were anxious to stop the activities of French-flagged privateers from the island, as well as to limit the possible spread of revolutionary ideas from there, or, as Foreign Minister Grenville put it, the "infinite dangers to which our Islands and your Southern Provinces would be exposed from an unrestrained commerce with St. Domingo."[21] With the two sides thus in concord on the broad principles, it was decided that a working agreement should be fleshed out in Philadelphia. The British chose as their negotiator a man very familiar with the situation, Thomas Maitland, now a general.

Shortly after Dr. Stevens had departed for Cap François, Maitland arrived in Philadelphia. There he, British minister Robert Liston, and Timothy Pickering—the president being at home in Quincy—sat down to draft an agreement. It turned out, however, that the British government had, in spite of Rufus King's remonstrances on the point, stuck to their old mercantilist policy, and instructed Maitland to demand that the trade be monopolized through a joint trading company. They even wanted to carve up the market, with the Americans limited to raw materials supply and the British taking all the manufactured goods trade. Pickering, for his part, was adamant in protecting Yankee principles of free trade. He also had the negotiating advantage, because Maitland, who was concerned that Dr. Stevens might already be making a preferential deal with Toussaint, was as a result in a hurry to conclude a deal. He and Liston soon agreed that they had little choice but to depart from their instructions on the point.

With that hurdle cleared, the two sides agreed to control the trade by administrative means, leaving its actual composition to market conditions. Provided that Toussaint removed the privateer threat, they would encourage American and British merchants to supply the island, but only subject to strict joint U.S.-British traffic controls, to be enforced by the Royal and American navies. Arriving vessels would be allowed at only two ports: Cap François or Port au Prince. Once there, they would either sell their cargo or get documentation—"passports"—from American or British representatives, allowing them to engage in coastal trade to the many smaller ports that supplied the plantations. By these means, the waters around the island would be kept clear of locally commissioned French privateers, all British and neutral shipping in the area would be strictly controlled, and—very importantly—the inhabitants of St. Domingo would be effectively kept off the sea, except for a few ships to be provided with British or American passports.

The importance of this last point was reemphasized by the first of the jointly drafted "Points of Understanding" which General Maitland carried to St. Domingo to guide him in his negotiations with Toussaint. It read, "It is understood that Great Britain and the United States have a common interest in preventing the dissemination of dangerous principles among the slaves of their respective countries, and that they will mutually and sincerely attend to that interest, to guard both against the dangers here alluded to in course of the proposed intercourse with St. Domingo."[22]

The American government hoped to straddle the horns of its dilemma. It would open trade with St. Domingo, but it would control that trade so tightly as to minimize the twin dangers of renewed unlicensed privateering on the one hand, and the spread of ideas of black emancipation on the other. St. Domingo would be placed, in effect, under quarantine. Pickering, in briefing Stevens on the results of the Philadelphia talks, was explicit. The agreed measures, he wrote, were "deemed necessary for the security of the commerce of both nations, and of the tranquility of our Southern States and of the British West Indies, which it was considered would be endangered by an unrestrained intercourse with St. Domingo. Both the commercial regulations and those calculated for the political safety of Dominions of each Nation, abounding in Negro population, must depend for their establishment on the orders of General Toussaint. . . . The design of these articles is obvious: the security of St. Domingo and the British Islands, and the United States, against any mischievous intriguers and revolutionaries."[23]

It remained, of course, to negotiate these conditions with Toussaint, including the limitations on the island government's naval capabilities. But Pickering and Maitland assumed—correctly it turned out—that Toussaint's desire for supplies plus British and American support would oblige him to swallow that pill.

The accord reached in Philadelphia in late April, Pickering insisted, had to be subject to approval by the absent president. It was with a sense of evident satisfaction, then, that Pickering was able to report to Stevens several weeks later that the president had approved. Nonetheless, Adams's approval had been a bit less than wholehearted. After stating that he could see "no rational objection" to the articles (which implied that he may nonetheless have harbored some reservations), the president offered that "On the whole, I think the negotiation has been conducted with caution and prudence, and that the result has my fullest approbation."[24]

Pickering saw the agreement as a first step. He continued to believe that Toussaint had political ambitions, much greater than mere reestablishment of the trade. If that were the case, the United States would not stand in his way—even though it was now official policy not to make any overt moves supporting the island's independence. But the official policy was a bit late in any event; there had already been enough winks and nods during the Bunel mission to give Toussaint the hint that he would face little opposition from the American administration if he chose to move. Briefing Rufus

King on the results of the talks in Philadelphia, the secretary of state stretched the truth a bit when he wrote:

> At the same time, we considered the terms as perfectly compatible with the ultimate dependence of St. Domingo on France. It is not, however to be denied, nor have we aimed at any concealment, that we have strong expectations that Toussaint will declare the Island independent. Unquestionably, he has long contemplated that event. But it is absolutely false, what Hedouville declared in his last proclamation, that the United States has intrigued with Great Britain to bring him to that measure: We have, in fact, not intermeddled In any matter whatever in the political affairs of St. Domingo. If Toussaint declares its independency, it will not be owing to the intrigues, nor the advice, nor even the suggestion of the United States.[25]

Maitland had been right; Stevens in Cap François had in fact negotiated a separate arrangement with Toussaint. But Maitland need not have worried. Stevens's negotiation had been limited to the threshold issue of privateering, and had scarcely touched on the regulation of the trade, much less the quarantine aspects.

Stevens had rapidly established a confidential relationship with the general in chief, assisted by the offer of the supplies he had brought with him. With the very grudging concurrence of French agent Roume, Stevens and Toussaint had worked on the language of an official decree designed to rein in the privateering abuses by releasing all captured American ships, protecting American property in the future, and canceling all previously issued letters of marque. The decree was published and put into immediate effect, but it had one glaring loophole. It called in all privateers and cancelled their previous commissions, but did not explicitly state that no new commissions would be issued. Toussaint promised Stevens that such would be the case, and Stevens urged, in his report to Philadelphia, that the assurance be accepted. Pickering did not agree, insisting that Congress would require written obligations from Toussaint. But by the time his response reached Cap François, the matter had become irrelevant, in view of Maitland's arrival with the new negotiating instructions.

General Maitland arrived at the port of Arcahaye, where Toussaint and Stevens had traveled to meet him. The arrival of British men of war and officers, of course, caused a flurry of anxiety on an island that had so recently been occupied by the redcoats, but Toussaint brushed it aside in the interest of concluding the agreement. He did not quibble long over the terms that had been proposed at Philadelphia, and on June 13 (ironically, a year to the day since the American law suspending commercial relations with France had initially been approved) a convention was signed. Toussaint pledged noninterference in Jamaica or other neighboring states, and made further changes in the earlier decree reining in the privateers. The two naval powers, in return, pledged to resume supplies to the island under the terms of the Philadelphia understandings, which they would enforce.

Stevens, who had not signed the agreement but would be the agent for both powers for the foreseeable future, hastened to inform Pickering that he had accomplished his first goal: the trade would be protected. The president, he urged, could now declare the trade open and issue regulations that would implement the agreements reached with Toussaint and the British.

On June 26, President Adams issued a proclamation in which he declared that the conditions of the Toussaint Clause had been met and that trade with St. Domingo—or at least the ports controlled by Toussaint—could be safely opened. A customs circular of the same day spelled out the terms under which American ships could trade there; that is, those of the Philadelphia understandings. In order, presumably, not to inflame French sentiments more than absolutely necessary after weeks of extravagant press speculation about the Maitland-Toussaint talks, the fact that the Americans had colluded with the British in achieving the accord was not mentioned.

American merchants had been anticipating the agreement (Pickering, for one, had been advising his friends that it was coming) and were eager to get down to business with the St. Domingo rebels. On the day the agreement became effective, a number of ships were already lying off Cap François, ready to sell their goods. The flow of American assistance to Toussaint had begun.

THE ST. DOMINGO STATION

The USS *General Green*—soon to play a role in the St. Domingo story—was fitting out for duty in the West Indies, and the Boston papers advertised for men to serve:

> All able bodied and ordinary Seamen who wish to serve their Country, on board the U.S. Frigate *General Greene*, Christopher Raymond Perry, Commander, now lying in at Newport, may have an opportunity of entering, by applying at the House of Mrs. Broaders in Fore Street, where a Rendezvous is opened for that purpose, and where the Terms will be made known.

> Where the INJURIES and INSULTS of our Country are considered on the one hand, and the glory of avenging them on the other, it is presumed that any pressing solicitation to enter the service will be unnecessary.[1]

In fact, the navy had few problems in recruiting; enthusiasm for the war was high, and the government was offering premium wages.

Secretary of the Navy Benjamin Stoddert already had most of his few available fighting ships in the West Indies. Even before the presidential proclamation, Stoddert had urged his captains to call at Cap François if possible, noting that General Toussaint was eager to see

American ships in those waters. However, the *Norfolk* and the *Ganges* had been the only U.S. Navy ships to call, when they had dropped off Stevens in April 1799. Most of the other ships, with orders to fight armed French government vessels but to leave French merchantmen alone, had gathered in the Lesser Antilles, where the naval activity and chance for prizes was the highest.

With the presidential proclamation taking effect in August, and the U.S. Navy partly responsible for enforcing its provisions, it became necessary to have a more or less permanent naval presence in the area of Cap François. The St. Domingo station was established, a naval agent was sent to Cap François, and warships (including the *General Greene*) began to patrol the area more regularly. The ships had orders to arrest French privateers, as well as any American merchantmen who were still trading with the island illegally, something which Stevens had complained about (rather righteously) as "one of the most iniquitous attempts to frustrate the intentions of the American Government as perhaps was ever formed."[2]

It was autumn, however, before the U.S. Navy was a permanent presence in the waters around St. Domingo. By that time, French privateers had already been scared away from the island, under the combined dissuasion of Toussaint's decree and U.S. and Royal Navy presence. The trade was once again safe, and soon a daily average of seven American-flagged merchantmen were calling at Cap François, either to sell their goods or pick up the required passports for port calls farther along the coast.

The increased naval presence was not all a blessing for Dr. Stevens, however. The officers and men in the young navy were eager for action, and for prizes, and found the business of patrol and checking of ships' documents to be tedious. They were unhappy that Stevens had issued passports to ships controlled by Toussaint's military, and wanted to arrest the ships, until Stevens was able to convince them that Toussaint needed a few vessels for communications and ferrying troops to different coastal locations.

There was also considerable confusion and some anger over the presence of French merchantmen, some of them armed, that had managed to reach the colony through the British blockade. Many navy officers wanted the armed French ships to be considered fair prizes. This caused a flurry of negotiation for Stevens, who had, for starters, to remind navy officers tactfully that they were not instructed to wage war on French merchantmen. He then negotiated appropriate documentation with Toussaint and an incensed Agent Roume (who was quite rightly protecting the interests of the French merchants), and finally had to convince his superiors in Washington to clarify the navy's instructions. Pickering, who would have preferred to seize the French ships, eventually agreed that they should not be molested, since the ports under Toussaint's jurisdiction could be considered "naturally neutral" in the wars between the northern powers.[3] (This justification probably had the benefit, in Pickering's eyes, of granting to the Toussaint government still another attribute of sovereignty.) It was the end of the year however before the imbroglio was cleared up. The navy agreed to honor special passports issued by Stevens for eligible French merchant ships, while Stoddert issued new orders to his commanding officers that eased the blockade of Toussaint's ports, and prohibited hot pursuit of French ships leaving harbor, or captures within three miles of the coast. Some naval officers were still unhappy, complaining that the new rules simply allowed the Royal Navy to take the prizes, instead of them.

On the whole, the arrangements were working very well. Under the protection of the British and American navies, American trade with the island was booming, contributing to a limited economic revival. Unfortunately, and in spite of the good business climate, Dr. Stevens was experiencing difficulties with some of the American businessmen at Cap François. Jacob Mayer, the consul, had accused him of making personal profits from sale of the goods that had been brought out on the *Norfolk*, and had poisoned some minds against him. More important than this sordid squabble, however, Stevens's relations with Toussaint remained firm and trusting, in spite of efforts by pro-French officials to prejudice the general against the U.S. Navy. Roume was part of the latter problem, and more; he had issued a few irregular letters of marque and tried to sow dissension between Stevens and Toussaint. But it was increasingly clear that he was more of a nuisance than a threat, and that Toussaint was able to neutralize his schemes. Stevens was pleased with the results of his mission so far, assuring Pickering that he had "the most perfect confidence in the Attachment of Toussaint to the Government of the U.S. and his sincere Desire to establish a beneficial and permanent Commerce between the two Countries."[4]

President Adams, on the other hand, was not fully convinced that the St. Domingo strategy would work out to be in his country's long-term interest. He was truly perplexed by the contradictions and uncertainties in the situation, and unsure of the wisdom of the policy that his administration had chosen to follow. Just after signing the proclamation, he had tried to express some of his concern to his zealous secretary of state: "The result of the whole is, in my mind, problematical and precarious. Toussaint has evidently puzzled himself, the French government, the English cabinet, and the administration of the United States. All the rest of the world know as little what to do with him as he knows what to do with himself. His example may be followed by all the islands, French, English, Dutch and Spanish; all will one day be played off against the United States by the European powers."[5]

President Adams had gone along with his cabinet's recommendation on the matter, and had allowed Pickering to conduct the key negotiations without close guidance, yet he was worried over the risks of the policy. His greatest immediate concern was not that the policy would harm his attempted rapprochement with the French; he knew that there were bigger issues at play that would determine the course of that initiative. He was concerned, rather, that the American enthusiasts for the colony's independence not get out ahead of Britain, which he believed harbored strong reservations on the subject. British cooperation would be necessary for long-term security in the region, he thought, even though their past actions in St. Domingo had created "much mischief for themselves as well as for us." The United States, he warned Pickering, should "do nothing without the consent, concert, and cooperation of the British government in this case. They are so deeply interested that they ought to be consulted, and the commerce of the island is not worth the risk of any dispute with them."[6]

Adams remained skeptical about the trade benefits that had been predicted from the policy. Three months after signing the proclamation opening the trade, he wrote to Pickering, in a letter full of misgivings about the policy's implementation, "I wish, as you do, that the trade to St. Domingo may turn out to be worth the cost. To speak in the style of a Frenchman, I have never felt any very sublime enthusiasm on that subject."[7]

While the president fretted about the details of implementation, and the necessity of coordination with the British, his sense of unease seems to have been based more on strategic considerations. "[T]he evils in store seem not to be foreseen," he had written to Navy Secretary Stoddert just after signing the proclamation.[8] He had in mind, particularly, the risks that the possibility of independence for St. Domingo and the other West Indian colonies might pose to American security. The evil that Adams most feared was not the security threat feared by the southern Republicans—that is, the possible export of radical egalitarian ideas to American slave quarters. That did not unduly perturb an antislavery New Englander like the president. He feared, instead, the external threat: that small, weak, and poor Caribbean states, first of all St. Domingo, could become platforms for adventures by the European powers in the area, or permanent seats of piracy against America's vital commerce in the region. Sounding almost the same alarm as that voiced earlier by the Republican spokesman Gallatin, the president ordered Stoddert to direct the navy against pirates in the area, noting his "apprehension that the West Indies Islands would soon become a scene of piracy. The dissolution of all principles of morals, government and religion . . . the proclamation of liberty to the negroes of the West Indies Islands, and the policy of one or more nations of Europe to erect predatory power in the West Indies, to be employed against the United States, as [are] the Barbary powers. . . . have long ago raised suspicions and forebodings, that the most desperate wretches in Europe would be allured to the Islands, give direction to the mass of bone and sinew which is now at liberty and idleness, or trained to military discipline "9

Concern about how the policy might play out, however, by no means meant reconsideration. With the president's party already badly split over policy toward France and other issues, there was no question of giving ammunition to the opposition by expressing, in public, any concerns about St. Domingo that the chief executive may have held in private. The Republicans had already begun to attack the Stevens mission as a misuse of public office, citing Jacob Mayer's complaints over the manner in which the shipment of supplies had been sold. The situation demanded that no doubts be expressed in the message Adams was expected to give to Congress in December. He asked his cabinet members for input on how his message should handle the St. Domingo issue. Treasury Secretary Wolcott, for one, admitted that "the whole subject of the arrangement with St. Domingo had from the first excited considerable curiosity, suspicion and dissent," and recommended that the message be bland and historical, so as not to excite the "divided opinions of the people." Pickering, predictably, argued for a self-congratulatory statement on the opening of the trade.[10] The president took Wolcott's lower-key advice, and the single, short paragraph in his address simply noted that trade had resumed in safety, and privateering had ceased.

In St. Domingo, Dr. Stevens had no doubts whatsoever about his role or the objectives of his mission. With the privateers banished, trade resumed, and the U.S. Navy on station, he had established the basis for a lasting commercial relationship with Toussaint's St. Domingo. The next step, as he saw it, would be to help Toussaint solidify his hold on power, and set the stage for independence. He and the general in chief had developed a trusting and confidential relationship which remained sound in spite of the abrasions and mini-crises of the wartime situation. Stevens lost few opportunities to praise Toussaint in his dispatches to Philadelphia, or to point out that his success was essential.

In June, the long-threatened civil war between Toussaint and Rigaud sputtered to life with Rigaud, according to Stevens, having made the first move. The hostilities at first were small in scale, which was fortunate for Toussaint, as his troops were desperately short of supplies until they began to flow from America. To help tide the army over, Stevens jumped to Toussaint's aid, arranging with the British (and with Philadelphia's approval) for a shipment of arms from Jamaica. Stevens also reported that French Commissioner Roume, even though nominally supporting Toussaint as general in chief, was secretly aiding Rigaud, as well as creating problems for American merchants, and all with the French government's approval. Stevens made it clear to Pickering which side he thought the United States should take. "It will readily occur to you, Sir, that if Toussaint should prove unsuccessful, all the arrangements we have made respecting commerce must fall to the ground. The most solemn treaty would have little weight with a man of Rigaud's capricious and tyrannical temper."[11]

The outbreak of the civil war had created another complication for the U.S. Navy. Instead of French privateers, it now had to deal with gunboats and small armed ships commissioned by Rigaud, or operating as virtual pirates, that swarmed the Bight of Leogane and attacked American and other shipping. Toussaint had complained, in a letter to President Adams in mid-summer, that if he was to be deprived of a navy of his own, he needed the Americans to control the corsairs. He asked that several U.S. Navy warships be sent to his aid, adding rather loftily that "In acceding to my request, you will have the glory of having cooperated, and having your nation cooperate, in the Extinction of a Rebellion which is repugnant to the eyes of all the Governments of the World."[12] Although Adams never responded directly to the request, the need to protect American shipping gave Toussaint, in practice, what he had asked for. It was also more than Congress had knowingly authorized in the Toussaint Clause. When the U.S. Navy authorized its vessels to fight the corsairs, it meant that they were effectively fighting on Toussaint's side.

The situation was of course ambiguous, so much so that U.S. naval officers on duty off St. Domingo remained suspicious over the prevailing documentary confusion and periodic requests for exemptions to existing rules. Stevens's efforts to justify his flexibility were at least honest, as in this letter to Captain Little, who had tried to arrest a ship that had been issued a somewhat suspect passport: "You must be aware, Sir, that my situation here is difficult and unpleasant, and that it requires much address to reconcile the jarring interests of the two prevailing Parties that, at present, share the Government of the Island [meaning France and Toussaint.] In a revolutionary Country like the present, circumstances are continually rising. . . . I shall often be forced to do what I do not approve of, and which, for want of knowing all the Circumstances that have actuated me, may appear to others as highly improper."[13]

All the same, Stevens got along reasonably well with the naval commanders, and retained the backing of Pickering and Stoddert at home. He did not invariably support Toussaint's requests. For example, he did draw the line at allowing U.S. Navy ships to transport any of Toussaint's troops, as the general requested on more than one occasion. But, as a result, he was logically obliged to support Toussaint's desire to have at least a few warships of his own, to be used in the coastal trade for transport of men and supplies. He was able to work out an arrangement with Silas Talbot, captain of the *Constitution* and current head of the naval station, whereby Toussaint's ships would be allowed to operate only if they bore one of the consul general's passports and were on an approved list.

The situation had, indeed, become almost absurd: warships fly-ing the French ensign, and commissioned by a recognized, even though not fully loyal, French governor (Toussaint), were conduct-ing operations against the forces of a second nominally French offi-cial (Rigaud), but were allowed to operate in waters, still legally French, only with the consent of the U.S. and British navies, and under documents issued by the consul general of the United States.

All the same, the war ground on. Slowly but surely, the pressure of Toussaint's army on land and the U.S. Navy at sea was pushing Rigaud back. The war between the armies, dubbed the "War of the Knives," was horrendous. It had become a race war, mulatto versus black, the vengeful mulatto chauvinist Rigaud against Toussaint's best general, the implacable and bloodthirsty Dessalines, with grue-some atrocities on both sides. At the end of the year Toussaint, now well supplied and confident, ordered a major offensive against Rigaud's strongholds on the southern peninsula. He suffered a set-back, however, when the supplies he had sent to the south coast on six of his ships were captured at sea and condemned by the British, who had feared that they were designed for use against Jamaica. When Toussaint asked Stevens to make American naval vessels avail-able in substitution, Stevens refused to take such an overt step of assistance, but did ask Commodore Talbot if he could help in some other way.

At sea, the civil war was characterized by the seizure and robbery of American ships by Rigaud's corsairs, sometimes accompanied by murders or worse. The navy was largely engaged in protection and convoy duty, and the occasional skirmish or punishment raid. Dr. Stevens was involved firsthand in one of the few renowned naval engagements of the war. He was a passenger on the U.S. Navy sloop *Experiment*, in the Bight, when the convoy it was protecting was attacked by twelve gunboats. In an eight-hour battle, the *Experiment* succeeded in sinking two of the gunboats, but lost three of its escorted ships—though one was recaptured the next day.

The last battle of the civil war was the siege of the southern port of Jacmel, where the mulatto army under Alexandre Pétion had been putting up a spirited defense against Dessalines and his army of almost ten thousand men. In the end, the defense crumbled in February 1800 when the U.S. Navy took sides. Commodore Talbot, it seems, had taken a broader view of what help he could offer to Toussaint's army than had Dr. Stevens, and his instrument had been the *General Greene*. As one of the ship's officers wrote to his family, "We were ordered by Commodore Talbot to make a cruise around Hispaniola . . . for the purpose of aiding Gen. Toussaint in the capture of Jacmel. We cruised off the port for a considerable time, to intercept supplies for Rigaud. That had the desired effect. . . . We engaged three of Rigaud's forts warmly for 30 or 40 minutes, in which time we obliged the enemy to evacuate the town and two of the forts, and retire to their strongest hold; this fort however soon hauled down its colors."[14] The civil war dragged on for almost another half year, but Rigaud's defeat at Jacmel assured Toussaint of victory. There was no longer any force on the island that could contest his authority, and France and French armies were far away.

In France, however, things had changed as well. To begin with, the Directory was gone. Corrupt and unpopular, its early military victories had been followed by Napoleon Bonaparte's disastrous campaign in Egypt, and an inconclusive war against the Second Coalition. Bonaparte had returned in November of 1799 to put an end to the resultant drift. His Brumaire coup d'etat resulted in the drafting of still another constitution, and the establishment of a ruling Consulate of three members, of whom only the First Consul— Napoleon, *bien sûr*—had real power. As the Directory had done away with the Revolution, now the Consulate did away with all but the barest forms of the Republic. France had reverted to autocracy.

And second, the peace talks with America had finally gotten under way. A bad crossing in stormy winter weather had delayed the American emissaries' arrival in France by ten weeks, with the result that it was March 1800 before the talks actually began. The change of government in Paris was a surprise, but no impediment to the delegation in carrying out its instructions. Talleyrand, after all, was still minister of foreign affairs, and the new regime showed them all appropriate honors. The head of the French delegation, indeed, was Joseph Bonaparte, Napoleon's brother.

The peace talks may have gotten off to an amicable start, but neither side was prepared to concede much. Adams, who had to contend with a cabinet that opposed his peace policy, sternly instructed his troublesome secretary of state that he would approach the French with a "pacific and friendly disposition," and expected his cabinet's cooperation. In a move probably designed as much to keep his subordinates quiet and under control as to maintain leverage during the negotiations, he also informed Pickering that operations in St. Domingo and elsewhere were to continue "as if no negotiations were going on."[15]

On the subject of St. Domingo, the two delegations had predictably different instructions. The Americans had been given a full set of documents on the arrangements with Toussaint, but for background use only. They were not to raise the subject except in the most general of terms, by demanding the right to trade freely with all of France's colonies. The French, on the other hand, were instructed that they could take the Americans' expected demands on trade privileges under consideration, but if the subject of St. Domingo came up, they were to complain about American policy in strong and explicit terms: "The United States Government, as if trying to offend in every manner possible, has publicly received the Agent of an Agent of the Republic as the representative of an independent power, and has dealt with him. Today St. Domingue offers the scandalous spectacle of an American Commissar giving to

French merchants, or refusing, or selling at a high price, the rights to trade with a French colony."[16]

Maybe it was just as well that St. Domingo never emerged as a major element in the negotiations. By mid-summer the talks had become deadlocked over two other issues: whether or not the Treaty of 1778, and France's rights under it, was still in effect, and whether the Americans could expect any reparations for the losses their merchants had suffered from French naval seizures. Napoleon, just returned from a decisive victory over the Austrians at Marengo and brimming with confidence, insisted on rejecting any reparations. With this major negotiating target ruled out by the triumphant First Consul, the Americans debated whether to pack their bags and go home.

In America, too, change was in the air. The political atmosphere, already superheated and vicious, had become even more tense with the approach of the elections, due to climax with the meeting of the electoral college in early 1801. The Adams administration was under attack; the war taxes, the loss of business with France, and the abuses of the Sedition Act had sapped its earlier popularity. It was also being eroded from within, with Hamilton and the arch-Federalists having deserted Adams in favor of the candidacy of Charles C. Pinckney. The president, finally stirred to action in May over the persistent—and now blatantly active—disloyalty of his cabinet members, had fired the Hamilton moles McHenry and Pickering (Walcott somehow stayed on). His action, however, confirmed the deep split within his own party. In the meantime, the Republicans were gaining ground, and a key block of electoral votes had become available to them in New York when an alliance of Aaron Burr, the Livingstons, and the Clintons had beaten the Hamilton group in that state's elections.

Toussaint had followed up his victory in the south by consolidating his position in the capital city. Even before the fall of Jacmel in late

February 1800, Stevens had been predicting momentous changes. In a short note to Pickering, partly in code and with his usual extravagant use of capitalization, he whispered,

> Every Thing announces a speedy Dissolution of those Ties, which once connected this important Colony with the Mother Country. While I was uncertain of the real intentions of Toussaint, I was loath to say any Thing to you about them. Now that I think that I know them, it is my Duty to announce them to you. He is taking his measures slowly but surely. All connection with France will soon be broken off. If he is not disturbed, he will preserve appearances a little longer. But as soon as France interferes in this colony, he will throw off the mask and declare it independent.[17]

In April, Toussaint engineered a coup. Letters of denunciation emerged mysteriously in Cap François, accusing Commissioner Roume of treachery and indecision, and demanding his resignation. When Roume resisted, the "popular" denunciations only spread to other areas of the colony, and expanded their demands: not only should Roume resign, but supreme authority in the colony should be vested in Toussaint. The general declined the honor, for the moment. Instead, he placed Roume under virtual house arrest, but then demanded that he authorize, in the name of France, a takeover of the Spanish side of the island which had been nominally ceded to France years earlier. Roume, intimidated, agreed after an initial refusal. It was virtually his last official act; Toussaint's rapid moves had neutralized him entirely as a factor in the island's politics.

Stevens reported these theatrical developments with deadpan prose, but could not hide his (premature) enthusiasm for Toussaint's victory: "But it is no difficult mater to foresee how this Business will terminate. He will accept the unanimous Invitation of the Colony, and from that Moment it may be considered as forever separated from France. Policy, perhaps, may induce him to make no open Declaration of Independence, before he is compelled. But this apparent and temporary Attachment to the Mother Country will only ensure the Separation of the Colony more effectually."[18]

Toussaint had declined the title of supreme authority on the island, but he had the substance of it anyway. Roume, after almost a year's imprisonment, would eventually be sent home to France. Rigaud's last foothold would be reduced by August, and he himself would also depart for France. And in January 1801 the Spanish authorities in Santo Domingo surrendered control, with only token resistance, of their end of the island.

The former servant of the Breda plantation had become the undisputed ruler of the entire island. His people were free, and he wished to protect their liberty, but his position was uncertain and his enemies numerous.

Timing can be everything. Toussaint had gained control of his country, and then of the whole island of Hispaniola, just as events elsewhere were beginning to conspire against his success.

The United States, on the face of it, was still strongly supportive. Congressional authority to continue the trade with St. Domingo had been renewed in March. By late summer, the president had authorized the opening of trade with all ports on the island controlled by Toussaint—those in the old Rigaud enclave as well as those on the old Spanish part of the island. The U.S. Navy had fought on Toussaint's side in the civil war and was still on patrol in the island's waters, protecting a lively trade with America. And yet the great champion of St. Domingo in the American cabinet, Secretary Pickering, had been fired. Consul General Stevens, who had been cleared by his superiors of wrongdoing in the case of the goods shipment, had nonetheless asked to be replaced—ostensibly for health reasons (he had contracted malaria). And even though he stayed on for many more months, Stevens never again had the kind of access and influence in Philadelphia he had had while reporting to

Pickering. Toussaint then added still another element of dissonance into the slipping relationship when he insisted, over Steven's objections, on raising the duties on American imports.

There was also a deeper-seated problem in the relationship with America. St. Domingo was no longer, after years of war and the breakdown of the old plantation economy, as attractive a market as it once had been. A decade of fighting had created demand for American munitions and supplies, it is true, but that was not a permanent situation, and in the meantime the colony's exports had become less competitive. Cheap St. Domingo molasses was a thing of the past, and many of the American rum distillers had switched away from its use, or to making whiskey. The island's plantation-based export economy had collapsed entirely during the years of fighting; it had reached its nadir in 1795 when exports amounted to no more than 3 percent of their prewar levels.[19] Toussaint, in need of export earnings to finance his defense effort and rebuilding, had striven to revive the plantation economy through labor contracts and profit sharing with the workers. But the effort was not fully successful, since the freed slaves resisted return to the plantations and often preferred to engage in subsistence farming or to flee into the interior. The situation was so bad that Toussaint had been obliged to issue a decree in 1800 mandating the return to their plantations of all laborers who were not "gainfully employed." His draconian measures brought about a limited rebound of the export economy, but production of the key commodities remained way below the pre-revolutionary levels. In 1801, raw sugar production was less than 20 percent of its 1789 amount, while refined sugar and coffee production were only slightly better at 35 and 55 percent, respectively.[20] In short, the profit motive, which had been the primary motivator of America's traditional relationship with St. Domingo, was gradually but surely eroding.

With France, the bridges were all but burnt. Business and conservative interests were once again ascendant in Paris, and all wanted a return to France's old colonial policies and practices. Toussaint feared a French attempt to force his submission. In fact, it had been news of a major French force headed for the Caribbean and fear that they would establish a beachhead in Santo Domingo that had motivated his takeover of that part of the island. And when a new set of French commissioners from the Consular government arrived, the insults and bad feeling produced were mutual. The French officers were "insulted and ill treated," according to Stevens, who also reported that Toussaint had felt that the fact that he had been officially reinstated as general in chief by the new government in Paris was by far outweighed by the insulting and patronizing tone of the official communication which informed him of that fact. "In reading this Letter to me," Stevens reported, "he expressed his utmost Displeasure, and all his subsequent Acts shew that he is determined to throw off all Kind of Subordination to the French Government."[21]

Napoleon Bonaparte, the new First Consul, thought otherwise, it can be assumed. But for the moment he was occupied with the continuing war in Europe, and St. Domingo was not a priority matter.

And then France and America made peace. The American delegation, deciding not to abandon the progress they had made, settled reluctantly for a convention without reparations. Talleyrand facilitated the closing phase of the negotiations, and Joseph Bonaparte hosted a great celebration at his castle at Mortefontaine, where the convention was signed at the end of September. While the convention resolved fewer issues than had been hoped, it removed the causes of the near-war. It was approved by Congress in early 1801 with only one proviso: that the Treaty of 1778 be permanently annulled. Although the convention was not fully ratified until just before Christmas, hostilities were effectively over much earlier. Early in 1801, Stoddert gave the ships on duty at St. Domingo orders to continue their patrols, but to take no new prizes, and in March the ships were called back, many of them scheduled to be laid up in a drastically reduced peacetime navy.

The United States was no longer a combatant, and its trade with St. Domingo was no longer a special, protected case. Trade to the island would once again be subject to the normal (if not entirely agreed) rules for neutral shipping in wartime.

By March, another major change had taken place. The American election had finally been decided, after a dead heat in the electoral college and thirty-six ballots in the House of Representatives. The Federalists, fatally split, had been defeated, and Jefferson had finally beaten Burr in the long House battle. Opponents of the Toussaint Clause would form the next administration, and soon they would also sweep into control of Congress. Toussaint no longer had any well-placed friends in the U.S. government.

JEFFERSON EQUIVOCATES

"**W**e are all republicans, we are all federalists," Jefferson said in his inaugural message to Congress. It was, to be sure, a nice rhetorical flourish, but it was also a true sentiment. The new president hoped that the defeat of the arch-Federalists meant a permanent political eclipse of their views, ones that he considered to be profoundly antirepublican, even monarchical. Moreover, the margin of his victory had been very close (as well as made possible largely through the split between the Adams and Hamilton camps), and consequently he needed to conciliate the Federalist middle-of the-roaders. It was, indeed, a good time for fence-mending, after the vituperation and animosity of the past few years.

The Republican victory, narrow as it was, nonetheless marked an important political turning point. The country itself was changing. Republican victory in the 1801 congressional elections would confirm it: the political center of gravity in America was shifting westward, away from the coastal cities, toward the small farmers of the Piedmont, and even to the new states and territories across the mountains in the "western waters." And the new voters were largely Republican; they wanted a small government, low taxes, and cheap land. Even the seaboard states were changing politically. Not only New York had gone Republican in the presidential elections; so had South Carolina, where Charles Pinckney, the only Republican in that otherwise staunchly Federalist family, had led the upcountry voters

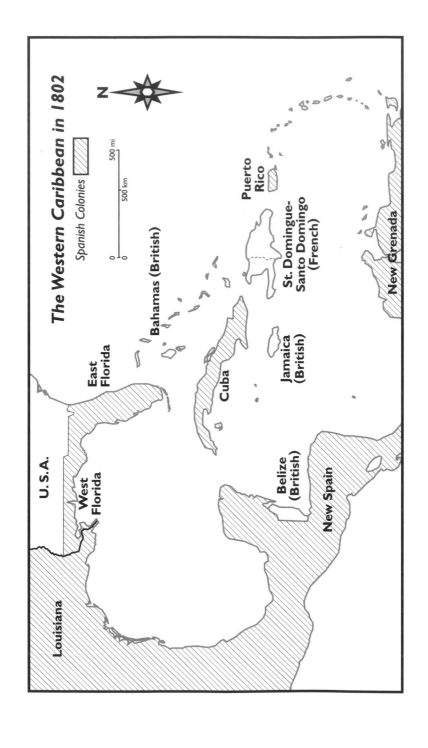

The Western Caribbean in 1802

Spanish Colonies

500 mi

500 km

Louisiana

U.S.A.

West Florida

East Florida

Bahamas (British)

Cuba

Jamaica (British)

Belize (British)

New Spain

Puerto Rico

St. Domingue-Santo Domingo (French)

New Grenada

against the old Charleston establishment. It was not yet fully evident, but the Federalists' day was over, and with it the political dominance of the merchant and financial interests of the seaboard cities.

Washington, the new federal capital, was itself a symbol of the change. Still a small settlement emerging from the woods, where one could go duck hunting a half mile from the president's mansion, it was a far cry from urban and urbane Philadelphia. The presidential mansion as well as the unfinished Capitol building were still leaky, drafty works in progress, and the city not much more than a scattered collection of houses and shacks linked by avenues that existed more on the elegant city plans than in reality. Washington was also, most decidedly, a southern town, where a slave market operated just down the hill from the Capitol and slaves tended tobacco fields within sight of the emerging symbols of the transplanted government.

Both Jefferson and Secretary of State James Madison would, as Virginians, identify readily with the imperatives of the western Republicans. And one of the key issues for the settlers in the western territories was assured access to the sea for the goods they produced. Freedom of navigation on the Mississippi was essential; there was no other practical way for the settlers west of the mountains to get their goods to market. But free use of the river was a foreign policy issue, since the west bank was under Spain's colonial administration, and both sides of the river were in Spanish hands around New Orleans. Even the rivers leading to the Gulf of Mexico from the areas that are now Alabama and Mississippi were blocked by Spanish control of West Florida, a strip along the coast. The Americans had won a diplomatic victory in 1795, when Thomas Pinckney had negotiated a treaty with the weak Spaniards that gave Americans a favorable border with Florida along the thirty-first parallel and permission to warehouse and export their goods through New Orleans. But that "right of deposit" was not really a right, but rather a concession offered by the Spaniards for a limited amount of time.

Spanish Louisiana was a weak neighbor with a decadent royal government at home in Madrid, and yet it had a hold on the westerners' trade lifeline. It was a situation sure to create problems as the restless, ambitious, and energetic Americans flowed across the mountains into the new, cheap lands of the West.

A new factor—cotton—was driving the demand for land, especially in the lower Mississippi valley and the Old South. The invention and popularization of the cotton gin in the last years of the previous century had suddenly made short staple cotton profitable, and had set in motion powerful social and political changes. Cotton acreage in the South was expanding dramatically, and exports to the insatiable English market had become a major source of income. But cotton was a labor-intensive plantation crop; the expansion of slavery necessarily went in lockstep with the expansion of cotton cultivation. As a result, the "peculiar institution," which had been under both moral and economic attack just a decade earlier, was experiencing a revival.

The renewed importance of the slave economy in the South would increase the palpable sense of insecurity among plantation owners. Concern that their slaves were being infected with the egalitarian ideas emanating from Toussaint's revolt—and from the more than ten thousand West Indian slaves already brought into the United States—grew as news spread of the first serious American slave conspiracy in years. It did not really matter that the Gabriel Revolt, near Richmond in the summer of 1800, was never proven to have any foreign connection. It was nonetheless widely believed to have been inspired by Jacobin subversion. Undoubtedly, there was cause for plantation owners to worry—the idea of liberty was indeed contagious. Nor was concern about this threat to domestic security a purely southern phenomenon, as northern capital was moving south to help finance the cotton expansion, and the northern money men wanted no impediments like slave unrest to harm their profit projections.

These were some of the key interests that would shape the nation's domestic and foreign policy for the next decade and more.

Jefferson owed his election, and soon would owe the election of a friendly Congress as well, to a loose coalition of small farmers, frontiersmen, and plantation owners centered on the South, the Mid-Atlantic, and the new western states. These constituents were instinctively antiestablishment, republican, with a distaste for all but the most essential government. They had little use for merchants, bankers, or shippers, except as necessary adversaries, nor did they hanker for a large navy. Many of them owned slaves. In short, they formed an entirely different profile from the people whom Adams, Hamilton, and Pickering had represented. The country's policies would soon reflect the difference.

When Thomas Jefferson stepped into the presidency in March 1801, he did not need to make major changes in the St. Domingo policy that he had so much disliked. President Adams had already done that for him. A peace with France had been signed, the navy had been pulled out of the Caribbean, the embargo on France had expired, and with it the need for the special exception of the Toussaint Clause. Jefferson was content to let trade with St. Domingo continue as though the island were still a part of the French realm, as it legally was. That was good economics and good politics. The trade made money for America, and many of the producers of the export goods were Republicans from the Mid-Atlantic states. What's more, not interfering with the trade also removed one possible source of friction with the angry and frustrated Federalists. But Jefferson had no sympathy for the colony's independence; he intended to do nothing that could be seen as prejudicing France's rights on the island, and he would keep a distant and correct relationship with the Toussaint government.

Jefferson wanted a good relationship with France. He, like most Americans, had most certainly lost enthusiasm for the French Revolution, but he still saw what remained of French republicanism as a necessary counterweight to British monarchy and its friends in the United States. Even before a new French envoy to Washington had arrived, Jefferson had taken the trouble to assure Consul Letombe that he wished to return to the "old basis of amicable relations so advantageous to both nations."[1]

The new French representative in Washington, Louis André Pichon, was well chosen by Talleyrand to facilitate an amicable dialogue. He was already well and favorably known, as he had been the intermediary in the back-channel discussions that had led to the peace talks and he knew America from earlier service during the Genêt mission. The young and enthusiastic Pichon—though only a chargé d'affaires rather than a fully accredited minister—was soon a major actor in Washington's small diplomatic circle, with exceptional access even in the informal protocol established by the new president. Assured as he was of a good reception, Pichon wasted no time in raising the delicate subject of American policy toward St. Domingo.

Less than a week after arriving in Washington, Pichon had already had two conversations with Jefferson touching on St. Domingo. The president, clearly, was not thinking of independence for the island. As Pichon reported, Jefferson said that his administration recognized French rights in St. Domingo and "could not favor any measures contrary" to them. But, Pichon reported, Jefferson also had observed that Toussaint wanted to use the British to balance pressure from France, and was "trying hard to maintain himself between us [France] and the English, in order to obtain a guarantee for the liberty of the blacks." Consequently, Jefferson suggested that as long as the European war lasted, the French should avoid any kind of pressure that might cause Toussaint to take drastic steps in self-defense, because, if backed into a corner, he might put the island in the hands of the British rather than surrender. As for the United States, Jefferson said, it would seek to "maintain U.S. trade advantages without harming the interests of France, or supporting those internal or external movements that could hurt the interests of France."[2]

In spite of these assurances, which indicated fairly clearly that America would henceforth take a hands-off attitude toward St. Domingo's political fate, Pichon still felt it necessary to go on the record. In a formal note to the new secretary of state, James Madison, on the measures necessary for putting the Mortefontaine pact into effect, Pichon expressed his hope that the president "will have seen fit to take measures putting an end to the unfriendly proceedings (to say no more) which have taken place in the French colonies, with the sanction of the American Government."[3]

One of the measures about which Pichon was complaining was the (admittedly irregular) assignment by the Adams administration of an American consul general to Cap François. On this point, Jefferson was more than ready to comply. In fact, as the Republicans had attacked the Stevens mission during the past election campaign as corrupt, and Stevens's partiality to the Pickering line was well known, it was an essential move for a new policy. Very shortly, Pichon was assured that "the agent for that island will be replaced immediately by a person whose instructions will be to respect the rights and interests of your nation, and to refrain from giving any cause for complaints." All the same, Pichon was warned at about the same time that the United States had its own interests in St. Domingo and that it would be pragmatic as to how it protected them. Maintaining the trade was America's prime interest, Madison had told him, and the administration consequently had to "take things as they were, and to consider Toussaint as having full authority on that island."[4]

The new American approach was becoming clear: the United States would send a new representative to Cap François, and he would continue to deal with Toussaint—but only as French Governor General (however hollow that title might in fact be). He was to promote American trade, and not secession.

The president's choice for the new envoy was noncontroversial: a man with no political background at all. Tobias Lear's main claim to position was loyal service; he had been personal secretary to George

Washington for many years and now, following the great man's death, was deserving of a suitable reward.[5] He was nominated and approved without controversy, at least from Americans. But in deference to French sensitivities—transmitted by Pichon's warnings on the subject—Lear was not commissioned as consul general as Stevens had been, nor even as consul, but simply as general commercial agent. That innocuous title, Jefferson and Madison hoped, would satisfy the immediate operational needs and yet not offend the disputing parties. They were wrong.

Lear arrived in St. Domingo in late spring, finding Dr. Stevens still in residence and offering a ready welcome. The two men hit it off remarkably well, with Stevens briefing his replacement thoroughly and introducing him to Toussaint and the other authorities in a professional manner. (So well, indeed, that Lear was soon writing testimonials to Washington as to Stevens's character and probity!) But Lear did not hit it off as well with the general in chief. Toussaint, angered at American disrespect—the new envoy, he sniffed, had arrived with no diplomatic credentials to present, no letter for him from the president or anyone else in authority, in fact he was no real envoy, just a commercial agent—was curt and unfriendly. He returned the copy of Lear's commission unopened, while "expressing his disappointment and disgust in strong terms, saying that his color was the cause of his being neglected, and not thought worthy of the usual attentions."[6] Stevens, it seems, smoothed over the incident for the moment, but it was not a good beginning to Lear's mission.

Toussaint had been angry with American policy ever since he had learned of the peace negotiations with France. War between the powers to the north had been highly advantageous to his cause; it had weakened France's hold on the island, made it possible for him to defeat the Spanish and British occupiers, and encouraged the Americans to give him crucial support against the French and their instrument, Rigaud. But now the Americans had sold him out with their peace agreement, and he was aware of rumors that the British and the French might also be seeking some sort of accord. The international environment was no longer so favorable.

At home, Toussaint was at the peak of his power. In a space of five years he had driven away the foreign armies, defeated his internal opposition, and extended his authority throughout the island. He had also outmaneuvered all the French officials who had sought to control him, including the now thoroughly crushed Philippe Roume. At the end of summer, Toussaint released that last French commissioner from his long house imprisonment, and allowed him and his wife to leave for France. With the economy reviving (aided by the participation of French planters and American merchants), the towns gradually rebuilding, and new administrative structures taking form in a somewhat ad hoc manner, Toussaint decided it was time to give a new form to the colony's government. No longer would the administration be run by the French Ministry of Marine; France's new constitution explicitly did not apply to the colonies until implementing legislation could be negotiated. Toussaint determined to take advantage of the opening to draft a law for St. Domingue; it would have a form unique to the colony's circumstances, and one that protected the personal freedom of its citizens. The step would, he realized, be seen as a challenge by the authorities in Paris to whom he still professed (however insincerely) his allegiance. Even so, Toussaint would take it. But he was not yet ready to take the bigger step, that of declaring full independence.

A special commission, drawn largely from the rubber-stamp Assembly, was appointed to draw up a new organic law, although the guiding hand of their work remained Toussaint's. The curious ambiguities of the resulting document show the inconsistencies and contradictions both of his character and of the situation. Intelligent and humane, he sought the rule of law and morality, and the absolute abolition of slavery. But at the same time he needed, and had long sought, control and authority. As a result, the document that emerged proposed a highly autocratic system. The colony's government was to be headed by a powerful governor, with Toussaint given a life appointment and his eventual successors to serve for five years. Order and discipline were, in his eyes, essential. The mandatory labor system was sanctioned, the military assigned a major role in the government and in administering the plantations, and Catholicism reinforced as the only legitimate faith. Although the law was to go into effect immediately upon its passage by the Assembly, it provided at least a minimal recognition of French sovereignty. St. Domingue would still be a colony of France in name, and the new law—a virtual constitution—was to be submitted to France—meaning Bonaparte—for final approval.

Toussaint knew that approval would not be easy. Ever since Roume's arrest, he had been governing the colony by virtual fiat, simply informing his nominal superiors in France of his decisions. It had been audacious behavior, and he could scarcely expect that French authorities would now welcome his unilateral declaration of a new organic law, or constitution, for their key colony. Yet he persisted. To show popular support for his move, he arranged an impressive display of the pomp of his new regime in early July. At a large public rally on Cap François's Place d'Armes, and punctuated by parades, fireworks, a thanksgiving mass, release of prisoners, as well as a subsequent dinner for six hundred guests, the new law was read to the throng, while it, as well as the general, were lauded and applauded.

Toussaint hoped somehow to persuade a French government, one that he had repeatedly undercut, slighted, or ignored, that his declaration of virtual autonomy was something they should welcome. Perhaps he felt it necessary to bring the issue out into the open; perhaps he had a fallback plan in case of an outright French refusal; his motivations are nowhere near as clear as the extent of his provocation. In any event, the man he chose to be his spokesman in Paris was given a near-impossible job. Engineer General Charles Vincent, a French native who had remained in Cap François and was a personal friend of Toussaint's, was deputized to carry a copy of the law to France for approval. Vincent was chosen in spite of the facts that he had opposed the law to begin with, and objected to the presumption of taking a printed, rather than draft, version to the capital. Interestingly, it appears that Toussaint also sent a second and separate envoy, one Citizen Nogere, to keep an eye on Vincent.

In late summer, both Vincent and Roume appeared in the United States on their separate ways to France. The energetic French chargé Pichon, who had been in regular correspondence with Toussaint and followed events in St. Domingo closely (if not always accurately—he had prophesied in June that Toussaint would declare his independence), met with both. Vincent, he reported, was still hopeful that there could be some reconciliation between his government and his friend Toussaint. As for Roume, Pichon reported, he was a badly shaken man. But Roume did give advice that corresponded to information Pichon obtained from still another visitor, Consul Edward Stevens. Stevens, in a long and surprisingly frank conversation with the chargé, pointed out that some of Toussaint's subordinates were chafing under his control. Roume had also suggested that France's best tactic to keep Toussaint under control would be to divide him from his lieutenants.

Stevens, if Pichon's usually accurate reporting can be trusted, seemed fairly disenchanted with his old interlocutor. Toussaint, he confided, had developed an "inflated ambition [that] stops at nothing, and he is surrounded by flatterers," who had given him a false view of his situation. Stevens said that Toussaint had a grand view of his destiny, and that he seemed determined to break with France when the time was right. If France wanted to regain control of its colony, he volunteered, it should come forward with a strong military force, accompanied by a declaration of peace, amnesty for most of the soldiers, and money to buy off the subordinate chiefs.[7]

Roume and Stevens were on to something. Toussaint's rule was not universally popular. Tobias Lear for his part, reporting to

Washington on the subject, had alluded to the weakness of Toussaint's popular base when he wrote that "Toussaint is certainly an extraordinary man. He appears to be adored by all the inhabitants; whether this proceeds from fear or love I cannot yet tell; but all speak of him as a just man." Later in the same dispatch, Lear mentioned one of the causes of the islanders' fear when he noted that "Great attention is paid by the Military and Civil officers to keep the Cultivators employed steadily at their work, and in some places not a little severity is used."[8]

In St. Domingo, grumbling about Toussaint's rule had indeed begun to spread. Many cultivators resisted the mandatory work contracts, and sentiment for redistribution of plantation lands in favor of small-scale farming was growing among officers of the army as well. Toussaint's Catholic, moralistic approach was also creating problems; the suppression of voodoo meetings, brothels, and gaming houses had sapped his popularity, while illicit continuation of those same activities was only increasing another problem—that of official corruption. In October, a sudden revolt of disgruntled plantation workers exposed the depth of the problem and forced Toussaint into draconian measures. Among the officers arrested and summarily executed for alleged leadership of the revolt was his own nephew and close advisor General Moise. The revolt had been both a personal and political blow to Toussaint.

Shortly afterward, the bad news arrived that the British and French had reached terms on a peace treaty, to come into effect early in 1802. The French, no longer tied down by the war, would then be free to deal with their troublesome colony.

Still more bad new came from France, where poor General Vincent, after many efforts, was finally granted an audience with the First Consul. This would be his only chance to convince Bonaparte of the relative virtues of Toussaint's new constitution, and it resulted in a short, unsatisfactory interview. Napoleon had already made up his mind how to deal with the breakaway leader whom he had called a "gilded African." Vincent was allowed to speak his piece, then curtly dismissed without a response. Not long thereafter he found himself posted to virtual exile in Elba.

Napoleon had been remaking the map of Europe. The 1801 Treaty of Luneville with a defeated Austria, and now the March 1802 Treaty of Amiens with an exhausted Britain, allowed him to preside over a pacified continent. The peace, he knew, would not last. But it would allow him to regroup, and to employ peaceful means of competition against his great opponent, Britain. In the east he would work to undermine British interests in India and the Ottoman Empire, while in the west he had plans to revive and fortify the French Empire. For that objective, the basic scheme had already been proposed by Talleyrand, Fauchet, and others during the Directory: it was the project to rebuild French power in the Caribbean and the Americas by reacquiring Louisiana from the Spanish.

St. Domingo was central to the plan, and protecting its wealth and that of the other French West Indies colonies had always been one of the prime incentives. The islands had been somewhat of a strategic liability in the recent war; difficult to defend and more difficult to supply from France against the might and reach of the Royal Navy. Their resulting dependence on American supplies had created another vulnerability for France, by bringing its colonies into the economic orbit of the new American power.

But, it was argued, possession of Louisiana could resolve that problem. It would provide France with a nearby base from which she could supply food and raw materials to the sugar islands, cut out the pushy American traders, and allow the mother country to reestablish the profitable *exclusif* regime. Possession and fortification of Louisiana would also eliminate the threat that it might be seized by Britain in the inevitable next round of fighting. Moreover, a strong French presence on the Mississippi would put a limit to the expansion of the aggressive young United States into the Mexican colonies of France's weak ally, Spain. It might even encourage American westerners, who would need French goodwill to get their goods to sea past New Orleans, to make common cause with France rather than their east coast compatriots.

It was grand strategy, of the kind that suited the man who would soon make himself Consul for life. Napoleon endorsed it readily. He had already authorized the first, necessary step over a year earlier when—one day before signing the Treaty of Mortefontaine with the United States—he had signed a secret treaty with Spain. In the Treaty of San Idelfonso, his Spanish allies had promised to retrocede the Louisiana colony back to France, in return for certain concessions and a promise that France would not dispose of it without Spain's assent. Little had been done yet to put the treaty into effect, but negotiation of the Peace of Amiens with Britain had now made it possible to move.

Toussaint's control of St. Domingo was of course a problem, but one that Napoleon expected would be manageable. The growing independence of the black ruler, and, as Bonaparte saw it, his cheekiness, had long galled the haughty conqueror of so much of Europe. He was determined to bring the rebel leader to heel. Moreover, Bonaparte had decided, on the advice of his economic advisors as well as his Creole wife, that reestablishing the colonial system was essential if the whole venture was to be profitable. That meant, quite simply, reimposition of slavery as well as the *excusif,* as if the Revolution had never taken place. Cooptation of Toussaint was therefore out of the question; he would have to be crushed.

Returning St. Domingo to full French control was, then, the necessary first step. Reestablishment of the immensely lucrative plantation system on the island was central to the whole plan. Its revenues would pay for the Louisiana enterprise, and more, and its needs would provide the basic market for Louisiana's raw material exports. Louisiana without St. Domingo would only be a drain on French resources, as it had been for Spain.

Crushing Toussaint, however, would have to be handled carefully, particularly in view of the important trading relationships that both Britain and the United States had built up with his regime. Talleyrand realized that it would be necessary to keep the extent of French ambitions clouded, and to sound out the extent to which the other powers might have objections. Although rumors had surfaced about France's secret retrocession agreement with Spain, Talleyrand was adept enough at the diplomatic lie to keep questioners from determining Napoleon's full intentions with respect to Louisiana.

But, with early preparations for a military expedition to St. Domingo under way even before the ink was dry on the draft Treaty of Amiens with Britain, France's intent to bring her errant colony back under control had become increasingly clear. Great Britain, Talleyrand and Napoleon reckoned, would pose no problem. The warlike William Pitt had been replaced as prime minister by the weak and complaisant Henry Addington, who had given signals that Britain would take a hands-off attitude—and perhaps even welcome a suppression of Jacobin ideas in the West Indies. (In fact, the French had initiated contacts with the British even as the Treaty of Amiens was being negotiated, assuring British noninterference with the naval expedition.) How the new American administration would react to France's plans, however, still needed clarification.

Although the new Jefferson administration had already given general assurances that it would respect France's rights on the island, Pichon needed to get a more explicit statement of their attitude toward the planned expedition. With the peace agreed to at Amiens not scheduled to take effect until early 1802, Pichon feared that Toussaint would declare the colony independent in the interim, and that American merchants would support the move. After a trip to New York, where he found a suspicious silence on the part of merchants usually knowledgeable abut the situation in St. Domingo, he asked Secretary of State Madison to clarify the U.S. stance. The ever-cautious Madison was annoyingly Delphic. He said that the United States could agree to France's reestablishing its authority over its colony, but qualified that with a statement that "the United States will take things in this colony as they are, without judgement; they only want to continue to trade, . . . they do not want to get into a problem with Toussaint."9

Not only had Madison not clarified his government's position on independence, he had suggested obscurely that France should know "what would not work" in St. Domingo, and then had changed the subject abruptly—implying a linkage?—in order to bring up questions about France's (still rumored) plans for reclaiming Louisiana. Pichon, unsatisfied by Madison's reticence, saw that he would have to clarify the secretary's clarification with the more loquacious and convivial President Jefferson.

Nine days later, on July 20, Pichon got his chance to draw the president out on American attitudes toward Toussaint's possible independence. In a relaxed, private conversation, Jefferson in fact raised the subject himself, commenting that his administration had heard reports (Lear's first dispatches had not yet reached the capital) that Toussaint would soon "declare himself." When Pichon asked how the government would view that possibility, Jefferson said that his administration would not favor such a declaration. But, Pichon's report continued, Jefferson then commented that "as long as France is in no position to act, the United States could do nothing; the trade with St. Domingo was very important to the United States, and if the [U.S.] government were to try to cut it off, it would get into an unnecessary conflict with Toussaint, and would be seriously compromised in public opinion." Pichon agreed to that point, adding that the United States should not cease trading with the island, since that would leave it totally dependent on the British.

But what, Pichon then asked, would be the U.S. position if France was once more in "a position to act" toward its colony; would there then be a "concert," or agreement, between the United States and

France on the issue? Jefferson agreed that there would be "no diffi-culty. But in order to make the concert complete and effective, you will need to make peace with England. Then, nothing could be eas-ier than to furnish your army and navy with everything, and to starve Toussaint. . . . There is no support for Toussaint in the United States; isn't the example dangerous for two thirds of the States?"[10] In addition, Jefferson concluded, Great Britain saw an independent St. Domingo "as we do," that is, as a possibly destabilizing and pirat-ical state in the Caribbean.

Pichon had what he wanted: a seemingly clear statement that the United States would not support an independent, black, and revolu-tionary state in St. Domingo, and would not oppose—and might even assist—France's efforts to regain control. In his report to Talleyrand, Pichon surmised that Jefferson's attitude had been strongly influenced by the domestic security scare occasioned by the recent Gabriel Revolt, and the subsequent Great Fear that had rocked his own slave state of Virginia as well as other southern states.

Jefferson had given the French a green light to proceed against Toussaint; he could have had no doubt that Pichon would report their conversation in that light. He could not stop the French expe-dition, in any event. Nor did he want to. If the potentially disruptive black regime were to be forcibly returned to the mother country's control, neither Jefferson nor his Republican supporters in the slaveholding South would be troubled. For strategic reasons, as well, it seemed at the time that a reinforced French presence in the Caribbean would be useful as a counterweight to the British naval superiority that had developed there during the recent fighting. The president wanted French goodwill for many reasons, and his promise to Pichon was a means to that end.

All the same, the president did not, as yet, know what scale of action the French had in mind, or what their chances of success would be. After all, Toussaint and his colleagues had already worn down two European armies—the Spanish and the British. In the circumstances, it was essential to keep open not only America's trade with St. Domingo, but America's political options there as well. With the outcome by no means certain, the president was prepared to envisage scenarios other than a clear French victory.

One possible outcome that Jefferson entertained seems to have been a sort of continued autonomy for the colony. (It should be remembered, in this context, that Jefferson had been predicting since the events of 1793 that white rule in the West Indies would inevitably come to an end.) In a November letter to his friend (and governor of Virginia) James Monroe, in which he was discussing the possibility of sending some of the slaves implicated in the Gabriel Revolt into a West Indian exile, Jefferson seemed ready not only to accept a black state of St. Domingo, but to consider the security risk as a manageable problem:

> The most promising portion of them [West Indian black inhabitants] is in the island of St. Domingo, where the blacks are established into a sovereignty *de facto*, & have organized themselves under regular laws & government. I should conjecture that their present ruler might be willing, on many considerations, to receive even that description which would be exiled for acts deemed criminal by us, but meritorious, perhaps, by him. The possibility that these exiles might stimulate & conduct vindictive or predatory descents on our coasts, & facilitate concert with their brethren remaining here, looks to a state of things between that island & us not probable on a contemplation of our relative strength, and of the disproportion daily growing; and it is overweighed by the humanity of the measures proposed, & the advantages of disembarrassing ourselves of such dangerous characters.[11]

At about the same time, Jefferson indicated that he had some reservations about his earlier statement of support for a French expedition. His comments suggested there might be still another outcome to the problem. Meeting with Pichon, he began by reiterating his earlier assurance that his administration would take no steps inimical to good relations with France. But he immediately detracted somewhat from that pledge, by pointing out once again that he wished to avoid any quarrel with Toussaint. In addition, he was careful to point out that American trade with St. Domingo had been deregulated since the end of the quasi-war, and he no longer had any authority to interfere with the trade—implying that "starving" Toussaint might not really be feasible. And finally he suggested, as if in passing, a totally new proposition, one that implied continued autonomy for the island and liberty for its inhabitants. As the surprised French chargé reported it, the president asked, "Why not declare the island independent, under the protection of France, the United States, and England? The island will need an oriental government; after Toussaint, another despot will be necessary. Why don't the three powers get together to confine this infection to the island? And as long as we would not permit the blacks to have a navy, we would avoid danger and moreover carry out a very profitable trade with the island."[12]

Pichon avoided a direct response to this rather bizarre proposal, offering simply to forward it to Paris "for reflection." It was never heard of again. Nor did Jefferson ever return to the idea of a tripartite guarantee; it was apparently a trial balloon launched by a president who was not at all above improvising his foreign policy as he went along.

The two communications do show, however, that Jefferson was no longer as ready to support the upcoming French expedition as he had told Pichon he was some four months earlier. Pichon understood this, and reported to Paris in early December that he thought that the Americans would help France regain control of its colony, but only because Jefferson feared the prospect of a black-ruled state in the region. The merchants already favored Toussaint, Pichon warned, and the government wanted above all to keep the profitable trade open. Consequently, any effort to close off the island's trade would sacrifice such goodwill as France enjoyed and simply lead to large-scale smuggling.[13]

The mystery surrounding France's plans for Louisiana was in part responsible for Jefferson's second thoughts. Faced with uncertainty as to French intentions in the Mississippi River valley, and how the St. Domingo expedition might tie in with them, he had become cautious. Perhaps a reinforced French presence in the Caribbean was not such a good idea, after all, if it could create new possibilities for subversion or limit American ambitions in the West.[14]

Moreover, Jefferson appears to have doubted whether France could really turn back the clock in St. Domingo. He told Pichon that the blacks would fight hard if the French tried to reimpose slavery, and he saw it as quite possible that an autonomous or even independent black regime could survive on the island.[15] That prospect was not necessarily one he welcomed, but it was a realistic one, and his main concern in that event would be to limit possible security risks to the United States from such a state in the neighborhood.

It would require, in short, a renewed quarantine. In that respect, it was a perspective not so different, all in all, from the view of the situation that had been held by John Adams when he had been president.

THE LECLERC EXPEDITION

Napoleon may not have been ready to show his hand with respect to Louisiana, but his determination to reestablish French authority over St. Domingo had already begun to be clear by October 1801, when terms of the peace with Britain were initialed. Previous plans for the island, which had involved sending still more commissioners and a small number of troops to rein in Toussaint, could now be scrapped. Once the Royal Navy had been neutralized by the peace accord, France would be able once again to send a large expedition into the Caribbean and bring about the submission of its straying colony. (A second, but smaller, expedition was prepared to subdue black rebels in French Guadeloupe.) For St. Domingo, an imposing force was put together, numbering over twenty thousand fighting men, including veteran troops, scores of senior officers, and a number of returning mulatto leaders, among whom were André Rigaud and Alexandre Pétion. The huge fleet set sail shortly before Christmas, even before the peace accord was put into effect. As Captain General, Napoleon had chosen the dashing but light-weight Charles Victor Emanuel Leclerc, whose major specific quali-fication for the assignment seems to have been that he had bedded and then wedded Napoleon's favorite and scandalous sister, the beautiful Pauline Bonaparte.

Napoleon's instructions to Leclerc were highly detailed, setting forth a phased plan for rapidly reimposing French rule. The First

Consul expected that coordinated land and sea operations would assure French control of the major towns and agricultural areas within three weeks; a second phase would successfully pit the French troops against organized rebel forces; and a final, more prolonged phase would root the remaining rebels out of the mountains. The instructions were also appallingly cynical, calling for a program of deception and entrapment. The island's black leaders were to be treated with respect only until the French had succeeded in occupying the principal points; following that they were to be subjected to increasing demands, divided one from another, and ultimately all were to be arrested and sent to France. The same fate awaited all whites who had assisted Toussaint and his colleagues. (If Toussaint resisted but was captured, the instructions continued, he should be summarily court-martialed and shot.) By the third phase, all the blacks in the pacified areas were to be disarmed and sent to work.

The instructions, for the moment, were silent on a key point: whether slavery was to be reestablished. Napoleon surely had already made up his mind on the issue, but he did not want to commit his views on this fateful step to paper as yet. When, and how, the blacks were to be deprived of their new liberty would depend on events on the ground. But the trend of Bonaparte's thinking was evident from this admonition: "The captain-general shall suffer no wavering in the principles of these instructions, and any individual who should undertake to argue about the rights of the blacks, who have caused so much white blood to flow, shall under some pretext be sent to France, whatever his rank or service."[1]

Napoleon was also confident (or at least wanted his brother-in-law to think he was) that the Americans would not stand in his way, indeed that they would help. "The Spanish, the English and the Americans," Leclerc's instructions read, "view with equal anxiety the black republic. . . . Jefferson has promised that, from the moment that the French army arrives, every measure shall be taken to starve Toussaint and to aid the army."[2] The latter statement, quite clearly, was a willful exaggeration of Jefferson's earlier remark to Pichon, and ignored the various caveats the president had expressed. The overstatement would be costly. Given that four months would have passed before Leclerc could put the president's promise to the test, and that Leclerc's instructions themselves called for a deliberate campaign of falsehoods and deception, Napoleon either had an improbably high opinion of Jefferson's probity or was engaged in wishful thinking. His instructions to Leclerc contained no incentives for the Americans to cooperate. In fact, the instructions were coercive, calling for immediate confiscation of all ships and cargoes destined for the rebels, plus a speedy return to the *exclusif*—steps which would surely cause major problems with American traders. And yet, Napoleon apparently expected that Jefferson was prepared to, or indeed even could, oblige American merchants to stop their profitable business with the rebels and instead supply a French army that aimed to drive them out of the trade as soon as possible.

News of the Leclerc expedition began to reach St. Domingo in late autumn, but did not cause immediate alarm. The focus was on more local issues. Napoleon's intentions were as yet unclear, while the recent rebellion of the troops and the execution of General Moise had shaken Toussaint's regime. The ground was changing, but there was still an atmosphere of business as usual, with French planters returning and American traders present in large numbers—in fact, Tobias Lear reported, most American goods were so plentiful that prices were weak. The administration's stand-off attitude toward the Toussaint government, on the other hand, caused Lear to complain, as late as November, that the United States risked losing its influence: "Not a single line of intercourse between the Government of the U.S. and this.—Not a Single line of Communication to me from my Government (on which head I have been often questioned, and have been obliged to exercise my utmost ingenuity to parry the question). No public Ships or Vessels belonging to the U.S. on the coasts or in the harbors as heretofore—and altho' the reasons for this have been full and repeatedly given when it has been asked—Has the change in your Administration destroyed all your ships?"[3]

By mid-December, however, news that peace between France and Britain was near, and that a major French expedition might be expected, changed the mood. Lear reported that everything had been put on hold until France's intentions became clear, and he worried that a heavy French hand—and particularly any effort to reimpose slavery—would have "dreadful" consequences. In mid-January 1802, he was even more emphatic, predicting that the blacks would never submit to a reimposition of slavery, and that they would destroy everything they could rather than surrender. Even so, he reported, the Toussaint government appeared to be taking no active steps to prepare for resistance, taking the public stance that France had every right to send troops to its colony.[4]

As little as two weeks before the French landing, Toussaint, somewhat surprisingly, was still trying in public to calm the fears of his countrymen. In a public address, he criticized those who, he said, were "trying to kindle the fire of discord" by accusing the French of "liberticidal intentions." "Never will it enter my heart," he assured his countrymen, to suppose the French capable of such acts.[5] He was, almost surely, putting on a brave front and trying not to inflame the situation until he saw what French intentions were, but he could not have been so optimistic in his heart. "We are doomed," he is supposed to have said to his colleagues when they saw the French fleet heave into sight off Santo Domingo.

Lear had received no official response to his messages about the imminent arrival of the French until the end of January 1802, by which time some units were already landing at the other end of the island. Madison's coded letter at that point informed Lear officially of the peace agreement, and instructed him, in essence, to do nothing that would annoy the arriving French. "It is equally inconsistent with our duty and policy to take any steps that would controvert or

offend the authority of the French Republic over St. Domingo, or
have the appearance of intermeddling in any manner in its affairs,"
Madison rather stuffily insisted. Just in case Lear had not gotten the
message, Madison sent still another at the end of January telling
him that the president was anxious that France have no pretext or
cause to claim that the United States was not showing "due respect
for its authority."[6]

The official line was clear. The American government would not
help Toussaint and his armies; it would not hinder Leclerc and his.
But the government had, for all purposes, ceased being the determining party a year earlier, when the Peace of Mortefontaine had
been signed. It was the American merchants who had become the
more important actors with respect to St. Domingo, and their reaction remained to be seen.

Proclamation

Inhabitants of St. Domingue! Whatever may be your origin and your
color, you are all Frenchmen; you are all free, and equal before God
and the Republic.

France, like St. Domingue, has been prey to faction and torn by foreign and civil wars. But all is changed!! Every people have embraced
Frenchmen and have sworn to them peace and friendship! All
Frenchmen have likewise embraced each other, and have sworn to all
be friends and brothers. Come ye, also and embrace Frenchmen, and
rejoice to see you friends and your brothers of Europe.

The Government sends you the Captain General Le Clerc. He car-
ries with him great forces to protect you against your enemies, and
against the enemies of the Republic. If it should be told to you that
these forces are intended to tear from you your liberty, answer, the
Republic has given us our liberty. The Republic will not suffer that
it should be taken from us. Rally around the Captain General; he
restores you abundance and peace. Rally around him; he who shall

dare to separate himself from the Captain General will be a traitor to his country, and the vengeance of the Republic shall devour him as the fire devours your dried sugar canes.[7]

BONAPARTE

The landings went swiftly, but not always according to the plan. In Santo Domingo, where the expedition first made land, in Les Cayes, Jérémie, and in other locations, the French troops landed virtually unopposed. The mendacious Proclamation was distributed, the black leaders and their troops went into hiding, and the French troops rallied the local militia and officials to their duty. Most of the whites and mulattos, who weeks before had been eager to do business with Toussaint's officials, began to trim their sails to correspond with the new reality of power.

But in other towns—St. Marc, Leogane, Port au Prince—the black forces withdrew only after setting fire to warehouses full of supplies.

And in Cap François, things did not proceed at all as planned. Henri Christophe, the local commander, informed the arriving French that he would not permit them to land until he had instructions from Toussaint, and he threatened to burn the city if the French forced a landing. A tense standoff ensued, with the French fleet being kept out of the harbor by contrary winds, while a delegation of leading residents (among them Lear) attempted to obtain guarantees from both sides that lives and property would be protected in case fighting broke out. When Christophe ordered that the town be evacuated, Lear arranged that the American residents be permitted to take refuge on the seventy-odd U.S.-flagged ships in the harbor. Lear's long and colorful account of the events of the day, which was quickly leaked to the American press, describes the scene: "In passing through the town from Christophe's to the wharf, a most melancholy scene presented itself—women and children, passing in all directions, in the most distressed conditions, to look for a place of safety, without knowing where to find it—and hundreds of black women, with whatever they could carry, proceeding out of town in various directions."[8]

In the end, there was little fighting, yet the city was not spared. When an exchange of fire between a French vessel and the harbor fort was mistaken as the beginning of the invasion, Christophe had the town put to the torch, starting with his own house. He then withdrew with his army into the countryside, taking as hostages many of the white residents who had not already fled. That night, from their point of relative safety on the ships, the Americans watched the ill-fated city burn once again.

The next day, Leclerc and the army debarked. An undamaged villa by the sea was found in which Pauline could hold court, the few remaining buildings in town were requisitioned, tent cities sprang up, and soon a sort of garrison normality began to assert itself among the ashes. Lear had a private meeting with Leclerc, in which the latter promised to respect the American's commission and responsibilities.

Leclerc had need for Lear's mediation with the American merchants, as among his first acts were ones that angered them greatly. First he banned any ships from leaving the island. Then he began to confiscate any goods that were consigned to the rebels. And finally he demanded that all goods on board be sold to the army at concessional prices, with three-quarters of the payment to be made in French promissory notes. The French quickly found, to their exasperation, that the Americans were not at all complaisant, demanding full value (and perhaps more) for their goods, and refusing to accept the French notes. Before very long, the dispute got heated, with the French sequestering more goods and detaining a few captains arbitrarily. Lear, in spite of the fact that he found some of the American captains to be "intemperate," was obliged to defend their interests, and suddenly U.S.-French relations on the island had a decided edge.

Leclerc was impatient; he had a war to fight and was convinced that the American merchants—whom he disdainfully characterized as Jews—were part of his problem. As he wrote to the minister of marine shortly after arriving, "It is the Americans who brought the muskets, the cannons, the gunpowder and all sorts of munitions. It is they who instigated Toussaint to go on the defense, and I am entirely convinced that the Americans have formed a plan to promote the independence of all the Antilles, because they want to enjoy a monopoly of the trade there, as they have done with St. Domingue."[9] Similar anti-American attitudes, it seems, were common among the French officers, who often did not hide their feelings that, once they had taken care of the rebels, they would settle scores with the Yankees. The arrogance of the French officers was even annoying, it seems, to the local French. An American resident reported that "The Creoles shake their heads and predict much ill. Accustomed to the climate, and acquainted with the manner of fighting the Negroes, they offer advice which is not listened to. Nor are any of them employed, but all places of honor and emolument are held by Europeans, who appear to regard the Island as a place to be conquered and divided. . . ."[10]

When news of Leclerc's high-handed actions reached the American maritime cities, it was grist for the mills of the Federalist press. Bitter at their electoral loss, still smarting from Napoleon's refusal to pay reparations for shipping losses during the quasi-war, and furious at Jefferson for his accommodating attitude toward the French, the Federalists jumped on Leclerc's actions with glee. Fulminations about Leclerc's seizures and arrests were interspersed with the most negative interpretations of French actions, designed, in the end, to embarrass Jefferson and his Democratic-Republicans. The French arriving on St. Domingo, one newspaper asserted, "are considered by the blacks as tyrants who have been sent to re-forge their chains," while Leclerc's Proclamation was run with the following editorial spin: "They had for their object to cajole the blacks in subjection. But Toussaint had more sense, and knew the tenure of French professions much better than Europeans who have been the dupes of

French policy for a number of years, and preferred freedom in the mountains although accompanied by deprivations and danger, to slavery. . . . Leclerc has added a new article to the catalogue of crimes—that of even doubting the good intentions of Bonaparte!"[11]

Regardless of his political and public relations problems, Leclerc was marking successes in the campaign against the rebel armies. Fighting had broken out across the countryside after the French landings in the ports. The black armies often employed hit-and-run tactics that resulted in the destruction of towns, plantations, and crops, but the French had gradually pushed them back into the hills in the center of the country. French successes, however, had been costly. Fighting in difficult country against disciplined and hardy (if outnumbered and outgunned) foes, the French suffered heavy losses even as they continued to win the battles. Toussaint and Dessalines, in particular, fought brutal, no-prisoners, scorched-earth campaigns. It had become, in short, a bloody race war. In March, a particularly tenacious defense by Dessalines's troops of a hilltop fort called Crête-a-Pierrot caused horrendous casualties on both sides. The French could scarcely afford many more such victories, while the black armies, fighting for their freedom and their pride, were motivated to persevere. A French officer, writing after the war, described his opponents: "It was remarkable to see the Africans, half naked, with musket & sabre, giving an example of the severest discipline. They set out for a campaign with nothing to eat but maize, established themselves in towns without touching anything exposed for sale in the shops or pillaging the farmers who brought things to market. Supple & trembling before their officers, respectful to citizens, they seemed only to wish to obey the instinct for liberty which was inspired in them by Toussaint."[12]

Leclerc's successes in the field apparently prompted him to take a still harder line in the capital city. He had learned of the unfavorable press treatment he was receiving in the United States, and tended to confound it with what he saw as an obstructionist U.S.

government position. He was fed up with the uncooperative Yankees, ready to lash out, and found Tobias Lear to be a convenient target. In early April, he summoned Lear, telling him that there were charges that he had been advising American traders not to bring cargoes to St. Domingo. In any event, Leclerc said, he had not received agreement from Paris to continue honoring Lear's credentials. So, in the absence of a bilateral agreement officially sanctioning his consular position, Leclerc concluded, he would have to ask Lear to surrender those official functions. Lear, who had already received guidance from Madison on this contingency, saw that it would be counterproductive to try to stay; he did not have the support of all the American traders, was under instructions not to challenge French authority, and had already sent his son home for a planned vacation. He told Leclerc that he would leave the island within ten days.

Lear's mission had not been a success. He had hit it off with neither Toussaint nor Leclerc, and American influence in St. Domingo had dropped precipitously. Yet it was scarcely his fault; American interests and France's new regional ambitions were bound to clash. Lear, at a minimum, had been an observant reporter of the French effort to subdue Toussaint and his supporters, and had provided Washington with some useful analysis. The French forces in St. Domingo, he had reported in March, did indeed have their eye on occupying Louisiana in a subsequent phase, but their forces were likely to be bogged down in St. Domingo for some time. "It is true that a force is destined to take possession of Louisiana," he had written, "That this will be done I have no doubt, but in the present state of this Island, all the force which remains here will be kept for the present."[13] Two weeks later, he would amend that to read "for some time." The war against Toussaint and his generals, in short, would not be easy, and while it dragged on, French ambitions in Louisiana would have to wait. For Jefferson and Madison, Lear's analysis was a welcome piece of news.

In spite of Talleyrand's continued obfuscations, the extent of French ambitions in the Americas had gradually become clear to Jefferson and Madison. Back in September of 1801, before Leclerc and his army had set sail and while the rumors of Spanish retrocession of Louisiana were still amorphous, they had felt it necessary to warn the French that the United States would have concerns about any Louisiana project. The new American minister in Paris, Chancellor Robert Livingston, was instructed to present a roundabout, but still not overly subtle, warning. The United States, he was to tell Talleyrand, would be "sensitive" to a French (or, for that matter, British) presence in the Mississippi valley, because any extension of Europe's wars would then inevitably spill over into the southern states, "whose numerous slaves have been taught to regard the French as the patrons of their cause." Realizing that American sensitivities alone would scarcely deter the impetuous First Consul, Madison instructed Livingston to suggest, in addition, that a French presence in the valley might even drive America into alliance with Great Britain. This rather weak demarche, in the end, was not made by Livingston until February 1802, and in a bowdlerized form at that—Livingston omitted the implied threat, and wound up simply asking for the Floridas as compensation for a French occupation of Louisiana. It fell flat because, as Livingston reported, even though most of his informants thought the Louisiana project to be "a great waste of men and money . . . it is a scheme to which the First Consul is extremely attached, and it must, of course, be supported."[14]

By the time Livingston saw Talleyrand, the Americans finally had proof of the extent of the French plan. Rufus King, in London, had obtained a copy of the Treaty of Idlefonso, in which Spain had promised to cede Louisiana. At the same time, Livingston reported from Paris that the St. Domingo expedition was only the first step, writing that "the armament destined, in the final instance, for Hispaniola, is to proceed to Louisiana, provided that Toussaint makes no opposition."[15] Livingston's "provided," written before the

Leclerc expedition had crossed the ocean, identified what would be a very important condition. Toussaint did resist. And, as the next few months showed, Toussaint's opposition had more effect on Napoleon's timetable than did American diplomacy, which the French simply shrugged off.

Madison expressed American frustration over France's arrogance when he wrote to Livingston in April 1802, "The cession of Louisiana to France becomes daily more and more a source of painful apprehensions. . . . Notwithstanding accounts from St. Domingo that part of the armament to that island was eventually destined for Louisiana, a hope was still drawn, from your earlier conversations with Mr. Talleyrand, that the French Government did not intend to pursue the object. Since the receipt of your last communication, no hope remains but from the accumulating difficulties of going through with the undertaking, and from the conviction you may be able to impress, that it must have an instant and powerful effect in changing the relationship between France and the United States."[16]

Jefferson could not simply count on Leclerc's "accumulating difficulties" to derail the French project. He felt it necessary to try a new diplomatic approach as well. In April, he decided to supplement the Livingston channel of communication (the chancellor spoke no French, was known to have an overly direct manner, and had so far not swayed Talleyrand). Jefferson asked the French businessman Pierre-Samuel Du Pont de Nemours, a man well known in both capitals, to use his broad contacts in Paris to convince senior French authorities of the seriousness with which the American government held the view that the Louisiana project would cause grave difficulties with the United States. Jefferson also sent a long explanatory letter to Livingston, in which he voiced his concern and anxiety, and tried to warn the French that their actions could throw America into the arms of Britain:

The cession of Louisiana and the Floridas by Spain to France works most sorely on the U.S. On this subject the Secretary of State has written to you fully. Yet I cannot forbear recurring to it personally, so deep is the impression it makes in my mind. It completely reverses all the political relations of the U.S. and will form a new epoch in our political course. Of all nations of any consideration France is the one which hitherto has offered the fewest points on which we could have any conflict of right, and the most points of a communion of interests. From these causes we have ever looked to her as our natural friend, as one with which we never could have an occasion of difference. Her growth therefore we viewed as our own, her misfortunes ours. There is on the globe one single spot, [the] possessor of which is our natural and habitual enemy. It is New Orleans, through which the produce of three-eighths of our territory must pass to market, and from its fertility it will ere long yield more than half of our whole produce and contain more than half our inhabitants. France placing herself in that door assumes to us the attitude of defiance. Spain might have retained it quietly for years. Her pacific dispositions, her feeble state, would induce her to increase our facilities there, so that her possession of the place would be hardly felt by us, and it would not perhaps be very long before some circumstance might arise which might make the cession of it to us the price of something of more worth to her. Not so can it ever be in the hands of France. The impetuosity of her temper, the energy and restlessness of her character, placed in a point of eternal friction with us, . . . render it impossible that France and the U.S. can continue long friends when they meet in so irritable a position. . . . The day that France takes possession of N. Orleans fixes the sentence which is to restrain her forever within her low water mark. It seals the union of two nations who in conjunction can maintain exclusive possession of the ocean. From that moment we must marry ourselves to the British fleet and nation. The idea here is that the troops sent to St. Domingo were to proceed to Louisiana after finishing their work in that island. If this were the arrangement, it will give you time to return again and again to the charge, for the conquest of St. Domingo will not be a short work. It will take considerable time to wear down a great number of soldiers.[17]

Such strong talk, however, tried to mask a weak hand. Jefferson's talk of alliance with Britain, contrary to his longstanding policy as it was, appears to have been largely a bluff—an effort to create leverage over the French rather than a serious option. The president knew moreover that he could not actually stop the French from occupying Louisiana if they obtained title to the colony from Spain. It appears he was hoping that, if he could not dissuade the French from their project, his repeated objections would at least build a case for obtaining some kind of compensation if they carried it out. The previous autumn, Livingston had been instructed to fish for compensation in West Florida, and although he had achieved little, that was still an objective. Jefferson now began to think of obtaining New Orleans—the choke point on the river—either in compensation or by purchase. But he had very little to offer Napoleon, or with which he could threaten him meaningfully.

By default, Toussaint's ability to hinder and delay Napoleon's plan by tying up Leclerc had become an asset to America's diplomacy. It bought time, and time was on Jefferson's side. The peace agreement signed at Amiens already looked unlikely to hold up for long, and a renewal of the European war might well cause Napoleon to reevaluate his American ambitions. In that light, it would be foolish for the Americans to help Leclerc solidify France's tenuous hold on St. Domingo.

Jefferson was embarking on a policy that involved carrying water on both shoulders. He would have to keep the French satisfied that the American government was not assisting the St. Domingo rebels, while at the same time allowing the private sector to do exactly that—and conniving implicitly with the bankers to avoid every appeal for help from Leclerc as he strove to solve his supply and financial difficulties. The policy was also expedient domestically, as it protected American security while keeping the merchant interests quiet. But for sheer diplomatic duplicity, it rivaled the work of the master, Talleyrand.

ST. DOMINGO AND LOUISIANA

Even as Jefferson struggled to find an amicable way to counter, delay, or frustrate France's ambitious strategy, America's day-to-day relations with Leclerc and his expedition had slipped from bad to worse.

Leclerc's dismissal of Lear was regretted quietly in official Washington, but resented strongly in maritime circles, where the action was seen as a first step toward closing American merchants out of the trade entirely. In response, the Federalist press attacks against Leclerc became still more pointed, with one paper running a letter that advised, "On no account make shipments to this place. The government (if such it may be called) is the most capricious, equivocating, ill natured and vindictive set of knaves that ever were cloathed with authority."[1] Hearing that the French might seek a loan from the Jefferson administration to help pay the costs of their expedition, the Federalist papers went on the offensive, demeaning France's credit standing and asking how such a loan could possibly be justified under the new administration's budget austerity.

Leclerc, in turn, managed to impart some of his growing indig-nation over the situation to his brother-in-law, Napoleon, who then berated Livingston for the liberties taken by the American press. The squabble had begun to escalate, in spite of the efforts of Madison and Pichon to play it down. (Pichon, in fact, was in a difficult place with his own government over the issue, as he had been quite frank in voicing his opinion that Leclerc had acted intemperately.)

A key turning point came in late March, when Leclerc and the French admiral Louis Thomas Villaret-Joyeuse informed Washington that they had put an embargo on all shipping to the island that did not clear through Cap François or Port au Prince. The objective, clearly, was to block shipping to any non-French controlled ports and to "starve" Toussaint's armies, as they believed Jefferson had promised to do. They asked that the U.S. government support their action by issuing regulations that would help implement the trade blockade.

Jefferson could not agree to the French demand. To begin with, the trade with St. Domingo was important economically, and he was unwilling to restrict it—some of the key exports, after all, came from the increasingly Republican Mid-Atlantic states. American traders had always tried to sell goods into markets where the demand was highest; they would fight bitterly any effort to tell them where to go, particularly if the restrictions had been demanded by a foreign power. The trade should remain open. Added to this economic interest was the new foreign policy and strategic imperative against giving any assistance, direct or indirect, to Leclerc's mission. Why should the administration help the French if it would only enable them to establish themselves in Louisiana more readily? In this, the administration saw eye-to eye with the Federalists, whose press had been asking the same question. The problem, then, was not the decision to turn down the French demand. It was how to present it to the French without inflaming the situation.

Madison and Jefferson devised a *yes—but* sort of answer, which recognized the French policy and agreed, on an official level, to respect it. But, they insisted, the American government could not control the trade by edict; it would have to propose legislation to do so and was unwilling to put such a contentious issue up for congressional debate. In the meantime, the merchants would be informed of the French measures and should respect them, but the government could not oblige them to do so. In short, it was up to the French to enforce their own trade ban; the U.S. government would not do it for them. And American traders (with their long and successful history of smuggling and evasive documentation) would be free to take whatever risks they thought acceptable. As Pichon reported it, Madison told him that "The United States will show all respect due to the authority of the French Republic and the measures it adopts to reestablish tranquility and happiness in a part of its possessions so known for unhappiness. If some American Citizens allow themselves to engage in an illicit trade with that island, they will be acting in a manner contrary to the desires of the U.S. Government and will put themselves in a position of responsibility before the authorities. . . ."[2]

This answer, in spite of its effort to show compliance, did not please the French at all. Nor, evidently, had Livingston's rather more direct approach. Writing to Talleyrand, the American minister asserted American rights: "It is obvious that, when peace diminished the value of military stores in the American Market, that the merchants would naturally seek another.—That now war existed between St. Domingo and the Parent Country.—That none was expected & that Toussaint was acknowledged by France as their governor—nor had the Government of France ever, til after the arrival of General Leclerc, expressed even a wish that the commerce be restrained, a commerce to which France is indebted for her islands not having lapsed into the hands of the British."[3]

Napoleon's reaction was to fume that "instead of prohibiting American Citizens from trading with the rebels of St. Domingue, the United States Government limited itself to declaring that it would give no protection to those engaged in the trade."[4] Nor was French resentment in any way diminished when Madison, in his conversation with Pichon, suggested that if the French truly needed American supplies, they were welcome to come and get them in American ports—at the very time that American merchants were refusing to accept French payment terms!

The Leclerc expedition had had financial problems from the beginning. The sequestration of American cargoes in St. Domingo, and the payments in French notes, had been necessary because Napoleon and Leclerc were hard pressed for cash. The Americans had proven unhelpful; American merchants were unwilling to accept the French notes except at a steep discount, either in St. Domingo or on the mainland. When Pichon went to New York and Philadelphia in March to help Leclerc's commissary official buy supplies, he found that French notes, which previously had been accepted at a 30 percent discount, had become worthless. "I have an unlimited Treasury credit, but I have learned today with humiliating certitude that I cannot place my notes at any rate,"[5] he complained. He had bought some of the supplies that the army in St. Domingo needed with own his mission funds, but he had exhausted that source, and Leclerc's agents had no cash at all. And the American government, he reported, was unwilling to act.

Two months later, Pichon reported that some Federalist bankers had recommended that he ask for a U.S. government loan. One can question why he took their advice, which may have been malicious (given the campaign some of the Federalist newspapers had been waging against such a loan), but he did try. Both Madison and Secretary of the Treasury Albert Gallatin told him that the idea would have no support, and Madison had bitingly pushed the point: how could the U.S. government, he asked, consider a loan when it did not know the final objective of the Leclerc expedition? This new rejection caused Pichon to dismiss the administration as "timid."[6] He had already sent a scathing analysis of the president's politics to Paris, saying that "Jefferson's administration has dashed the hopes of some, and justified completely the fears of others. The principles which guide it are clear: a warm partisan spirit, ambition to retain power and to please the voters, a singular pretension to new ideas, a childlike vanity hidden behind a front of simplicity, and an affected self-denial."[7]

The young chargé's critical report shows disillusionment with the Republican administration, true, but it may also have been a step necessary to protect himself from the increasingly sharp attacks, originating from Leclerc's headquarters in Le Cap, on his performance and his alleged complicity with the American administration. Indeed, for the rest of his tour in Washington, Pichon was in an uncomfortable situation. Unenthusiastic about the Louisiana project, openly critical of Leclerc's management of the St. Domingo expedition, and convinced that the economic health of France's West Indian possessions required American goods and goodwill, he was increasingly at odds with the imperious unilateralism favored by Leclerc and his superiors in Paris.

Leclerc, of course, had good reason to be disappointed in the U.S. administration, although Pichon was not to blame. Where his instructions had told him to expect support, Leclerc had found indifference; where he had asked for assistance, he had been given ambiguous and unhelpful answers. By early summer, it was clear that the American government was not going to help him, while the American merchants were going to refuse French payments in paper—even as they continued supplying the rebels, who paid in products.

But in spite Leclerc's frustrations, the war was going well.

Toussaint had surrendered in early May. Why he did so is not clear to this day. His military situation, while difficult, had not been not hopeless; the army might have fought a guerrilla war for a long time. But he had been fighting for ten years, was over fifty-five years old, and perhaps had been softened somewhat by the ease of his time as head of government. The earlier defection of his northern army commander, General Henri Christophe, had been a heavy blow. He, like Christophe, had a bond of loyalty to France and a sense that St. Domingo could only prosper with a French connection; he had never been able to break the ties to Paris when he had had the opportunity. Now, he seemed to lack the heart to fight a long war against the might and authority of his mother country. And yet, he surrendered without any assurances on the principal point for which he had been fighting for so long: continued freedom for his fellow black citizens. Whether he expected such assurances, or intended to continue the struggle clandestinely, is unknown. When he did surrender to Leclerc, he simply retired with a group of his loyalists to his plantation and made no political statements.

Toussaint's defection caused a collapse of the rebel armies. Soon the other major leaders, in particular Dessalines, rallied to the French tricolor. Some rebel bands continued to oppose the French, while other units simply melted away into the towns or to the maroon settlements in the hills. The French pursued their advantage hard; they even insisted that their new allies prove their loyalty by hunting down their old colleagues. In Dessalines, always an angry man and never one for half measures, they had a particularly effective and brutal agent for this gruesome business.

It soon appeared that Leclerc, though months behind his planned schedule and at the cost of many thousands of soldiers, would succeed in his mission.

Then it all came unglued. French military casualties began to mount seriously, though this time not from combat. The problem was the onset of the wet season, bringing with it illnesses, particularly yellow fever. At the same time, political tensions were undermining Leclerc's military successes. With scores of planters returning to the island from their overseas refuges and calling for retribution, rumors began to circulate that the government planned to deport all black and mulatto soldiers, even those who had remained loyal. Then a heavy-handed French effort to disarm all black islanders only increased the tension. The ex-slaves began to fear seriously that their freedom would be the next thing to go.

In early June, Leclerc, treacherously violating his own safe-conduct order, had Toussaint arrested and shipped off to an imprisonment in France from which he would never return.[8] The betrayal of this inspirational leader, who had fought for the freedom of the slaves and yet tried to stay true to France, further galvanized the opposition to Leclerc. Distrust and hatred of the French was redoubled, even among those blacks who had opposed Toussaint's leadership. For the more radical of those leaders, like Dessalines, a moderating influence, moreover, had been removed.

This tension finally reached a breaking point in July. Rumors had been heard for some time that the government in Paris would rescind the 1794 abolition decree. Those stories, finally, were proven to be correct. France, which had already jettisoned the revolution, now seemed to have abandoned the principles of liberty and equality as well. True, St. Domingo was spared for the moment, as the new law stipulated that a return to slavery did not immediately apply to the colony, or to Guadeloupe. But what real consolation could such a delay be to those fearing the loss of their freedom? It was clearly only a matter of time before the old colonial system would be imposed again in all its brutality. (Leclerc, in fact, had received authority from Paris in the same month to reestablish slavery whenever he saw fit, but he wisely chose not to do so.)

When a ship came into Cap François bearing news that the French military expedition to Guadeloupe had crushed the slave rebellion there, and then reinstated slavery in that colony, the word spread like wildfire. It would be better, St. Domingo's ex-slaves concluded individually and collectively, to die fighting for their freedom than to have it taken away without a struggle.

Leclerc's victory over Toussaint was undone. "With this state of things, Citizen Consul, the moral force I had here acquired is destroyed," he wrote to his brother-in-law.[9] By October, the major black as well as mulatto leaders had deserted France and were in open revolt across the island. When their example led many of France's native troops to desert as well, the situation for the French became serious. The army was hemorrhaging, both from battlefield casualties and from the rampant spread of disease. Leclerc's army was reduced to about four thousand men, and the general himself eventually fell ill. He died in early November, and the beautiful Pauline had to end her unhappy ten-month stay on St. Domingo by accompanying her husband's body back to France.

Jefferson, who was following the situation carefully because of the connection with Louisiana, had been insightful when, back in June, he had written, "What has been called the surrender of Toussaint to Leclerc, I suspect was in reality the surrender of Leclerc to Toussaint." He was, however, premature. In spite of Leclerc's death, the war was by no means over. Still another American, this one resident in Cap François, described the continuing struggle as follows: "The negroes have felt during ten years the blessings of liberty, but a blessing it certainly is, however acquired, and they will not easily be deprived of it. They have fought and vanquished the French troops, and this strength has increased from a knowledge of their oppression, and the climate itself combats for them. . . . The country is entirely in the hands of the negroes, and whilst their camp abounds in provisions, everything in town is extremely scarce and enormously dear."[10]

Indeed, the most brutal and inhuman phase of the fighting was yet to come. Leclerc's replacement had been the second in command, Donatien de Rochambeau, son of the French count who had fought years ago alongside Washington (and who had just barely avoided the guillotine during the Terror). The younger Rochambeau had served in St. Domingo earlier, with Sonthonax, but had quarreled with the commissioner over the latter's abolitionist policies. His politics on that score were unchanged, and his approach to the black rebels was one of naked coercion. Reinforced with over twenty thousand new troops, and employing mass executions, hunting dogs, and mass drownings as weapons of terror, he would seek over the next year to stamp out the rebels with the utmost severity. Unfortunately for the tens of thousands who died in this dreadful war of extermination, his opponent Dessalines, who had been elected to that leadership by fellow rebel generals, was equally brutal and determined. Atrocities on both sides were commonplace, life was cheap, and the new French recruits died from disease as regularly as they did from the fighting.

While the campaign in St. Domingo dragged on long past its planned completion date, Napoleon continued impatiently to plan his takeover of Louisiana. The first step was to get clear title to the colony. That was finally achieved in October, in spite of some heroic efforts by the Spanish foreign minister to delay or divert a deal that he though unfavorable to his nation's interests. The month before, Napoleon had already named General Claude Perrin Victor to lead the troops that would take over the colony from the Spanish. A plan to send off Victor in the fall had had to be scrapped, however, because of the pressing needs of Leclerc on St. Domingo. Leclerc's and then Rochambeau's demands seemed insatiable; all the available ships were used in sending some ten thousand reinforcements in November, and then another fifteen thousand in January 1803. As a result, it was not until December that Victor arrived in Helvoet Sluys, Holland, to begin gathering the force for Louisiana.

The Americans, in the meantime, had been watching the situation with increasing anxiety. Pichon reported, as early as July, that American public opinion overall was turning against France. Both the agricultural and the commercial interests, usually antipathetic, now had common cause for distrusting France. Farmers and westerners were concerned about the possibility of having such a turbulent and even dangerous neighbor as Napoleonic France on the west bank of the Mississippi. In that respect, Pichon's reports even echoed Jefferson in contending that France should tread lightly in Louisiana, lest it push the United States into Britain's embrace. Meanwhile opinion in the maritime and commercial centers had already been shaped against France by the unsatisfied demand for reparations from the quasi-war and continuing friction over trade with St. Domingo and the West Indies. The situation was not helped by the "expressions of hate and antipathy that our officer in St. Domingue occasionally appear to express against the government of the U.S.," Pichon added.[11]

Rochambeau, sad to say, was no better at handling the Americans than Leclerc had been. He, too, complained to Paris about the criticism he was subjected to in the American press, as well as the fact that Americans continued to sell goods, particularly munitions, to the rebels whenever possible. As a result of his complaints, Madison in Washington and Livingston in Paris were repeatedly called on to deny any official American involvement, either with the press attacks or with whatever smuggling American merchants might be involved in. Taking refuge in what was probably a technicality, both denied knowledge of any contraband trade at all. (It surely existed, though statistics are unavailable. Officially reported American trade with the French West Indies in 1803 indeed dropped by almost half from the previous year, which allows one to suspect that cargoes were being declared for other destinations, but then smuggled to ports not controlled by the French. In the French-occupied ports, where payment was still made in the unwanted French notes, supplies were scarce.)

Rochambeau only compounded his problems with the Americans when, toward the end of the year, he levied high taxes on resident merchants and forced contributions from visiting merchantmen as a way to meet his desperate cash requirements. When some American captains refused to pay, he clapped them in jail until they bought their way out. He also demanded that Pichon arrange large loans in the United States, but the poor chargé once again had to face incredulity from the bankers and a total lack of support from Jefferson and his colleagues in the government.

Still another issue was creating friction between the French and Americans. Following a number of incidents in which American ship captains departing the West Indies for their home ports had been forced to take on board black men who were obviously being expelled from the islands, a fear grew that this reflected a dastardly new French policy of exporting their troublesome subjects to America. While it turned out that those acts neither reflected French policy nor were frequently repeated, the level of southern anxiety was such that they nonetheless resulted in American legislation early in the new year. The new act passed, along with the solemn notation that "much danger to the peace and safety of the peoples of the Southern States in particular is to be apprehended from admission of persons of this description" (i.e., blacks and mulattos from the French West Indies).[12]

What brought this kettle of ill feeling to a boil, however, was an act neither French nor American. It was an action by the Spanish intendant in New Orleans, who in October suddenly decided to cancel the warehousing and exporting rights enjoyed by Americans in that city ever since the Pinckney treaty had been signed in 1795. That the intendant, Juan Morales, had every right to do so does not explain the sheer recklessness of his act. It was, in fact, a product of the indecisive and corrupt government in Madrid. Originally directed by the king, the action was quickly opposed by the Spanish governor, the minister in Washington, and the foreign minister, whose joint efforts eventually brought about a royal reversal. But the damage had already been done. The Americans were incensed; the vulnerability of their Mississippi lifeline had been exposed—and by the despised Spanish, at that. Seeing a French hand behind the Spanish action, many Americans wondered what they could expect if Napoleon, who had finally gotten formal Spanish agreement to the retrocession that very month, were to become their new neighbor. Popular indignation rose across the United States against retrocession, Congress fell into an ugly mood, and in the Federalist coastal cities the drums of war against France began to sound.

Jefferson had to do something to ease the pressure. He did not want to get pushed into a crisis, much less a war, with France. The president, it seems, was resigned to the possibility of having the French in Louisiana, but still hoped it could be avoided—through their defeat in St. Domingo, renewal of their war with the British, or something, anything, else. The continued struggle in St. Domingo had at least given him time, as the French clearly would not be able to move into Louisiana until they had stanched that huge drain on their resources. The time could be used to negotiate, which might calm the uproar, and perhaps even find a solution that would remove the foreign stranglehold on the river's commerce. With that in mind, he nominated James Monroe, a fellow Virginian who was particularly popular in the West, to be a special envoy to the French government. Along with Livingston, he was instructed to negotiate either for a purchase of New Orleans or a permanent right of deposit at that port. Early in 1803, Congress approved the nomination and quietly authorized $2 million for the purpose (bribery of key French officials was considered, apparently, to be a viable option).

Jefferson attempted to speed along the dilatory Monroe with this advice: "As to the time of your going, you cannot too much hasten it, as the moment in France is critical. St. Domingo delays their taking possession of Louisiana, and they are in the last distress for money for current purposes."[13]

In Holland, General Victor's fleet became icebound in January. Although by this time he had almost his full complement of men, it would probably be weeks before he could sail. In order to keep the project moving forward, Napoleon approved sending an advance guard ahead, to take formal possession of Louisiana from the Spanish. The new French prefect for the colony, Pierre Laussat, and a small military detachment were given that mission and departed January 10. The main force (unless, of course, it was also diverted to St. Domingo, as the earlier detachments had been) would follow later.

Also in January 1803, Napoleon learned of the death of his brother-in-law Leclerc. It was a personal blow; he might not miss the vain Leclerc, but Pauline was his favorite sister. More to the point, it was a strategic setback; Napoleon did not have much confidence in the command ability of Rochambeau, and feared he was the wrong man to finish the job. He had already sent out almost fifty thousand troops to conquer the island, and still it held out. The Consul for Life (as he had had himself declared the previous summer) was not ready, however, to abandon his effort to build a counterweight to British power in the Americas. His orders to his minister of marine continued to insist on the earliest possible departure for General Victor's armada.

In late February the ice in the Dutch ports finally broke up. But before the troops could be embarked, new storms swept through. So many ships were damaged that it would take General Victor another month to get the fleet ready once again.

In St. Domingo, the killing continued. Rochambeau's naval forces could not control all the ports of the island, and supplies and munitions continued to flow to the rebels. The black armies wore away at his strength by their readiness to sacrifice their own men and women, and by constant guerrilla attacks—Christophe had even had the cheek to bring up cannons and bombard Cap François. In the French occupied towns, money and supplies were short, and prospects of obtaining more of either from America depressing. As a result of his latest taxes and arrests, Rochambeau's chances of obtaining financing in America had disappeared. The merchants and bankers had all but cut him off, and his repeated requests to the American government for credits or advances against the American debt to France were going nowhere.

It was becoming increasingly evident that Rochambeau could only win if he had still more men and, most importantly, cash money with which to buy vital supplies from the Americans. Napoleon had precious little of either to spare. And if Rochambeau could not win soon, and bring St. Domingo back under French colonial control, the Louisiana project would no longer make sense.

In March, Napoleon quietly reordered his priorities. Difficulties with Britain were piling up; he knew that the peace might not last much longer. In the event of war in Europe, the Louisiana project would be a diversion of scarce resources, perhaps even a great risk. And General Victor's troops, if they were not sent across the Atlantic, could more profitably be used to augment the threat to England posed by the French army already encamped at Boulogne. As for St. Domingo, it seemed to be a bottomless pit. Short of money and short of naval assets, Napoleon could no longer afford to reinforce or refinance Rochambeau. The army there would have to win on its own, and the whole American project no longer could have priority. For the moment, though, Napoleon kept this new appreciation of the situation to himself.

In mid-March, Prefect Laussat arrived in Cap François on his way to New Orleans to take possession of the colony in the name of France. But, at the same time in Paris, Livingston was writing excitedly to Madison that Napoleon had just threatened Britain that it would either have to evacuate Malta as it had agreed to do at Amiens, or face renewed war. Several days later, Rufus King reported from London that General Victor's army was being mobilized against England; its American mission had been cancelled. (The rumor was accurate, if premature; Victor's orders for Louisiana were not officially cancelled until May 3.) Napoleon, it appeared, was moving toward a renewed war in Europe. Would he also abandon his costly American plans?

Monroe finally arrived in Paris several weeks later in early April, but Livingston had already begun—in fact almost concluded—the negotiations. Napoleon was ready to sell New Orleans—and, most surprisingly, all of Louisiana as well. The $15 million price would also, finally, include reparations for American maritime losses during the quasi-war. The unexpected and fateful agreement was signed on May 1.

The story of the Louisiana Purchase, which doubled the size of the United States and turned the country into a continental power, has been told in detail elsewhere. But key to the success of the negotiations was the issue of timing. America was able to buy a vast and incredibly rich territory because Napoleon had lost the fight for time; his window of opportunity to establish a new French empire in America had all but closed. He turned away from America because the endless fight in St. Domingo had cost so much in time, money, and men that he could not justify continuing. Louisiana had become expendable because St. Domingo had not been reconquered. Toussaint and Dessalines, with an important assist from yellow fever, had finally won—and their success served both their people and the United States.

In short order, the truce of Amiens broke down and French-British hostilities resumed, both in Europe and the Caribbean. The Royal Navy immediately placed a blockade around the French-occupied ports in St. Domingo, and also sent supplies to the rebels led by Dessalines. Rochambeau, now completely cut off and under siege, was doomed. In some desperation, he wrote to Washington in late summer, begging the French there to help him get supplies: "For the last three months, we have been out of contact with Europe, and for more than six weeks, the English have blockaded the Colony's ports, intercepting all communications and prohibiting the entry of our ships. As a result, we are out of money, are close to seeing all our supplies run out, and our troops exposed to the most dreadful famine."[14]

By autumn, the French held only the principal seaports, and soon they began to lose them as well. Finally, hemmed in by land and sea at Cap François, Rochambeau surrendered at the end of November. Seven thousand men, all that was left of the tens of thousands of unfortunate French, Polish, and other troops who had been sent to St. Domingo, submitted themselves to the Royal Navy, rather than face the humiliation of surrendering to the native leaders. France would never again rule its old colony.

Years later on St. Helena, Napoleon told his memorialist, "I have to reproach myself the attack on this colony. I should have contented myself with ruling the island through the intermediary of Toussaint."[15] He did not conjecture, however, as to whether such an alliance would have allowed him to hold on to his plans for Louisiana.

Another interesting piece of retrospection came just a year after the Louisiana Purchase. In a long article, Alexander Hamilton tried—for clearly partisan purposes—to minimize the importance of Jefferson's historic achievement. That his article was mean spirited did not denote, however, that it was entirely wrong. On the connection between St. Domingo and the Purchase, he wrote:

> On the part of France, the short interval of peace had been wasted in repeated and fruitless efforts to subjugate St. Domingo, and those means which were originally destined to the colonization of Louisiana, had been gradually exhausted by the unexpected difficulties of the ill-starred enterprise. To the deadly climate of St. Domingo, and to the courage and obstinate resistance made by its black inhabitants, we are indebted for the obstacles which delayed the colonization of Louisiana, till the auspicious moment, when a rupture between England and France gave a new turn to the projects of the latter, and destroyed at once all her schemes as to this favorite object of her ambitions.[16]

A RISKY TRADE

On January 1, 1804, at Gonaives, the victorious native generals who had expelled the French declared their country to be independent. It was to be a new start. Even the French name of St. Domingue was dropped; the new country was to be called by an old indigenous name, Haiti. The generals, most prominently Dessalines, Pétion, Christophe, Clairvaux, and Geffrard, swore to "renounce France forever, to die rather than live under its domination, and to combat with their last breath for Independence."[1] They also appointed Dessalines, their most dynamic and determined fighter, to be general in chief for life, for they knew that their struggle was by no means over, and that the defeat of Rochambeau's army did not mean that the French—or anybody else, for that matter—would readily accept their claim to nationhood.

The victory had been won at a terrifying cost. The brutality of the fight, already appalling under Leclerc and Toussaint, had spiraled virtually out of control under the implacable and racist leadership of both Rochambeau and Dessalines. Tens of thousands, perhaps even hundreds of thousands, had lost their lives in the battles, mutual atrocities, starvation, and displacements that had marked the last years of the struggle. More permanently, the infrastructure that had underpinned the island's earlier prosperity—irrigation works, mills, warehouses, port facilities—had been largely destroyed. Dessalines

and his colleagues, free, proud, and defiant, presided over a shattered and needy country.

Regular supplies of foodstuffs, munitions, and arms would be
required. The new rebel government needed to feed its armies, prepare against a possible French return, and maintain the workers on
those plantations that still operated (and on which Dessalines was
determined to keep the forced labor system). During the fighting,
the British (once the European war had resumed) and American
merchants had been happy to supply the rebel forces in spite of the
nominal French prohibition. The British had done so out of policy,
in order to deprive the French of their prize colony. Indeed, and in
spite of some anxiety about the effect that Haiti's independence
might have on their own sugar colonies, the British continued to
supply Dessalines's armies well after their declaration of independence. The American merchants, on the other hand, had no political
agenda. Their goal was business, and if they could get their cargoes
in and out of the rebel-held areas of the island under the protection
of the British fleet, all the better. The evacuation of Rochambeau's
forces seemed, at first, to make business all that much easier.

The French, however, had neither gone away nor given up. To
begin with, they still controlled the old Spanish end of the island,
and from their main base in Santo Domingo they posed a permanent, if at the moment somewhat toothless, challenge to native control of their old colony. The French governor there, General
Marie-Louis Ferrand, did what he could to make life difficult for the
new Haitian regime. Most significantly, he began to issue letters of
marque empowering French-flagged privateers to prey on neutral as
well as belligerent shipping to and from ports controlled by the
rebel regime, with little distinction being made as to whether they
had the right to seize legitimate cargoes or just war contraband. A
similar and even more loosely administered system began to operate
from Cuba. Ostensibly neutral Spanish officials there were allowing
French government officials, from among the thousands of angry

and vindictive refugees from St. Domingo who had fled to Cuba for safety, to commission additional privateers. Operating openly from the ports of Barracoa and Santiago, these privateers often had questionable if not downright spurious letters of marque, virtually no instructions as to which cargoes could be confiscated and which could not, and a strong tendency as a result to simply plunder their prey rather than submit themselves to the rigors of admiralty courts. Unarmed American merchantmen, not surprisingly, were high on the list of preferred prey.

Although the French privateers soon became a serious problem for American merchants, the profit from successful voyages continued to be very attractive, and insurance rates had not yet become prohibitively expensive. The goods got through. But the success of the trade only ensured that the French, already indignant in the time of Leclerc and Rochambeau, would become still more furious as they watched American goods enable Dessalines and his colleagues to strengthen their hold on the country.

French indignation was also fueled by the ferociousness with which Dessalines established native rule. The new general in chief had become convinced, by the failure of Toussaint's attempt to cooperate with the French as well as by Rochambeau's subsequent persecution of all blacks, that the new nation's best security would lie in black nationalism. In late February he began a systematic elimination of the remaining whites, beginning by accusing them of criminal involvement in Rochambeau's war crimes, and proceeding to wholesale massacres of those unlucky enough not to have fled the island. As news of the massacres spread, the British began to back away from their earlier support for Dessalines, even though they continued to provide supplies to the local market and the rebel armies. But the American merchants, unperturbed by such niceties, continued to trade wherever there was a market.

The massacres, however, did not go unnoticed in American public opinion. And when Dessalines (who in November would proclaim himself emperor) began to talk about spreading freedom in the region and invaded the Santo Domingo end of the island, many Americans—particularly in the South—began to worry that their fears of a renegade, Jacobin state in the region had come true.

The Jefferson administration had avoided any official comment and had taken no official stance on the rapidly changing situation in St. Domingo. Rochambeau's difficulties in obtaining credits and American supplies had been brushed off as a purely commercial matter, even though (or perhaps because) the lack of supplies had made his position in St. Domingo untenable. Even after the Louisiana Purchase had been agreed to, the American administration did nothing to ease Rochambeau's plight. The general, like Leclerc before him, vented his displeasure in his dispatches to Paris, but Jefferson and Madison remained outwardly disinterested. The administration was able to avoid official comment on Rochambeau's defeat, on the new flood of dispossessed French refugees who consequently arrived in American ports, on the Haitians' declaration of independence, on the massacres of the whites, and on Dessalines's invasion of Santo Domingo.

Silence, of course, did not mean lack of concern. And the main issue between France and the United States with respect to Dessalines's Haiti, as it had been with respect to Toussaint's St. Domingo, would be the trade in American goods, particularly war supplies, to areas controlled by a government that the French considered to be in revolt. The American protestations that they had no official knowledge of contraband trade had, from the beginning, been a smokescreen, and would no longer hold up. Sooner or later, Jefferson and Madison knew, the issue would demand action.

French chargé Pichon was also concerned. He had foreseen, back in the summer of 1803, that Rochambeau could not hold on in St. Domingo once the war with Britain began again.[2] Once that happened, he posited, the Americans would want to know what the

French government's attitude would be toward trade with a rebel-held island; he urged Paris to think ahead on the issue. His concern, it turned out, was justified when he learned that Dessalines had written to President Jefferson pleading for an expanded trade. At the time, of course, Dessalines was just the leading insurgent general, and his letter had no official weight, but it was nonetheless a portent. The general in chief had made no specific request, and his plea required no answer. He wrote,

> the people of St. Doimingue have thrown off the yoke of tyranny and sworn the expulsion of their executioners. . . . Trade with the United States, Mr. President, with an immense harvest in the warehouses and a still more plentiful one expected, presents an opportunity for the mariners of your nation. Their old relations with St. Domingue should have convinced them of the honesty and good faith with which their ships will be welcomed in our ports. . . . I will assure, with all the authority that has been confided in me, that United States ships will be safe and able to profit from our exchanges.[3]

Pichon, who learned of the letter only in October, asked Madison for an explanation. The secretary of state, according to Pichon's usually reliable reporting, admitted that the situation with St. Domingo was "a cause of embarrassment" to the administration. The president, he said, did not want to harm relations with France nor prejudice her "rights and dignity" over the issue. There would be no response to the Dessalines letter, he continued, even showing the letter itself to Pichon so he could verify its contents.

America, Madison went on, considered France to be still sovereign over the island, with authority to enforce its laws there. That said, the trade would inevitably continue, including with rebel areas. If the French objected to that trade, it was up to them to apply their laws to regulate it. But what, Madison then asked rhetorically, would be the case if France had to evacuate the island, and could no longer enforce its laws? The United States, he said, saw several possibilities, which depended to a great degree on British intentions. The British could try, once again, to occupy the island, they could make a preferential trade arrangement with the blacks as they had tried to do with Toussaint, or they could protect the island's independence. In any of these cases, Madison argued, the French government should have no interest in limiting the access of neutrals like the American merchants, who would keep the British from enjoying a trading monopoly. If France tried to cut off all trade, he concluded, it would just burn its bridges to its colony, to the benefit of the British and the insurgents.

Pichon, uninstructed on France's possible postevacuation views, reported to Talleyrand that he had avoided responding to Madison's exposition. But, he advised Talleyrand, the American trade would most surely continue, and the U.S. administration would simply hold to its position that American merchants were free to take the trade risks on themselves. He concluded his report on the conversation by advising that the French government should not make this a major issue; to do so would be "valueless and counterproductive."[4]

British intentions indeed could be, as Madison had pointed out, crucial. Their blockade had crippled Rochambeau's army in St. Domingo, and in so doing had served the strategic interests of both Britain and America; the former by depriving her enemy of its rich colony, the latter by thwarting any remaining French ambitions toward Louisiana. The Royal Navy's blockade both limited French supplies to the island and kept the rebels under an effective quarantine, while British tolerance of the American merchants indicated that the Addington government would not try to establish a monopoly over the trade. Even as French rule over the island came toward its end, the British showed no ambition for a renewed invasion; the huge losses they had suffered a decade earlier apparently had inoculated them against such an adventure. They even showed some interest in an American-British arrangement over the island, according to

James Monroe (who had been sent on to London after his success in Paris), but neither side pursued the suggestion and it was left to die.[5] In the end, the British played only a minor part in the growing American-French dispute over trade with independent Haiti, remaining content to see France excluded from the trade, to insulate their prize colony of Jamaica from the Haitian infection as much as possible, and to trade actively with the new Haitian regime in competition with the Americans.

None of the powers, of course, acknowledged the Haitian generals' declaration of independence. For the warring Europeans, the fate of a colony like St. Domingo was something to be determined by the bargaining that would accompany an eventual peace settlement, rather than by mere physical possession at some point during the worldwide war. The Haitian generals' declaration of independence was interesting, and their long struggle to break clear of France had certainly been impressive, but it was not considered final. The thought that a group of revolting colonists could somehow decide their own political fate was perhaps conceivable (had not the Americans proven it possible two decades earlier?), but it was certainly not seen as applicable to the Haitian case. The St. Domingo rebels, after all, could make no case for a history of effective self-government as the Americans had, and their military dictatorship could scarcely be defended on liberal philosophical grounds. Moreover, that they were leaders of a bloody and fearful slave revolt made recognition of their declaration of independence all the more unthinkable. France, Britain, Spain, the United States, all were powers that accepted slavery and benefited from it; there was simply no serious constituency in favor of recognizing the legitimacy of a such a rebellion.

In the United States, as André Pichon had often pointed out, the southern interests whom Jefferson represented had been consistently opposed to legitimizing the revolt of the blacks in St. Domingo.

In January 1804, anticipating news of Rochambeau's surrender at Cap François, Pichon reported that "US traders undoubtedly see [the French withdrawal] with pleasure, without worrying about the consequences of the emancipation of the colony, which is now open to speculation. Opinion, on the other hand, is divided as to the consequences; and the States of the South are anxious about the example which could be produced among the black slave population, the source of their wealth." The result of this division of American opinion, he predicted, would be a passive American policy; the government would look aside as the merchants traded with the rebels, even in contraband articles, and claim it was France's responsibility to police it.[6]

Pichon had evidently been well briefed by his friends in the American administration, for it was only two weeks later that Madison drafted what was to be the basic guidance for American diplomacy on this issue, and the policy was every bit as passive as Pichon had predicted. Explaining the administration's views to Chancellor Livingston in Paris, Madison urged him to try to convince the French of the logic of America's stance. Madison began with a description of the problem. "The Island of St. Domingo, having been evacuated by the French troops, and the black chiefs having declared it to be in a state of independence, the trade between it and the U. States falls under some delicate considerations," he wrote. Had the British seized the island, he continued in an almost regretful tone, American merchants would have been able to trade there under British rules. But the British had no such plans, nor was it clear that such a step "would be permitted by the black inhabitants."

The problem, Madison postulated, was what rights did France retain over trade with the island? "As it is not the purpose of the United States to discuss the controversy of France with St. Domingo, much less to espouse, at the expense of a war with the former, the station which has been taken or may be taken by the latter, the rights of France in the present case will be admitted to be the same as they were prior to the evacuation of the Island by her troops." Those rights, Madison stated, were to interdict contraband shipments to areas at war, to intercept trade to areas besieged by her forces, and to enforce her laws on the island with respect to trade by neutrals. "Thus far, and thus far only, her rights will continue to be admitted. She cannot of right require the Government of the United States to enforce her claim on the high seas with respect to contraband of war, or to blockade by prohibitory and penal statutes of their own. . . ."

"But with respect to a trade which merely exchanges a supply of the ordinary wants of the Island, for the surplus of its production, it cannot be for the interest of France to forbid the trade to a neutral and friendly nation," Madison concluded. To do so would only play into the hands of Great Britain. Moreover, "What would be the effect? To starve the inhabitants into a return under the French authority? Far from it. It would have no other effect than to turn their labor from the culture of articles exchangeable for imported food, to the culture of food for which their soil and climate are adapted, thereby rendering them more independent of all external authority and connections, and lessening the commercial value of the colony to France. . . ."[7]

The American policy, then, was a timid one, an effort to maintain the status quo without alienating France. The administration would acknowledge Haitian control of the colony, but not recognize Haitian independence, and would continue to consider France as the legitimate ruler. It would permit American merchants to trade with the island's inhabitants, and would make no effort to control their shipments. At the same time, it acknowledged implicitly that France might want to exercise its residual sovereignty to control the trade, but argued that it was not in France's best interests to exclude neutrals in doing so. The policy recognized the right of properly commissioned French ships to interdict contraband headed to

Haiti, and to control all commerce to defined blockaded areas. The American merchants trading with the island would do so at their own risk.

The policy was, in fact, an expedient compromise. Jefferson was trying to satisfy many different interests, domestic and foreign, in a fluid situation.

He wanted, as a point of departure, to protect a profitable business from being lost to British competitors. Many of his constituents and supporters benefited by exporting their products to St. Domingo. That his policy would also protect the interests of the New England merchants and shippers, mostly Federalists, was perfectly acceptable. He did not, he knew, need their immediate support, as his party was well positioned anyway to win the elections at the end of the year. But he did not want to push them into total opposition. The more extreme Federalists feared that their northeastern states were being marginalized politically and economically as a result of the Louisiana Purchase and, led by a group called the Essex Junto that included the president's old antagonist Timothy Pickering, were trying to form a potentially secessionist Northern Confederation. Aaron Burr, the vice president, had also emerged as the Junto's unlikely ally as he ran for election as governor of New York. In such circumstances, Jefferson could not afford to adopt a policy that hurt New York's, or New England's, maritime interests; he needed to permit—even encourage—legitimate, noncontraband trade with St. Domingo. His constituents among the plantation interests in the South, for their part, could probably tolerate the trade itself. But they were unlikely to tolerate any action that appeared to recognize the rebel black regime in Haiti. The apprehensive planters, increasingly dependent upon slave labor as a result of the cotton boom, lost few chances to vilify the Haitian revolution and to insist that the administration do nothing that might open the door for Haitians—or their Jacobin ideas—to come to the

United States. Jefferson, who had feared the "combustion" of revolutionary ideas emanating from St. Domingo ever since passage of
the Toussaint Clause, shared their apprehensions if not their outspoken rhetoric.[8]

As far as foreign relations were concerned, Jefferson's main concern in shaping the St. Domingo policy was not to aggravate France
unduly. The European struggle was gradually heating up, with
Napoleon (who would proclaim himself emperor in May) threatening to invade England, and France and Britain each attempting to
harm the other through indirect means (such as trade sanctions)
that squeezed neutral powers such as the United States. It was not
the time to aggravate the testy French ruler. Nonrecognition of the
rebel Dessalines's regime thus had a foreign policy as well as a
domestic policy rationale. Jefferson would, to placate Napoleon,
make an effort to be seen as respecting France's rights in its old
colony, even while doing nothing to enforce them.

Beyond simply placating France, Jefferson was prepared to seek
French goodwill actively. The turnover of Louisiana was by no
means complete, and a convention for the settlement of maritime
damages from the quasi-war was still under negotiation. Moreover,
the status of West Florida was also in dispute with both the French
and the Spanish. Jefferson and his Republican supporters were
determined to obtain the territory, but Spain claimed it still owned
it—right up to the Mississippi River—and was prepared to be
obstructionist to make its point. Jefferson believed that only French
leverage on the neutral but weak Spanish would get them to accept
American claims to the disputed territory. From that perspective,
St. Domingo's trade was not worth a quarrel with France (perhaps
even a war, as Madison's instructions to Livingston had suggested) if
it would cost America a chance to expand into the Floridas.

Jefferson's policy, not surprisingly, given the domestic and international constraints, had thus come in many important respects to
parallel that of President Adams: nonrecognition of the rebels,

quarantine, and support for the trade as long as it did not inflame relations with the belligerents. A major difference was that Adams had thought the St. Domingo trade not worth a quarrel with the British; Jefferson was concerned about the French.

It would be months before Madison's instructions could reach Paris, be presented to the French government, and an official reaction be returned to Washington. In the interim, and pushed by trouble-some new developments, André Pichon took up the issue. The problem was that the damages, and abuses, caused by the French privateers had become serious. Not only were a large number of armed French-flagged ships plying the Caribbean without proper commissions, but they were confiscating legitimate as well as contra-band cargoes. Moreover, both the freebooters and the legitimate privateers often seized any American ships in the area on the allega-tion that they were bound for St. Domingo, no matter what their papers said—and justified their actions by citing the Americans' known tendency to declare false ports of destination.

Pichon decided to take the initiative, complaining to the American government before they could do so to his. He probably also hoped to head off what he feared might become a direct dia-logue between the administration and the Haitians: he knew that Toussaint's old emissary Bunel was back in the United States as an unofficial envoy from Dessalines, and he was worried that Dr. Stevens might also be involved in promoting unofficial contacts.[9] So, in early March he went on record with an official demarche, in which he laid out French objections to the fact that Americans were trading with the island, particularly in arms, as if it were any other destination. The island, he insisted, was in a state of revolt against its legitimate government, and the American trade was highly irreg-ular. He did not, however, call it illegal—he had no instructions on the point and was not yet prepared to go that far. In what he prob-ably assumed would be a telling argument to the Virginian president and secretary of state, Pichon drew the following parallel: "Suppose that the black population of the Southern States of the United States, after having revolted, were to take over the Ports of those States. If, in such a circumstance, there were all kinds of well advertised voyages to those ports, from France or the French colonies, in a similarly tolerated trade; it would undoubtedly appear to the US as not conforming to respective neutral obligations of states, and the feeling that would be excited can easily be imagined."[10]

Pichon also consulted with Madison about the privateers operating from Cuba, and found Madison (probably to the chargé's relief) inclined for the moment to blame Spain for the irregularities there. Madison said that he had already talked to the Spanish minister, the Marquis de Casa Yrujo, requesting him to get the Spanish captain general in Cuba, Salvado Joseph de Someruelos, to rein in the French officials who were running privateering operations from Cuba's theoretically neutral soil. By summer, Pichon also got involved more directly, documenting to Paris the irregularities that were occurring in application of French maritime law in the Caribbean, and writing himself to the Cuban captain general. Someruelos did eventually issue an open letter to all residents of Cuba—Spanish and foreign— in which he reminded them of Cuba's neutral stance and warned them against taking up arms. The decree had only limited effect, however, and became irrelevant in any case when, early in the following year, Spain joined the war on France's side.

Even before Chancellor Livingston was able to make a full presentation of the American case in Paris, however, the situation had escalated. Faced with the loss of a growing number their ships to the French-flagged privateers, and ballooning insurance rates, American shippers had taken it upon themselves to arm their vessels. The administration was doing nothing to stop the practice, claiming that it was done in self-defense. The legality of the ship owners' action was nonetheless questionable—after all, in Toussaint's day the

U.S. government had felt it necessary to specifically authorize similar measures. From New York, Baltimore, and other major ports,
Pichon reported, merchant ships—often carrying contraband—
were sailing to St. Domingo in convoys, sometimes heavily armed,
and often manned by returning Haitian blacks (Dessalines had
offered a forty-dollar reward to any captain repatriating a Haitian).
As a result of these new measures, Pichon, protesting the matter in
official correspondence with Madison, had begun to characterize
the entire American trade with St. Domingo as illegal: "American
businessmen are publicly arming ships in the ports of the U.S., destined to support by force a trade which is contrary to international
law, and to trouble the effort of those cruisers of the French
Republic that have been authorized to prevent it. These armed ships
also aim to cover the shipment of munitions to the rebels of that
colony. . . . It is clear that American Citizens, under the very eyes of
their government, are conducting a private, piratical war against a
power with which the United States is at peace."[11]

Jefferson was not convinced; the government would as yet do
nothing to prohibit the trade.[12] But Pichon was not given a categor-
ical "no," and in fact the administration's answer was ambiguous.
Madison admitted in a subsequent conversation, Pichon reported,
that the administration was somewhat embarrassed over the turn
the issue had taken, particularly so since the protection being given
to a possible contraband trade might be "contrary to U.S. interests."
The stream of negative reports from the island about Dessalines's
continuing eradication of the whites was also, it seems, influencing
the administration's view of the situation. Pichon reported that he
had lectured the secretary of state against doing business with the
Dessalines regime, arguing that "While the blacks are violating all
their promises, declaring and executing a war to the death against
the French, how can it be possible, even as French blood flows in
all the towns, that we see the Americans, protected by our enemy
the British, enjoy all the privileges of a friendly nation?"[13]

But the Americans, in turn, had good reasons of their own for indignation against the French. If their merchants had armed their ships in self-defense, that was because the exactions of the French-flagged privateers, official and unofficial, had become truly onerous. To add insult to the injury caused by these virtual pirates, the French governor of Guadeloupe had now issued a decree in which he virtually declared all American captains trading with St. Domingo to be, themselves, pirates, and subject to corporal punishment. The decree caused such a storm of negative comment that the concerned Pichon tried to reel in the edict through his own correspondence with the governor. He also pointed out to Paris, once again, that French law was not being applied consistently in the Caribbean, and that U.S.-French relations were suffering as a result. But his effort with the governor proved unsuccessful, and in any event he was given no encouragement to continue by Madison. In short order, several American captains were arrested and condemned to death. No executions actually took place, but the threat—and the insult—infuriated the American merchants and required an official American response.

In this strained atmosphere, it was little wonder that Livingston's demarche in Paris was coolly received. Based as it had been some months earlier on the hope that the French government would find American noncontraband trade with the Haitians both legal and in the French national interest, it had largely been overtaken by events and the growing invective. Livingston made the arguments urged on him in January by Madison, including an additional request— that the French allow American commercial agents to be assigned to the French-held part of Hispaniola, to help monitor the trade and protect the interests of American seamen.

Livingston did, however, have a proposal to make that took account of more recent developments. He proposed that the United States and France negotiate a convention in which the U.S. government would, in return for French acceptance of U.S.-St. Domingo trade, institute a system by which all American ships bound for the West Indies would be required to post a bond, which would be forfeited if any contraband was landed in St. Domingo.[14]

It was the end of summer before Livingston finally got an answer from the French foreign minister. The French, it seemed, were still sorting out some of the specifics of their policy. Talleyrand did concede one point: that some French administrators might have been applying maritime law in an inconsistent manner. If that were the case, Talleyrand prevaricated, "they do not have imperial sanction." The emperor, he promised, would investigate and correct any abuses found. (In late October, indeed, Talleyrand informed the minister of marine that Bonaparte wished the colonial governors and officials on Cuba to be instructed to regularize their procedures for issuing letters of marque and taking prizes. He also indicated that the emperor had given, and then retracted, permission for American commercial agents.)[15]

But as far as the basic issue of American armed trade with St. Domingo was concerned, Talleyrand conceded nothing. International law, he insisted, prohibited neutral nations from using warlike measures, and "the present communication between the United States and the rebel colony of St. Domingue can only be seen in the Antilles with astonishment and irritation. In a situation in which that unhappy land has become the tomb of its proprietors, and a scene of the most horrible atrocities, is it admissible that a friendly and peaceful nation believes it can allow itself to establish relations of assistance, supply and trade? . . . Is there an interest in helping such men to survive?" The U.S. government should recognize, Talleyrand concluded, that its merchants could not arrogate to themselves the right to take up arms, or privately compromise the relations of their country with foreign nations.[16]

There was no mention of a convention to regulate the trade.

The French, it was clear, were in no mood to forget their loss of St. Domingo, or what they saw as American duplicity in that drama. They were determined to stop America's trade with their rebel colony.

THE CLEARANCE ACT DEBATE

I n May 1804, as the bellicose and confident Napoleon Bonaparte was crowning himself emperor of a stable and prosperous France, the Addington government in London collapsed from its own weakness, and the great statesman and Francophobe William Pitt the Younger was called back as wartime prime minister. In ill health and deep in debt, Pitt had lost much of his fire but none of his determination. Within weeks, he moved forcefully to strengthen English defenses and lay the groundwork for still another great coalition against the old enemy, France. The struggle between the two great powers was moving to a new level of intensity, in which the rights of the few remaining neutral nations, such as the United States, would be subordinated by the belligerents to the great demands of their war effort.

The Americans had much to lose from the sharpening of the conflict and the squeeze on neutrals, because so far they had gained much from the war. The Dutch, the Danes, and the Swedes had all been squeezed out of the neutral shipping business, and Spain would soon follow when it sided with France. The Americans had filled the gap; the U.S. fleet was still growing and American captains, benefiting from their neutral status, were active in every trade. They were particularly successful in carrying the exports of the French West Indies to Europe and vice versa, taking advantage of a British ruling that considered those products no longer to be enemy goods if their shipment to or from Europe was indirect, that is, via an American port. Most Americans benefited from the increase in trade. The port cities were bustling, farmers were selling their surpluses, shipbuilders and seamen were fully employed, bankers, merchants, and insurance companies prospered, and the government collected customs duties at rates that made it possible for Secretary of the Treasury Gallatin to pay down the national debt. The Haiti trade was, of course, only a small part of this general prosperity, but it was not insignificant, especially to the manufacturers of arms and gunpowder, who otherwise had few available outlets for their goods.

Neutral vessels were required by international law and practice to submit to search on the high seas by belligerent warships or properly commissioned privateers, and any cargo they carried (and sometimes the whole vessel), if considered contraband, was subject to seizure and confiscation by an admiralty court. As the war heated up, the belligerents' searches became more and more aggressive. British warships maintained regular patrols just off many American ports, stopping and searching as much traffic as they could. Toward the Caribbean, French privateers were more active, swarming in particular around Charleston. One British practice which was especially galling to American sensitivities was their insistence on the right to press into the Royal Navy any British subject whom they found serving on an American ship. Admittedly, many British tars had slipped off to join the booming American merchant fleet, where the pay and treatment was generally better than on English ships, but not all were deserters from the Royal Navy as the British tended to claim. Moreover, British officers were so often arrogant in their manner, and arbitrary in whom they chose to impress as alleged British subjects, that the American administration was obliged by the public outcry to defend American rights in the issue.

The Jefferson administration as a result found itself increasingly occupied in the diplomatic and legal defense of American neutral rights, whether from improper seizures, conflicting interpretations of contraband, violations of American territorial waters, British impressments, illegal privateers, or whatever. The merchants were, in general, happy to shift the burden of defending their rights to the government. They most definitely did not want the United States to take sides in the war, which would put an end to their profitable middleman business. The Haiti trade, however, was one place where they had determined to defend their interests without support from the government. There, they had taken matters into their own hands by arming their ships against the illegal privateers— although a few had gone too far, actually engaging in combat with proper French cruisers. But even then, most of the merchants wanted the government role limited to a diplomacy that would not prejudice their neutral status—as can be seen by a protest made by Baltimore merchants when they thought (erroneously) that the federal government intended to provide U.S. Navy protection to American vessels going to the island.[1]

Jefferson's diplomacy on maritime affairs was largely reactive. He and Madison had good reason to defend the right of American shippers to carry such commerce as the European war had, fortuitously, made available. The Haiti trade, in spite of the greater legal question marks that surrounded it, was simply a part of this calculation. It was something to be defended, but was not an objective of policy in itself.

The president's main foreign policy objective, as his first term drew to a close, continued to be to consolidate America's hold on his great prize, the Louisiana Purchase. That meant firming up the territory's boundaries, particularly along the Gulf Coast, where Spain's stubborn defense of its claim to the strip of East and West Florida was blocking American settlers' access to the sea, and threatening hostilities. Jefferson's first term had been a success, due in large part to the Louisiana deal. Gaining the Floridas would, he thought, provide for a successful second term, should he win the year-end election. That prospect, indeed, seemed increasingly likely, given the opposition's confusion following Burr's defeat for governor of New York, the collapse of the Northern Confederacy idea, and then the death of Hamilton in his duel with Burr.

But getting the Spaniards to relinquish the Floridas, Jefferson calculated, would almost surely require getting the French to apply pressure on their proud but weak ally.

Napoleon and Talleyrand were not in a mood to oblige the Americans. The war against Britain took absolute precedence, and Spanish support (and the Spanish fleet) would be essential for the planned invasion of England. In the circumstances, they had no interest in leaning on the Spanish in order to satisfy what they saw as American greed for more territory in Florida. American greed in the Haiti trade was already annoying enough. But there was no reason, either, to actually tell the Americans that France would not help them, since dangling the bait of a positive response before their eyes would keep them attentive to French requirements. Talleyrand, that master of ambiguous responses, would simply keep the importunate Americans guessing.

Months before, Talleyrand and Napoleon had decided to strike a more difficult stance with the Americans. The man chosen to replace Pichon, whom they suspected of having become too sympathetic to the American point of view, would have no problem in taking a harder line. He was Jean Marie Turreau, a general with solid republican credentials and a no-nonsense air, who neither liked Americans nor spoke much English. He would crack the whip when necessary. Talleyrand's instructions to him on the issue of the St. Domingue trade, certainly, did not look toward compromise. The emperor, Talleyrand said, considered that all American help to the rebels of St. Domingue was directed at France itself, and that "the existence of an armed Negro people, occupying places that they have despoiled by the most criminal acts, is a horrible spectacle for all the white nations;

all of them should feel that, by allowing them [the blacks] to continue in that state, they are sparing incendiaries and assassins."[2]

General Turreau arrived in Baltimore in mid-November, and presented his credentials to the president several days later. Brimming with self-confidence and resplendent in his official uniform, Turreau, with his "profusion of gold lace," managed to put off the determinedly republican Jefferson (who, earlier, had received the new and rather stuffy British minister Anthony Merry in his bedroom slippers). It was not the moment, anyway, for a business discussion. At a dinner following the ceremony, the two men exchanged remarks on the outcome of the French Revolution, with the president musing that it would have been best had the process stopped with the 1798 constitution.[3]

Had the discussion turned to the business of Haiti, Turreau would have had powerful new arguments to use against America's connections with the Dessalines regime. Reports had recently arrived that the Haitians had caught an American, Captain Tate, in the act of trying to smuggle out a number French citizens who were fleeing from the massacres. Both the French and Tate had been summarily executed, in an outrage to American sensitivities that had already created a "furor" and was to provide fuel to the anti-Dessalines Republican press for years to come.[4]

On the other hand, Turreau would have been disturbed—to say the least—had he known that the U.S. government was attempting to make an informal overture to Dessalines. The channel was not through Dessalines's unofficial agent, Bunel, who had been watched closely by Pichon during the months he had been in America. Madison and Jefferson had, instead, been listening to an American merchant named Jacob Lewis, who had for some time been urging that there be some contact with Dessalines. Dessalines was refusing to give trading preferences to the British, and was in dispute with them over a number of issues, to the extent of closing some ports to their ships. Lewis had argued that the U.S. government should take advantage of the situation and find some way to reassure Dessalines, informally, that the United States sought no preferences and wished to keep open the noncontraband trade. In September, Lewis had returned to Haiti, had seen Dessalines in Gonaives, and, with some informal (and undocumented) guidance from Madison, had had a general discussion about the trade. Nothing, however, had resulted from the effort, and it was soon forgotten.

Turreau, in any event, had no need to make representations about the Haiti trade. The American administration had already decided to take action on it own.

When Madison had told Pichon, back in June 1804, that the administration was "embarrassed" over the trade, he and the president were already considering ways in which they could manage the growing crisis over the issue. Several weeks later, Madison wrote instructions to the new American minister-designate to Paris, John Armstrong, which read, in part, that he should give "early and steady attention" to the issue when he got to the French capital. "The arming of vessels, by American Citizens, avowedly for a trade with St. Domingo, is a circumstance sincerely regretted and would certainly be controlled if within the legal authority of the Executive," Madison wrote. He added that the administration would have hoped to have seen a legal ruling blocking the sailing of any armed ships that did not give security against engaging in contraband trade, but that no such case was then before the courts.[5]

What Madison did not write in the instructions was that the administration, in the absence of a court case, was considering how else it could get the "legal authority" to control the trade. Its first choice was to try to get the authority through a treaty with the French, which would then become the law of the land. Livingston, as noted earlier, had already been instructed to seek such a convention.

When it became clear, several months later, that Livingston had failed to get Talleyrand to even discuss the idea of a treaty, it meant

that the administration would have to seek legislation on the issue—
something which Madison had often told Pichon it was reluctant to
do, because of the potentially damaging results of a public debate.
However, the acerbity of Talleyrand's response to Livingston, and
the imminent arrival of the hard-liner Turreau, indicated that early
action would be preferable if a larger confrontation over the issue
was to be headed off. The president confided to John Quincy
Adams, at the end of October, that he was determined to put an end
to the trade.[6] That probably overstated the case, but what was clear
was that the president felt he had to take some action that would be
responsive to French demands and his own reading of international
law. With that aim in mind, the president included a section in his
November 8 message to the reconvening Congress in which he set
the stage for a legislative proposal: "Complaints have been received
that persons, residing within the US, have taken on themselves to
arm merchant vessels, and to force a commerce into certain ports
and countries, in defiance of the laws of those countries. That individuals should undertake to wage private war, independently of the
authority of their country, cannot be admitted in a well-ordered society. Its tendency to produce aggression on the laws and rights of
other nations, and to endanger the peace of our own is so obvious,
that I doubt not you will adopt measures for restraining it effectually
in future."[7]

Jefferson's reluctance to take the St. Domingo issue to Congress was
not ill-founded. Although his party could boast large majorities in
both the House and Senate, its members were not at all of one
mind on the subject. Republicans lawmakers from New England
and the Mid-Atlantic states had many constituents, or were themselves, involved in trade, and they would view any proposal that limited their opportunities with a gimlet eye. The Baltimore merchant
Samuel Smith was a case in point. A strong Republican who had
helped Jefferson greatly in the 1800 election, he was at one and the

same time a senator, brother of the attorney general, and a close relative of Jefferson's confidant Wilson Carey Nicholas, yet his business interests led him to resist government interference with the West Indies trade. He, and others like him, would need some convincing. The government needed to come up with a proposal that would not engender opposition from its own ranks, as well as the opposition side of the aisle.

It was not just the trade issues, however, that gave the administration pause in introducing the subject. The truly inflammatory issue could well be the subject of Haiti itself. The last congressional debate touching on the island's fate had been in 1798, when the question was whether the black rebels might gain their independence from what was then a hostile power. Now, six years later, the rebels had claimed their independence—but at the cost of war, dispossessions, and massacres that had seriously prejudiced American public opinion, and which had provoked a backlash in the slaveholding South.

In a Congress increasingly sensitive to the slavery issue, St. Domingo had become a metaphor for the horrors of revolution and possibilities of slave revolt, a sort of tocsin that the administration hesitated to ring lest it set off an unwanted debate on the very contentious issue of slavery itself. It may have been fear of such a debate that brought Jefferson to redraft his message to Congress so as to remove an inflammatory passage on St. Domingo's possible impact on domestic security. Madison and Jefferson had certainly convinced the sometimes gullible Pichon, in any event, that such a debate was potentially dangerous for them. The French chargé had written to Paris that congressional debate over who would get the suffrage in the new territory of Louisiana had already opened the argument over slavery in a way which risked striking off "sparks that, along with what has happened in St. Domingue, and combined with the partisanship that pervades, could light a fire which is frightening to think of."[8]

The Virginians Jefferson and Madison may have been exaggerating the danger somewhat. While the Haitian revolution was uniformly seen in Congress as dangerous to the nation's internal security, it was also seen on occasion as a positive moral lesson. Two speeches in the House, both by Republicans, illustrate some of the variety of opinion on the issue. In the first, on the question of whether or not to give the vote to inhabitants of the Louisiana Territory, Congressman John Jackson of Virginia had argued for an immediate granting of rights as follows: "Allow, for the sake of argument, that the people are slaves. This does not prove that they are not fit objects of a free government. Look at the ensanguined plains of St. Domingo; the oppressed there have broken their chains, and regained their long lost rights. There, notwithstanding the great debasement of the human character, the sacred flame of liberty is not extinguished." His Pennsylvania counterpart David Bard, on the other hand, while acknowledging the Haitian emancipation, argued that it was the very reason why Americans should fear their own slaves. In debate on a possible imposition of a tax on imported slaves, he warned.

> The negroes are in every family; they wait on every table; they are present on numerous occasions when the conversation turns on political subjects, and cannot fail but catch ideas that will excite discontentment with their condition. . . . If they are ignorant they are, however, capable of instruction, and capable of becoming proficient in the art of war. To be convinced of this we only have to look at St. Domingo. There, the negroes felt their wrongs, and avenged them; they learned the rights of man, and asserted them; they have wrested the power from their oppressors, and have become masters of the island. If they are unarmed, they may be armed; European Powers have armed the Indians against us, and why may they not arm the negroes?[9]

The administration had prepared its ground carefully. The legislation it proposed, in late November, was based on the idea of a bonding requirement for armed vessels, similar to the proposal Livingston had made the previous summer to the French. This was a less contentious step than a ban on the trade, and more open to negotiation of compromise language, yet it was a step that the French just might see as satisfactory. (Armstrong, the new minister in Paris, was instructed to tell the French that it should be seen as a sign that America was still seeking agreement on establishing an "innocent commerce" with St. Domingo.)

At the same time, the administration arranged that the bill be introduced in the House by a New Englander, the Republican William Eustis of Boston, a man who could not be accused of hostility to shipping or merchant interests. Eustis, in turn, saw to it that the first voice heard in debate, in defense of the bill, was Jacob Crowninshield, a Salem, Massachusetts, congressman with impeccable merchant credentials. In the face of these adroit tactics, the Federalist opponents were on the defensive from the beginning.

The bill proposed that no vessel carrying, or capable of carrying, cannons or other armament be granted permission to sail from American ports for destinations in the Western Hemisphere, or the Atlantic coasts of Europe and Africa, without posting a bond. The bond, for two times the value of the ship, would be forfeited if there were any evidence that the ship had engaged in illegal armed acts against the vessels or territory of any nation at peace with the United States. Ships that engaged in warlike acts would, in addition to losing their bond, be subject to confiscation.

The action was directed only at armed vessels. Unarmed ships would be exposed to no new requirements, and still might carry on trade, as they saw fit, with any port, including those in Haiti. Nor was there any effort to regulate the shipment of contraband goods; the administration continued to insist that it would be up to the belligerent powers concerned (in this case, France) to control contraband, not the U.S. government. Thus the trade would go on, while only its most egregious practice would be restricted in an effort to comply with international law and—most importantly—to placate the French. Eustis admitted as much to his colleague Senator

William Plumer. Still another supporter of the bill (in a moment of unnecessary candor) blurted out on the Senate floor that the "purpose of the bill was not so much to preclude the continuation of the trade with St. Domingo, but to give a sort of half-way satisfaction to France in excuse for the iniquity of that trade."[10]

In the House, debate on the bill proved to be businesslike and, though sometimes impassioned, did not stray into divisive territory, such as the slavery issue. Almost no Federalist representatives rose to attack the bill, so debate was largely among the Republicans, some of whom objected to specific provisions, but only one of whom challenged the basic premise of the bill. That challenge came early on and from, interestingly enough, John Wayles Eppes, the president's nephew and son-in-law. Eppes, who was a strong opponent of the trade, argued that the draft bill missed the point—that the armed trade with St. Domingo was illegal, and should flatly be banned. Eustis followed him, pointing out that "Every gentleman knows there is great difficulty in restraining a trade where the profits are high, although attended with more risk and danger than ordinary. [There are] but two ways the thing could be done on the present occasion. . . . either to interdict the trade altogether, or to pass the bill now on the table."[11]

With the issue thus drawn, a vote was called for, and Eppes's amendment to ban the trade lost convincingly. That done, the debate turned to the details of the administration's proposal. Opponents of the bill all but conceded that the armed trade was "iniquitous," or even "illicit," that the delivery of arms to the "brigands" was somehow improper, and that the American captains engaged in the trade were capable of questionable practices. They concentrated, instead, on trying to make the proposed measures as toothless as possible.

Jacob Crowninshield's opening argument for the bill had stressed the irregularities of the Haiti trade as the prime justification for regulation. Even though ships in the India trade also carried armament against pirates, as he mentioned in a later speech, he argued that the armed Haiti trade needed to be brought under control.

Moreover, he said, the flow of arms was not necessarily in America's interest, as they were going to "a class of people it is in the interest of the United States to depress and keep down, rather than put arms into their hands, to do such extensive mischief as is every day practiced in that island. . . ." This backhanded slap at the Dessalines regime was, surprisingly, almost the only mention of the situation on the island to emerge from the debate. It was mitigated only slightly by the later comment of another Republican, Joseph Clay of Pennsylvania, to the effect that even if there were to be a suspension of trade with Haiti, "the evils of having the present inhabitants for our neighbors would not be lessened." The trade, he pointed out, would still continue and others would make the profit.[12]

The debate in the popular press, on the other hand, was much more unbridled and considerably more partisan. If the outnumbered Federalists in Congress were largely silent, the Federalist papers were not. Boston's *Columbian Centinel* made perhaps the most extreme case, arguing that "The black people of Hayti, having solemnly declared themselves a sovereign, free and independent nation, having adopted a constitution, and having by their strength and valor demonstrated their power to maintain their Independence, ought to be considered and treated by neutral nations, as an Independent State. Their condition is not dissimilar to that of the people of the United States in 1778." To this fine moral argument the paper then, unfortunately, added a point that clearly disclosed its motivation, admitting "that the trade with St. Domingo is extremely lucrative may be inferred from the great risks which our merchants and mariners run. . . ."[13]

Even as the lawmakers in Washington were avoiding the issues, the papers exchanged impassioned volleys on the legitimacy of the Haitian regime and the legality of trade to the rebel country. The outspoken and often outrageous Philadelphia *Aurora* took the lead for the Republicans, declaiming that

A portion of our merchants, a number of individuals, in about a half dozen sea ports, taking advantage of the state of affairs in St. Domingo, and knowing the immense profits to be derived from an illicit commerce with its black inhabitants, undertake to arm their ships in order to resist any attempt of French vessels to prevent their entering certain ports. The question then first requires to be determined, are the revolters in St. Domingo, that ferocious banditti—either under the law of nations, or in the eye of humanity, or in the view of a just and honest policy—are they to be considered as an independent nation? . . . At present we consider them in no better light than land pirates—as something less to be respected, and from sound policy more to be discouraged, than the piratical states of Barbary. . . . [The merchants] disregard the government and laws of their country, for they undertake to wage war not against pirates, but against the commissioned vessels of a nation with which we are at peace. . . . Our government, then, is solemnly pledged by its response to the whole American people, not to suffer the conduct of the Mercantile class to produce a war from which the whole nation would suffer.[14]

The Federalist *Baltimore Federal Gazette,* in turn, responded with a lengthy article, citing legal authorities in defense of the thesis that arming neutral ships was admissible and proper under international law, and pointing out the that Danes and Swedes both allowed their merchantmen to arm. In a less analytical and more rhetorical mode, the *Centinel* thundered that "The facts of the case are—a war now exists between France and one of her remote colonies, who refuse her obedience. The colonists are in possession, have declared themselves independent, established a government, and maintain their independence." Their war is a public one and they act as distinct and independent peoples, the paper insisted. The United States should be neutral.[15]

The newspaper debate soon descended to finger-pointing. Republican papers dusted off the old St. Domingo bugaboo, citing the atrocities, and the execution of Captain Tate, as reasons why "motives of sound policy, arising out of the law of nations and of the principles of self preservation . . . call on us to discountenance, by all means, the barbaric Empire of St. Domingo." The *Aurora*, as usual, was the most outspoken, offering that "commerce with a horde of uncivilized and bloodthirsty revolters who, if encouraged, would devastate the West Indies and even threaten us with domestic danger. . . . The circumstances under which the revolters have gained the ascendancy in St. Domingo, and our own peculiar situation in regard to population of that description, render the question extremely delicate. . . ." Against this kind of populist charge, the *Centinel* could only reply, rather lamely, that "It does not, in any manner or degree, alter the nature of the case that one of the belligerents should put more inhumanity into their laws than the other into theirs, that one should be black and the other white, that one of them should be more civilized and the other less. . . ."[16]

Although the *Aurora* was eventually constrained to recognize that it could no longer call the entire Haiti trade illegal, when even the Jefferson administration accepted the noncontraband trade, its finger-pointing got closer to home. It could name the names, it threatened, of the merchants, the ships, the powder mills, and the details of shipments involved in the contraband trade. It also virtually accused unnamed merchants of dealing in stolen goods, charging that they had received payment for a shipment of seventy thousand pounds of powder in the form of silver plate confiscated from executed French planters. Perhaps because of such charges, perhaps simply because the Federalist legislators were no longer challenging the clearance bill, or perhaps because a concurrent political brawl—the Republicans' inept effort to impeach Judge Chase—had suddenly given them better copy, the Federalist papers eventually dropped out of the exchange over the St. Domingo trade. As the bill neared acceptance, the *Charleston Courier* summed up the Federalists' attitude with great irony and some chagrin: "This Bill we have all along considered as the effect of pusillanimity on the part of our government, who wanted courage to define and assert our national rights, and who chose rather to sacrifice a lawful and lucrative commerce than to gainsay a formidable friend and ally, the Emperor of the French Republick."[17]

Against this backdrop, the legislators in Washington continued to shape a bill that would offend the fewest. The administration, for its part, was not pushing too hard. Jefferson, riding on the success of his first term, had just been reelected for a second four-year period, and his priorities were, for the moment, elsewhere. The administration did not even send documentation supporting the bill to Congress, in the form of letters from the British and French, until the end of January, when the debate in the House was already over. Those diplomatic letters, indeed, added very little; the one from Pichon was dated the previous May, and the one from British minister Anthony Merry simply noted that the arming of neutral ships was prejudicial to the interest of Great Britain as a belligerent power. The most influential outside testimony, in fact, was a memorial from the merchants of Philadelphia, which explained carefully and persuasively (even the *Aurora* admitted that the argument made sense) their rationale for arming their ships against the piratical activities of ships "having or pretending to have" French letters of marque. Speeches by congressmen, pointing out that insurance had become alarmingly expensive because of those French activities, and that even commerce to New Orleans was no longer safe from illegal seizure, also had their effect in dampening support for a strong bill. Only one effort was made to strengthen the bill, by including the value of the cargo in the bonding requirement, and it was beaten back.

On Christmas eve, by a resounding 77 to 33 vote, the House passed the Clearance Bill. The pro-trade Republican congressmen having joined with the Federalists to shape a weak bill they could live with, the vote was a formality. The roll call showed a highly partisan result: the Federalists solidly opposed, and only a half dozen Republicans voted against the president's legislation. But the lack of teeth in the bill was a bipartisan product.

In the Senate, preoccupied as it was with the violently partisan struggle over the impeachment of Judge Chase, the bill nonetheless was still controversial, and a lively contest ensued. The House version was not acceptable to the senators, who sent the bill to the commerce committee for further revisions. As the committee was headed by the merchant Senator Samuel Smith, the bill emerged from those deliberations almost totally eviscerated. The Senate leadership, however, blocked the committee report and reverted to the original House version. Even though this was a small victory for the hard-liners, the bill that the Senate finally passed on February 22 had been watered down somewhat from the House version. The House, more interested by this time in closing out the session than in reopening the debate, quickly agreed to the Senate's changes. Sent to the president, the bill was signed into law on March 3, 1805.

The Act to Regulate the Clearance of Armed Merchant Vessels, as it was called, provided that any armed ship headed to the West Indies or the Spanish Main must post a bond for double the value of the vessel, its tackle, and its furniture, on condition that its arms not be "used for any unlawful purpose, but only for resistance and defense in case of involuntary hostility." It also required that the ship's armament not be sold during the voyage, or at a minimum be fully accounted for as a legitimate transaction. The owners and skipper of any armed vessel going elsewhere than the restricted areas would be required to take an oath that their vessel was not bound for the West Indies. Violators of the bond requirement could see their ships seized. The new law would be in force until the end of the next session of Congress, that is, until spring 1806.

The act was, in the end, a compromise on top of a compromise. President Jefferson had sought an action which would calm French outrage over the armed trade to Haiti and correspond more closely with his reading of international law, yet not cripple the noncontraband trade. He still hoped that the French would acquiesce in "innocent" trade with the Haitian regime, and help him in his drive to obtain the Floridas. Always improvising and optimistic in his rather unstructured foreign policy, he had, however, chosen to arm himself with a flywhisk to deal with an alligator of a problem. And then, after Congress had further weakened the flywhisk, he had very little with which to face the French alligator. Trying to put the best face on it, Madison instructed John Armstrong, two days after the act was signed, that he should seek to persuade the French that "an absolute prohibition was certainly more than could of right be required." Passage of the act, he wanted the French to believe, proved the friendly disposition of the United States, and might encourage them to allow an open trade regime with St. Domingo. More realistically, he told Monroe in London that the French might in fact be hurt by the act, since their colonies in the West Indies depended more on the American merchants for their defense supplies than did the British ones.[18]

While the administration was congratulating itself, for the record at least, on its success, one Republican who had voted for the bill was angry at the result. George Logan, a Pennsylvania Quaker with strong pacifist beliefs, was convinced that Jefferson had chosen a dangerous ploy with the Clearance Act. He though that France was not to be bought off by such a weak measure, and that the subsequent friction might lead to hostilities. Logan had intervened once before to avoid hostilities with France, undertaking a private mission of mediation to Paris at the time of the XYZ Affair. He had been excoriated by the Federalists at the time, and legislation had been passed making such private diplomatic missions illegal, but he was a determined and principled man. In the case of the Haiti trade, he saw nothing to convince him that it was worth a fight with the French. The defeat of the Smith committee report in the

Senate had given him confidence that he might find supporters among those Republicans who, like John Eppes in the House, despised both the merchants and their Haitian customers. He decided that he would demand not only the stoppage of the armed trade to Haiti, but the stoppage of all U.S. trade there.

On the day after the Senate vote on the Clearance bill, Logan put forward a draft bill designed to stop all commercial intercourse with St. Domingo. With the legislative session winding down, it stood little chance of immediate passage, but its disposition would be an important signal for the future. Amazingly, in a Senate that had just voted 20 to 8 to pass a weakened Clearance Act, Logan was able to marshal a substantial protest vote against his president's chosen policy. The vote on February 27 was a tie, and consideration of the trade ban was defeated only by the vote of retiring Vice President Aaron Burr, performing one of his last acts as an official of the American government. Logan took the narrow defeat for a victory. He knew that the Republican majority in the next congress would be even larger, and he intended to return to the charge.

THE TRADE SUSPENDED

The Clearance Act, of course, did not solve the problem. Virtually everyone involved in the legislation realized that it offered too many loopholes to be able to stop the armed trade. And even if it had done so, the French persisted in considering the entire trade with the rebels, armed or not, contraband or not, an unfriendly and perhaps even illegal practice. Indeed, some of Jefferson's supporters agreed with the French position, among them Congressman Eppes, Senator Logan, and even Secretary of the Treasury Gallatin. The influential Gallatin had called the trade "altogether illegal," and argued that the United States could only trade legally with the rebels if it took the step—both politically and diplomatically dangerous—of acknowledging their independence.[1]

But the act did at least buy time. The initial French response to the president's initiative, Armstrong reported from Paris early in 1805, was positive. Talleyrand, Armstrong also wrote, had even offered to promote with Bonaparte the idea of allowing innocent, noncontraband American trade with Haiti. The minister's offer, on the other hand, had been accompanied with the suggestion that he be paid a substantial bribe for rendering the service, making it seem just another duplicitous gesture by that master of insincerity.[2] There was no follow-up by either side.

The Americans, for their part, continued to press the French on the harmful effects of the previous summer's decree by Governor

Ferrand in Santo Domingo, virtually making all American trade with Haiti subject to seizure by the privateers. Jefferson, in fact, thought that he was making some headway with General Turreau on the issue, although it appears that he had misread the Frenchman's signals. Turreau was limiting himself to anodyne responses on the Haiti trade simply because he wanted to get new instructions following passage of the Clearance Act, not because he was softening his government's position. In the spring, he informed Talleyrand that his stock answer was simply to criticize the American government's "tolerance shown to such a shameful and guilty trade." But by early summer he was urging his government to take a stronger line. "[I]t has come time to throw down the glove or stay quiet," he reported, while noting his strong preference for the first action.[3]

What had caused Turreau to want to throw down the gauntlet, and seemingly also convinced the French government to do so, was a brazen bit of self-congratulation by some of the major contraband shippers. A large New York-based convoy, armed with over seventy cannon, had sailed for Haiti back in the winter, when the Clearance bill was still under debate. The voyage, completed early June, turned out to be a commercial triumph, and the merchants could not resist blowing their own horn. With their profits in the bank, and a toothless Clearance Act offering them the possibility of more such bonanzas, they celebrated their success. At a big public reception, attended by prominent Republicans as well as Federalists, they proposed a number of toasts which, to say the least, offended French sensitivities. "To the commerce of the United States: May its sails be unfurled in every sea and as free as the wind which fills them," they huzzaed. And then, "To the government of Haiti, founded on the only legitimate basis of all authority . . . the peoples' choice. May it be as durable as its principles are pure."[4] To Turreau, those were fighting words.

In his rump capital of Santo Domingo, Governor Ferrand did not wait for further instructions from Paris to toughen his stance. While he still had not punished any American captains as pirates as he had threatened to do, in June he issued a new decree declaring that any ship going to or from a rebel port would be subject to seizure and confiscation, and its senior officers punishable before French justice. He charged that American ships, even since the Clearance Act had been passed, still got American port clearance in spite of declaring ports in Haiti as their destination. He also accused American captains of transporting arms for Dessalines from one rebel port to another, in effect becoming "auxiliaries to the black rebels." His accusations were sweeping: "Several of the most respected merchant houses of New York, Philadelphia, Baltimore etc have for a long time past, kept up a continual intercourse with the revolted blacks, and have habitually supplied them with every sort of provision and warlike stores. . . . Powerful equipments of neutral vessels, for war and merchandise, have been made in the ports of the United States to protect this infamous commerce," his declaration railed.[5]

It was autumn of 1805, however, before General Turreau had the new, stronger instructions he wanted, along with Talleyrand's assurance that Napoleon had become incensed at the American behavior, which he had called "shameful."[6] The tougher new French position had already been exposed in Paris in early August, when Talleyrand sent a sharply accusatory letter to Minister Armstrong. In his note, Talleyrand minced no words, trying to destroy what was left of Jefferson's argument that the American government could not ban the trade:

> Even if the expeditions are the result of private speculation, the United States Government is nonetheless obliged to put an end to them by a variety of obligations. . . . No government can support a revolt by subjects of another power, nor in that state of affairs enter into commerce with them nor favor those who are in connection with its own subjects. . . . It is impossible for the United States to continue to close its eyes any longer to the effect of its commerce with St. Domingue. The expeditions for that island are made with

scandalous publicity; they are supported by armed ships; on their return they are celebrated and the results of their speculation boasted, under the acknowledgement and even the praise of the government. . . . His Majesty has charged me to ask, in his name, the Government of the United States to oppose any expedition, under whatever pretense or designation, to the parts of St. Domingue occupied by the rebels.[7]

Armstrong, the following day, sent a placatory note to the minister, urging him to realize that the New York convoy had sailed long before passage of the Clearance Act, and that the administration's sponsorship of the act was a signal of his government's good intentions.[8] Talleyrand, however, was having none of it. The following week, he fired back a still tougher message. "Certainly the Federal Government does not wish, in order to favor private citizens, to give new capabilities to the rebels and brigands," he posited. "Neither your government, nor His Majesty, can remain indifferent to it, and the seriousness of these facts demand that His Majesty consider as a fair prize any vessel that ships to or from the parts of St. Domingue occupied by the rebels. . . . This system of impunity and tolerance cannot continue, and His Majesty is convinced that your government will find it an act of friendship to put an immediate end to it."[9]

General Turreau was finally able to act on his new instructions in November. In a formal note to Madison, he set out charges that differed only slightly from those Talleyrand had enumerated to Armstrong. Although Turreau threw in a few gratuitous racial insults when he called the Haitian rebels "that race of African slaves, the reproach and refuse of nature," his closing demand was in fact somewhat less heavy-handed than his minister's. "The only way open for the redress of these complaints is to put an end to the tolerance which produces them, and which daily aggravates their consequences," he urged.[10]

Madison did not reply to the French minister's note.

Jefferson's foreign policy was in difficulty. Victory over the Barbary pirates had given him a welcome boost during the summer, but American relations with the major powers—Great Britain, France, and Spain—were increasingly troubled. Nor was he making any progress toward his major goals, the protection of American neutrality and the acquisition of West Florida.

In fact, the administration's tactics on Florida—swinging back and forth as they did between questionable legalisms, bluster, subversion, and attempts at diplomatic pressure—had created a near crisis in American-Spanish relations. That was not overly important in itself—Spain was in decline, its American empire beginning to crumble—but American pressure on Spain had eventually caused an annoyed France to openly support its weak ally. The French had finally made it quite clear, at the end of 1804, that they objected to the American tactics and would not support American claims to West—much less East—Florida. France's new imperial swagger, added to frictions over the Haiti trade and other minor but contentious issues, contributed to a rapid decline in American-French relations. Mutual suspicion reached such a point that in late summer Jefferson confided to Madison that he feared "hostile and treacherous intentions against us on the part of France," which were leading him to think seriously of arranging a backup alliance with Great Britain in case of a spread of the European war.[11]

Not that relations with Great Britain were appreciably better. Each of the European powers, intent on defeating its historic enemy, aimed to assure that neutral shipping served its own interests exclusively. But Britain's reach was greater, and after Admiral Nelson's great victory at Trafalgar in October, the Royal Navy truly controlled the Atlantic. The Pitt government was determined to destroy the neutral commerce, most of it American, that was allowing goods from the French West Indies to reach France and Spain and feed their war effort. In July, a British court had reversed long-standing British policy, ruling in the case of a ship called the *Essex* that transshipment at an American port would no longer be permitted in the carriage of West Indies goods to and from Europe; henceforth all such cargoes would be considered as in a continuous voyage, and subject to condemnation as enemy goods. Following this ruling, British seizures of American ships jumped sharply, and the very existence of the profitable transshipment business between the West Indies and Europe was threatened. At the same time, Royal Navy patrols and impressments of seamen off the American coast became still more aggressive. In response to these challenges to American pocketbooks and pride, American-British relations plummeted, and an outcry grew in the coastal cities for the government to react to the insulting and harmful British actions.

With Congress due to convene in December, Jefferson and Madison needed a strategy to deal with three pressing issues: the rapidly escalating crisis with Britain, the dispute with France, and Jefferson's own objective of obtaining the Floridas. It was evident that national pride and self-interest would demand a response to Britain's high-handed measures against American shipping. The problems with France, on the other hand, had lost priority, since the new popular indignation against the Royal Navy had dampened the outcry about the French privateers. Moreover, French demands on the Haiti trade—as the administration had already admitted by sponsoring the Clearance Act—had some merit, and the overall level of trade with the island was down in any event. Jefferson needed to deal with the two European powers in a way that would serve his objective of obtaining West Florida from Spain, and he believed that he could not achieve his goal without French acquiescence, at a minimum. In light of these considerations, an appropriate strategy called for confronting Britain, attempting to bully Spain, and dealing with the prickly, probably malign, but just possibly helpful French.

That meant, unfortunately, mollifying the French on the Haiti trade.

The Ninth Congress was a strongly Republican one in which the Federalists had been reduced to a small minority. Jefferson's majority in both houses of Congress, however, did not equate to a rubber-stamp approval of administration proposals, as the Republican numbers masked an increasing factionalism within the party. Many of the new, northern Republicans were engaged in industry and commerce, and often had as much in common with their Federalist opponents as they did with some of the old-line, small-government republicans or populists of the South and West from their own party. The perennial debate over slavery, which was becoming more acute as a result of the revolution in Haiti, the cotton boom, and the impending ban on slave imports, also divided the party. A debate over trade with Haiti was unwelcome because it could touch divisively on both sore points. But it was unavoidable, and the administration moved to make sure that it came out favorably.

Jefferson and Madison were satisfied to let Senator Logan take the lead, as he had said he would do when his motion to cut off the Haiti trade had been defeated in the previous session. The homespun-wearing and strongly pacifist senator was an ideal sponsor. He had credibility as an independent thinker who differed with his president over policy toward Spanish Florida (he thought Jefferson too bellicose) and slavery (he was an abolitionist). At the same time, he was a man of great personal integrity whose Quaker beliefs had led him to oppose the Haiti trade, both on legal principle and because of the risk of hostilities with France it seemed to entail. Logan introduced a bill on December 20, 1805, shortly after Congress convened. He was unable, however, to make a strong opening argument since, in the absence of any new statements of justification from the administration, he had been obliged to fall back on Jefferson's submissions to Congress of the previous year.

In introducing his bill, Senator Logan argued that the Clearance Act had not worked; trade to Haitian ports, he asserted, had increased since the act had been passed. A new act, he argued, was necessary to stop a trade that was both illegal and provocative. Then, in closing his remarks, he somewhat surprisingly raised the possible effect of the trade on the security of the southern states, asking, "is it sound policy to cherish the black population of St. Domingo, whilst we have a similar population in our Southern States," which were exposed to possible insurrection?

Logan was answered by the Massachusetts Federalist John Quincy Adams, who took issue with the idea that new legislation was needed. The Clearance Act was working, he asserted. Senator Logan's bill had been defeated in the previous session; why was it being brought up again when there was no new information that demonstrated the need for further measures? Adams was joined in this line of argument by another Federalist, James Hillhouse of Connecticut, but also by two prominent Republicans, Samuel Smith of Maryland and Samuel Mitchill of New York. Mitchill argued that the Senate should more appropriately be spending its time looking at the question of British aggressions against American shipping, rather than doing the French bidding on Haiti. The Haiti trade, he proposed, "is no great thing in itself, and we might do exceedingly well without it; but I dislike the idea of forbidding it, at the mandate of a foreign Power." Cutting off the trade, he and Senator Smith insisted, would not only help Great Britain monopolize the trade, "giving her the monopoly that she asked, and Dessalines refused her," it would also force the Haitians to take to the sea as pirates in order to earn their way by preying on American shipping.

With these interventions, the mercantile interest's basic arguments against the bill were set out: that the trade with Haiti was legal, and profitable; that any irregularities had been taken care of by the Clearance Act; that further French pressure should be resisted; and that the Haitians could be more dangerous if deprived of American trade than if kept supplied.

James Jackson, a staunch Republican from Georgia, was that day's main speaker in support of the bill. On the commercial aspects of the proposed legislation, he agreed that Congress should be looking at trade sanctions against Britain, and said that he would gladly support them; the British colonies would be starving within a year.

But the most dramatic element of Jackson's intervention was on the inflammatory issue of slavery. Responding emotionally to Senator Adams's question as to the necessity of a new bill, Jackson laid bare the connection that existed, for many southerners, between America's response to the Haitian revolt and the safety of their own slaveholder societies. He would be pleased, he said, to see the bill, or one like it, brought up every year, just as the many bills to limit the slave trade were raised on a regular basis. Haiti was a danger. When the European war eventually ended, it would be in the interest of all of the countries having colonies in the West Indies to "extirpate" the Haitians, or ship them off the island. If that were to happen, he warned, "The United States, by affording them succor, arms, ammunition, and provisions, must be considered by them as their allies," and that the rebel blacks would consequently seek refuge in the States. "One of those brigands introduced into the Southern States was worse than a hundred importations from Africa, and more dangerous to the United States." He compared Haitian independence to a situation in which "a parcel of runways" from Georgia or South Carolina, in the Okefenokee Swamp, were to declare themselves independent and obtain arms from abroad. When Senator Hillhouse suggested that Jackson's fears were overblown, and a "bugbear," the Georgian retorted that "this might be no bugbear [to the honorable gentleman from Connecticut], safe and remote from the scene of action in New Haven, but it was a serious bugbear to him, and would be to the whole southern country, where the horrid scenes of that island would be reenacted, their property destroyed, and their families massacred."[12]

While the anti-slavery Logan may have been somewhat embarrassed by support of this nature, it was helpful. The vote on enrollment of the bill had to be delayed for several weeks until the administration, at Senator Mitchill's request, furnished further documentation supporting its case.[13] In January, the bill was enrolled for further consideration, by a vote of 21 to 7. With only Senator Mitchill among the Republicans voting against it (Senator Smith apparently having been persuaded that the danger of hostilities with France was real if there was no action on the issue), the bill seemed assured of eventual passage.

The bill, which proposed a total ban on trade with all rebel-held ports of the island of Hispaniola, was entrusted to a committee headed by Senator Logan, where it could be expected to get respectful treatment. In the meantime, since the House had taken up the increasingly clamorous complaints against British maritime practices and was moving toward a partial trade ban against that country, that complication had been removed from the debate about Haiti. As a result, when the Logan bill reemerged from committee in mid-February, it had been toughened rather than watered down. Logan resubmitted the amended bill to the Senate, with the unfortunate comment that its passage had been "demanded" by the French. This injudicious admission of acceding to foreign pressure predictably drew the ire of the Federalists, but also angered many of those Republicans who had been prepared, reluctantly, to support the bill for party purposes. But it did not change the final outcome.

The final day's debate, indeed, was anticlimactic. The main speaker was Senator Samuel White, a Federalist from Delaware, who in a long, eloquent, and detailed speech, heaped sarcasm on the bill's proponents. He described the bill as surrender of a very valuable trade as a result of pressure from the French, and its proponents as men "who have taken for granted the very points in dispute, viz: that the blacks of St. Domingo are the slaves of the French, and are now in such a state of revolt that no nation has a right to trade with them." But the Haitians, he argued, were free men, freed by France itself, and their fight with France was part of a civil war, not a rebellion; they were "fighting to serve not only their independence as a community, but their liberty as individuals; to prevent their degradation from the exalted state of freemen to the debased condition of slaves, struggling against the manacles that have been forged for them by the lawless ambition of power." He concluded that the United States should remain neutral and keep the trade open, just as France had done with the American colonies when they were in a state of revolt against Britain. "Will it be said . . . that no nation is allowed to trade with them [the Haitians] for centuries to come? Or will the gentlemen hold them as rebels to all Eternity, and never suffer the rest of the world to have intercourse with them? Sir, those people will never be reduced by General Ferrand's war of proclamations. . . ."[14]

White's eloquence was to no avail. After his speech, the bill was put to a vote and passed, by a tally of 21 to 8. Senator Mitchill had joined the majority, and only one Republican (interestingly enough, the North Carolina planter David Stone) voted against it.

When the bill finally came up for debate in the House of Representatives, the outcome was not in doubt. The administration had managed to keep the Republicans in the Senate loyal on the issue, and the representatives were expected to follow suit. Debate was short but intense, even though it covered by now familiar ground. The Republicans again showed that they were not united in their views of the bill. Jacob Crowninshield once again took the pragmatic, commercial view when he said, "But, pass what law you please, you cannot stop the intercourse between citizens of the United States and inhabitants of St. Domingo. If they cannot trade directly from the United States, they will remove to some of the West Indies and continue the intercourse, or the intercourse will be continued by agents in those islands." His opinion was balanced however by that of his colleague John Smilie of Pennsylvania, who insisted that "Either give up the trade, or acknowledge the independence of Hayti. I am of the opinion that, while we acknowledge the rights of France over that island, we cannot trade with its inhabitants without the consent of France."

A sharper rhetorical exchange took place between Federalist Joseph C. Smith and Republican Joseph Clay. When the former declared that he viewed the bill "as a surrender of all the rights of self-government, as a sacrifice of the honor and independence of this nation on the altar of Gallick despotism," the latter retorted that "We cannot trade with them without acknowledging their independence. If gentlemen are prepared to do this, I shall consider it as a sacrifice on the altar of black despotism and sacrifice."

Clay had raised the most sensitive issue of all, that of black rebellion and black rule. He was followed by the president's son-in-law John Eppes, who snarled at the bill's opponents that "Some gentlemen would declare St. Domingo free. If any gentleman harbors such sentiments let him come forward boldly and declare it. In such case, he would cover himself with detestation. [This is] a system that would bring immediate and horrible destruction on the fairest portion of America." Eppes's bit of invective was, happily, ignored by the following speaker, William Ely, a Federalist from Massachusetts, who attempted with a rhetorical flourish to have the last word. "I have scarcely heard any reason why this bill should be passed," he taunted. "Hence, I am inclined to think that reason had little to do with the business, unless there are secret reasons. . . . Have the Haytians no rights? If they were once the subjects of a government that can no longer hold them, has that nation any right to call on us to starve them out, to starve these people into subjection to that Power?"[5]

The vote, which immediately followed the debate, was 93–26, with all the Federalists opposing and the Republicans maintaining party discipline. After coordination between the two houses of Congress on final wording, the bill would go to the president for his signature.

That old proponent of trade with St. Domingo, the former secretary of state and now senator from Massachusetts, Timothy Pickering, had of course voted against the bill. As a leading member of the ultra-Federalist Essex Junto, in regular opposition to all Republican policies, he could expect no favors from his old opponent from the days of Washington's presidency. Nonetheless, the Republicans' success at railroading the bill through Congress had made him indignant enough to write an impassioned letter to Jefferson. Attacking the bill, the role of Jefferson's son-in-law John Eppes in pushing the southern position, and the "insolent demand" of Turreau, Pickering urged the president not to sign the bill into law. He defended the Haitians and the excesses of their revolt, which he compared to the turmoil of France's revolution. He pleaded, "Are the hapless, the wretched Haytians ('guilty,' indeed of a 'skin not colored like our own'), but Emancipated, and by a great National Act declared Free; after having enjoyed freedom many years, having maintained it by arms, resolved to live free or die; are these men, not merely to be abandoned to their own efforts, but to be deprived of those necessary supplies which for a series of years they have been accustomed to receive from the U. States, and without which they cannot subsist? . . . Save your country, sir, while you may, from such ignominy and thralldom."[16] But he pleaded in vain; the president never answered his letter.

Senator Logan, in introducing his bill in the previous Congress, had admitted that his intent was to placate the French, and not to totally cut off the trade. But the act, as passed, was no mere sop: not only did it prohibit commerce between America and persons in parts of Hispaniola "not in the possession of France, and under the acknowledged government of France," it made it necessary for American skippers headed for any other port to post bond, assuring that they would not go to the proscribed areas. General Turreau, ever the hard-liner, complained that the act was not strong enough, that American citizens living abroad, for example, were not covered.[17] He was, to a degree, right, but he was asking for too much. The act would indeed cripple American trade with Haiti.

Several days after passage of the act, Turreau, who (in spite of his disdain for America, and the scandal surrounding his tumultuous marriage) had become an accepted part of Washington's social scene, met Senator Logan on the street. The Imperial Minister, resplendent in his coach, and the plain Quaker, who was walking, exchanged a few words of greeting. But when the Frenchman offered Logan a ride, the proud and independent senator thought it best not to be seen—Washington was already a town of political gossip—in the company of a foreigner whom he had just helped hand an important victory. He declined the offer. "I believe, sir, you are ashamed to be seen with Monsieur Turreau," the minister said. Logan, discreetly, did not respond.[18]

The new Act to Suspend the Commercial Intercourse between the United States and Certain Parts of the Island of St. Domingo was signed by the president and passed into law on February 28, 1806. It was to be in effect for a year, and would make the trade with any part of Hispaniola under control of the Haitian regime illegal.

The act had passed without the sort of public debate that had characterized the Clearance Act the year before. Except perhaps in the South, it was neither popular nor much noticed, apparently shrugged off as a slightly sordid bit of Washington political expediency. Even Boston's *Centinel,* so vehement the year before in defending Haiti, could only write cynically, "The Parliament of Paris could not have registered an Edict of Louis XIV with greater promptitude than the loyal Congress of the U. States have registered the edict of the Imperial Bonaparte and his faithful Ministers Talleyrand and Turreau, to annihilate the trade of the U. States with colonists who were made free by a decree of the French Convention. . . ."[19]

According to the young antislavery advocate John Quincy Adams, the act was "among the most disgraceful statutes ever enacted by the United States."[20] And yet, at the time, it was seen by the majority as a necessary and even expedient tactic in a difficult wartime situation, and one that—evidenced by its expiry provisions—was never expected to be permanent. The United States, already in controversy with Spain and facing a rapidly escalating crisis with Great Britain, could not afford a simultaneous confrontation with France.

Jefferson's move to cut off the trade was, in the circumstances, a convenient foreign policy maneuver. He undoubtedly saw acquiescence to French demands over the Haiti trade as a low-cost option to keep some freedom of maneuver vis-à-vis the major belligerent powers. The French had not been mollified by the Clearance Act; it was not such a big step to give them the other half of the loaf. And the president still maintained his hope for French help in the faltering negotiations with Spain (in vain, he eventually discovered, after the French had taken advantage of his gullibility).

It was also good politics. The most valuable part of the trade to Haiti had been, for some time, the contraband trade, but the merchants involved in it were, to a large degree, Federalists who opposed Jefferson's policies in any case. There was little political cost to displeasing them. That the trade in normal provisions to the island would also be cut off was unfortunate, but because Jefferson was simultaneously defending American commercial interests against Britain, he probably would not lose much support from the exporters or shippers by his stance on the Haiti trade. Party solidarity had been maintained; the northern Republicans had, in the end, opted to support their president and to avoid alienating their southern colleagues, who felt strongly about the bill. By the same token, Jefferson had solidified his southern political base by refusing to legitimate a trade that, by common accord, would in time amount to de facto recognition of Haitian independence. The step had entailed little political cost, since southern distrust and fear of the Haitian experiment was not balanced by enthusiasm elsewhere. In spite of the Federalist rhetoric, neither the president nor the majority of Americans—conditioned as they had been by a decade of stories about rebellion and atrocity in St. Domingo—could see much of a parallel between the Haiti of 1806 and the fledgling United States of twenty-five years earlier. There simply was no significant public support for what was seen as an autocratic, murderous Haitian regime.

But good politics do not always make good policy. The act, a tactical step by a president whose foreign policy was highly improvisational, had serious and negative long-term effects. It was, to begin with, not a temporary measure; its results were long-lasting. Events, unforeseen at the time, would prolong the ban until the trade itself had changed in ways that caused it to lose attraction. And the denial of recognition to the Haitian revolution became enshrined in policy. "The fatal influence that the independence of the Haytians would have on their own states" had been, according to Federalist senator William Plumer (who opposed the act), the main reason why the southern senators had supported it.[21] Whether their explanations to their northern colleague were fully sincere or not, the fact was that the southerners had taken advantage of the debate to block the possibility of Haitian recognition, by using the argument that normal relations with Haiti would create a national security risk. That argument would be employed time and time again over the coming years, and the southerners would not surrender the victory they had gained by passage of the suspension legislation.

EMBARGO AND NEGLECT

When the congressional session adjourned at the beginning of March 1806, President Jefferson could be satisfied with the foreign policy results he had achieved. To manage the crisis with Britain, he had been given some promising tools to work with. The Congress had passed a Non-Importation Act, which barred the import from Britain of a variety of manufactured products for which there were American or other substitutes. The objective was to hurt the British economy in retaliation for the damage to American shipping, perhaps gaining some negotiating leverage in the process while promoting domestic manufacturing. The British West Indian trade was not touched.

But in spite of a steady public uproar over the continued British seizures and impressments, there appeared to be no consensus on actually putting into effect the trade restrictions that Congress had just passed. There did seem to be general agreement, on the other hand, that the grievances against Britain just might be resolved by negotiation. Consequently, the administration had asked for, and Congress approved, a negotiating mandate. The president, temporarily waiving the terms of the Non-Importation Act, selected William Pinckney to assist James Monroe, the American minister in London, to conduct the negotiation.

To deal with Spain over the Florida issue, Jefferson had also gotten the mandate he wanted. Congress had approved negotiations to purchase West Florida, and had authorized a sum of $2 million to facilitate that goal. Since the plan required that the French government play a strong supportive role, the cost had been to yield to Napoleon's demands over the Haiti trade.

Jefferson and Madison nevertheless still clung to the hope that the French might eventually acquiesce in American trade with Haiti, at least in noncontraband goods. The previous year's suspension act had been a concession to the French government, they reasoned, and Bonaparte should see it in his interest to return the favor by pressing Spain over Florida, as well as by agreeing to an eventual renewal of American trade in order to avoid a British monopoly over trade with the breakaway Haitians. Jefferson wrote to John Armstrong in Paris that he now should have negotiating leverage as a result of the fact that the U.S. administration had suspended the entire trade with Haiti, "which could not of right be demanded from us." Madison made the same point, even though protesting a bit too much, and disingenuously, that the act had not been the result of French pressure. At the same time, he also told Armstrong to dust off the old 1804 instructions to Livingston, which had spelled out the rationale for an American supply link to the Haitians:

> In prohibiting the commerce in unarmed as well as armed vessels, the Act goes beyond the obligations of the United States. And altho' it must be understood to have proceeded from that consideration, and not from any rightful requisition on the part of France, and still less from a manner of pressing it, which might justly have had a contrary tendency, yet it cannot fail in itself to be grateful to the French Government, and may perhaps furnish you with an auspicious occasion of presenting, anew, the view of the subject. . . . A trade under certain regulations, in articles of subsistence on our side, and in the productions of the Island on the other, seems to be so obviously favorable to the true interests of France that a dispassionate reconsideration of such an arrangement may be reasonably expected to recommend it to an enlightened Government.[1]

As it turned out, however, almost none of Jefferson's expectations from the foreign policy mandates Congress had given him were met.

The British, to begin with, were in no mood to negotiate. To the contrary, they were more determined than ever to prosecute the war against France by all means. The collapse of the Third Coalition at the end of 1805, following Napoleon's crushing victory over the Austrians and Russians at Austerlitz, had left Britain isolated behind the defense of the Royal Navy. As long as the navy was shorthanded, impressments would be essential for the war effort, and American ships would continue to be the main target (justifiably, in fact, as a study the following year by Treasury Secretary Gallatin showed that over a third of the seamen on American ships were British subjects!). Moreover, popular sentiment in England increasingly viewed American and other neutral shipping as being in tacit alliance with the French enemy, and that keeping or even tightening the restrictions on that shipping was essential for the war effort. Even as the new American envoy, Pinckney, was sailing to join Monroe in London, the British had ratcheted up their restrictions. They declared that Europe, from Brest to the River Elbe, was under blockade, and that any American ships headed to those ports in the future were likely to be seized.

Monroe and Pinckney began negotiations in September of 1806. Seeking a rollback of the new rulings against indirect shipments from the West Indies to Europe, and an end to impressments, they found the British totally unbending. The Americans' expectation that they had negotiating leverage from the threat of implementing the still-postponed Non-Importation Act, which would cut off British exports to the United States, proved to be chimerical. The British were fixated on the struggle with France, which was escalating even as the negotiations with the Americans sputtered along. By late autumn, Napoleon had matched the new British blockade by declaring the entire British Isles under interdiction, with all neutral ships subject to seizure. In this climate, Monroe and Pinckney were unable to achieve what they had been sent out to do, and in desperation acceded to a draft treaty that met almost none of their negotiating objectives.

The text, representing only the most minimal of British concessions, was received in Washington only in March 1807, toward the end of the congressional session, and almost a year after passage of the still-suspended Non-Importation Act.

The draft treaty was such an embarrassment that President Jefferson decided not to send it to the Senate for ratification. It would have fared badly there, in any event, with even such good Republican senators as Samuel Smith vowing to oppose what was seen as an abject surrender to British demands. Almost two years after the British ruling in the *Essex* case, the American mercantile industry, which earlier had grown prosperous on the European war, was now in danger of being throttled by the competing edicts and blockades of the belligerent powers. And the administration, as yet, had devised no effective strategy to deal with the problem.

Jefferson's strategy to gain West Florida from Spain was showing no better results. The French, with the American concession on the Haiti trade given into their hands, declined to be helpful. Talleyrand was willing to make a show of offering French good offices at the talks in Madrid, but he was quite clear that the French would not support America's pretensions to the territory.[2] America would, over the coming decade and more, gain control over and then possession of the two Florida territories, but the French never played a positive role in the affair. Jefferson had surrendered the Haiti trade, it turned out, for a will-o'-the-wisp.

The president was also disappointed in his hope that he could talk the French into allowing Americans to trade with Haiti. Even so, he and Madison were dogged in pursing that rather elusive objective. In 1807, when tension with Britain had risen to the point that hostilities even looked possible, the secretary of state instructed the American minister in Paris to be alert to chances to bring up the matter of the Haiti trade. Going back, once again, to the guidance he had given Chancellor Livingston some three years earlier, Madison instructed Armstrong to offer that the United States regulate the trade in "arms and other warlike stores" as a replacement for the total suspension (which had just been extended by Congress). "In the event of a war, or even of a general stop to the commerce with Great Britain, the renewal of the intercourse with St. Domingo will become an object of great importance to the U. States," he pointed out, "The President desires that you endeavor to reconcile the French Government to discontinuance of its opposition to the intercourse in question."[3]

But the French were still smarting after having been expelled from their old colony, and were determined not to tolerate any supplies to the Haitian rebels. Governor Ferrand and his remaining garrison still flew the French flag in Santo Domingo, having repulsed Dessalines's effort to take over the rest of the island. Even if the French Navy was currently in no position to come to Ferrand's help, someday, Paris reasoned, they would be able to reclaim their property. In the meantime, keeping the rebel regime on edge and poorly supplied—even if under the wing of the British—was preferable to allowing the Americans to sell whatever the Haitians could afford.

In Washington, Turreau, ever vigilant, continued to insist that American merchants were finding ways around the suspension act, using false Scandinavian flags and destinations in the Antilles. He was right, and the Haitian rulers themselves gave credibility to his charges by urging American merchants to come to their ports "no matter which flag you fly."[4] But the number of American captains and cargoes that managed to elude the American regulations, and the still-problematic French privateers, was small. The problem was not just the restrictions, it was more profound. The nature and attraction of trade with the island, with the exception of the ever-profitable contraband trade, was diminishing due to events and trends in Haiti itself.

Dessalines was dead, assassinated by his fellow generals after attempting to extend the government-run plantation system to the south of the country. The man whose determination, vision, and ruthlessness had brought about the independence that Toussaint had dreamed of was brought down by those same characteristics. He turned out, as ruler, to be almost as dangerous to his fellow citizens as he had been to the French. Henri Christophe and Alexandre Pétion, who had good reason to fear his cruelty and vindictiveness, had conspired to have him killed in November of 1806. His empire was scrapped, and a new constitution drawn up through which the ex-slave Christophe was named president and the mulatto Pétion head of a powerful Senate. That power-sharing arrangement, not surprisingly, proved unstable; each general was too ambitious, and the strains between their respective communities too great, for cooperation. Within months the country had drifted back into civil war, with Christophe controlling the north from Cap François and Pétion the south and west from Port au Prince. That war, bloody, cruel, and ultimately indecisive, went on until 1812, requiring both leaders to maintain standing armies and to find war material. But much of the fighting was low-intensity warfare, and the logistical demands of the armies reduced to a minimum—as evidenced by this contemporary description: "Tis surprising with what little baggage large armies of eight or ten thousand men march. A knapsack with a few Bananas and a Calabash for water are their equipment, no baggage wagons, no luggage of any kind follow tardily after the army. Thus equipped, bare-footed, they move with a celerity really astounding. Hunger, fatigue, rain, heat of the sun has no effect on them; seldom are there any sick. In the field they are brave in the extreme, having excellent officers and well disciplined. No European troops in this climate could succeed for one campaign against them; united they are invulnerable."[5]

War, as usual, made for good business, and a small number of enterprising American merchant captains did succeed in circumventing the regulations, as well as the privateers, to sell in the Haitian markets. But the American trade suspension had assured that the British became the dominant suppliers, a situation that was solidified when the competing Haitian rulers both offered preferential trade arrangements to British merchants. The British kept out of the civil war itself, but their supplies and the Royal Navy were always in the background. On occasion they found it useful to cooperate with the Haitians, as was the case in 1809, when their marines helped a native army finally drive French governor Marie-Louis Ferrand and his troops out of Santo Domingo.

The continued, even if diminished, need for munitions, however, masked an accelerating trend in the nature of the island's economy and trade. Dessalines had tried to keep the sugar plantations, or at least those ones that could be put back into operation after the destruction of the war with the French, in profitable operation. His successor in the north, Christophe, had the same objective; he wanted to finance his state with the export earnings that sugar could best supply. But maintaining the plantations required enforcement of the unpopular system of obligatory contractual labor, and many workers fled—either into the backwoods settlements of free maroons, or to the rump state in the south. There, Pétion had abandoned the plantation system. The major landholdings were being broken up and redistributed to military and government officials, while elsewhere the ex-slaves simply occupied the land on their own. Those Haitians who had survived the years of war and genocide had no interest in returning to the regimentation of a plantation- and export-based economy; they had opted historically for a life of subsistence farming, for freedom rather than regimentation.

American merchants had complained, as far back as 1805, that export goods were in short supply in Haitian harbors. The great days of the sugar boom that had given birth to the profitable American trade were certainly over. Cheap molasses from the island had been replaced at American rum distilleries, and demand had fallen for those American foodstuffs that had sustained the sugar workers— and it would continue to decline as the Haitians turned to subsistence farming. James Madison's earlier prognosis had proven right, though with a reversal of cause and effect. Madison had warned that a cutoff in trade would drive the Haitians into subsistence farming, whereas it was the workers' flight from the plantations that was causing the export trade to dry up. As a result of the collapse of the old St. Domingo industry, sugar was now being grown in Louisiana, and production was rising rapidly in the British Caribbean colonies. With sugar beet cultivation beginning in Europe as well, such Haitian sugar as was being produced had to sell in a much more competitive market. Consequently coffee, which could be cultivated by autonomous smallholders, would become Haiti's primary export, supplemented by the growing hardwood logging business.

Trade with Haiti, in short, had lost the special allure that had fed its huge expansion in the last half of the previous century. The island had become simply another supplier of tropical products where, with the exception of the risky munitions business, profits were average. This was scarcely a scenario for growth, even in normal times or ones without an American trade suspension. But the times were by no means normal, and as the struggle between the European powers expanded into a war of hemisphere-wide trade sanctions, American trade was vulnerable to still more sweeping disruptions.

For over a decade, American merchants had prospered from the European war, at the sufferance of the belligerents. With the war reaching a crescendo, and Britain and France locked in a struggle to the end, that sufferance had run out. Restrictions on neutral shipping were being ratcheted ever upward, each power trying to deny supplies to its opponent. Napoleon had consolidated his hold over the continent by alliance with Russia, and forbidden all trade with the British Isles. The British, in turn, would issue a new set of Orders in Council that required neutral ships to land all their cargoes in Britain, with reshipment to the continent permitted only under British license and after payment of prohibitory taxes. As a result of those restrictions, American ships headed almost anywhere would be subject to seizure by one belligerent or the other.

Fueling the intense American frustration over this state of affairs was the British insistence on patrolling just off American harbors, and impressing seamen whenever they chose to claim that they were British subjects.

Jefferson's administration was in a dilemma. Neither European power was prepared to negotiate seriously over the American grievances, and war was no option. Jefferson occasionally blustered about the possible need to resort to arms, but he was neither prepared for nor wanted to pursue such a drastic choice. In this he was in tacit accord with the Federalists, who clamored for action yet actually wanted no hostilities that would disrupt what trade they could still conduct.

This simmering crisis was brought to a head by a piece of British arrogance. The Royal Navy's frigate *Leopard,* which had been a long-standing nuisance to American ships off the Atlantic coast, hailed an American frigate, the *Chesapeake,* in late June 1807, demanding that the *Chesapeake* turn over four alleged Royal Navy deserters. When the American captain refused the order, the British ship opened fire on the unprepared Americans, killing three sailors and then conducting a forcible search to remove the alleged deserters. This insult to a U.S. Navy ship, in sight of the port of Norfolk, was more than American pride could stomach. Even in the midst of that summer's flurry of excitement over the treason trial of Aaron Burr, the administration could no longer prevaricate.

Jefferson and Madison had long believed that American trade should not be a purely passive factor in American diplomacy. They recognized that their primary responsibility was to protect American commerce, and American rights as a neutral carrier. But they also believed that America's position as the leading neutral carrier, and as the primary supplier of necessary foodstuffs to the West Indian colonies of the belligerents, gave them potential leverage. Without American shippers, they reasoned, the belligerents would be deprived of tropical products, and their West Indian colonies would starve. Cutting off trade could coerce the Europeans, peaceably, into taking American grievances into account. The actual crisis seemed, to them, an opportunity to put the thesis to a test.

Admittedly, they had few other options. The country was not ready for war, and would not be even if more frigates and defensive gunboats were built posthaste. The navy was too small, after the first Jefferson administration's cutbacks, to convoy American merchantmen through hostile waters. And, following the fracas with France over the issue, the administration was scarcely ready to authorize merchants to arm their ships in self-defense. That left only two options: a complete rupture of trade, or a prohibition against American ships engaging in international trade. The first idea was too draconian; at least some level of imports and exports would be necessary, even if they had to be carried by foreign ships. A self-imposed embargo, Jefferson concluded, was the best available option. It would not only be a defensive option—after all, no American ships could get seized if there were none at sea—but also an offensive one, testing the thesis of peaceful coercion through denial of trade. A cutoff would not be directed at the British alone—they may have triggered the crisis, but their policies were only marginally more onerous than those of the French. He decided to seek a temporary embargo.

Minister Turreau, when he saw that the Americans were not going to go to war with the British over the *Cheaspeake* incident, vented his disdain and disappointment to Talleyrand. (He evidently did not yet know that the wily and duplicitous minister, guilty of one betrayal too many, had just been fired by Napoleon.) "France," Turreau groused, "has, and ever will have, nothing to hope from the dispositions of a people that conceives no idea of glory, of grandeur, of justice; that shows itself the constant enemy of liberal principles, and that is disposed to suffer every kind of humiliation provided it can satisfy its sordid avarice and its projects of usurpation over the Floridas."[6]

After an exchange of diplomatic remonstrances and declarations which made it obvious that the British were not going to be helpful in defusing the situation, Jefferson turned to the new Congress. Once again, he could count on a solid Republican majority to get his wish executed. All the same, he waited until December, until it was clear that there was no better option, to present his proposal. The delay also gave time to prepare the ground.

The ground was prepared so well that there was virtually no debate. On the same day that the president asked for legislation, a bill proposing an embargo on all American shipping abroad was presented in the Senate by Samuel Smith, the rules were waived by a party-line vote, the bill was read a second and third time, without amendments, and then was approved by a vote of 22–7. The Federalists were alone in opposition. The House was, relatively, more dilatory. Although the House bill was introduced contemporaneously with the Senate one, there was a modicum of debate and some unsuccessful attempts to add limiting amendments. Nevertheless, the bill passed virtually unchanged three days later, on December 21, 1807, by a largely party-line vote of 82–44. The president signed it a day later, a dubious Christmas gift to the nation.

Rarely has such an important act been put into effect with so little debate.

The embargo was a disaster, for the country and for Jefferson. As its effect rippled through the economy, it rapidly became highly unpopular, and the president's opponents were able to paint the policy as another bit of pro-French nonsense.

Some manufacturing centers were helped by the measure, but agricultural exports fell disastrously, and the seaports were hard hit by unemployment and stagnation. In New England and New York, the embargo brought about widespread economic distress, causing northern Republicans to side with Federalists, and revitalizing the separatist schemes of arch-Federalists such as Pickering's Essex Junto. Even the Mid-Atlantic states involved in the export and carrying trade were hit hard; Baltimore's business was crippled and

Senator Smith must have wondered why he had sponsored such a damaging bill; from that time on he drifted into quiet resistance to Jefferson's leadership. The Republicans, faced with defections over the policy and snowballing opposition, would pay dearly for the embargo idea in the 1808 elections.

The embargo also forced Jefferson to contradict his own principles concerning the desirability of a small, nonintrusive, government. As merchants and exporters tried desperately to find ways around the embargo, through Canada or whatever, the government found itself obliged to erect a web of regulations and prohibitions on coastal trade, fishing, river traffic, and other possible loopholes. Not unsurprisingly, corruption and smuggling kept pace, and before long military courts became necessary to enforce the unpopular measures. That, of course, only fed the hostility to government and Jefferson, and even his southern and western supporters began to see the embargo as a mistake.

Worst of all, the embargo had little effect on the belligerents, who managed somehow to find enough alternative suppliers to keep their colonies from collapse. True, there was some belt-tightening required, but it was wartime, and in the final analysis they largely ignored the supposed American leverage.

The embargo was finally dropped, over a year later, in favor of a complicated effort to get the belligerents to compete with each other in exempting Americans from their restrictions on trade. This gambit was embodied in the Non-Intercourse Act, which authorized the president to reopen trade with France or England if either one would respect American neutral rights. Although the effort was ultimately unsuccessful, the new act did replace the embargo when it was passed in March 1809, and at least eased the public mood enough to get Jefferson's chosen replacement, James Madison, elected to the presidency in spite of the split in the party that the embargo had caused. But the Embargo Act had already done its damage, and for the Haiti trade it had proven to be a virtual coup de grâce.

American trade with Haiti never recovered from the successive blows of the Clearance Act, the suspension, and then its successor the embargo. When America's foreign shipping resumed in 1810, attention had shifted to more promising, growing markets, such as the China trade. The prolonged suspension in the Haiti trade, and its decreased profitability, made it unfamiliar, unattractive, or both to traders who sought good profits. It would be years before the Haiti trade once again reached any level of importance, and even that was a pitiful reminder of the golden days before the French Revolution.

With the trade so diminished, there was no longer a powerful voice for Haiti in the United States. The business and shipping communities that had promoted a connection with the island had moved on; they or their representatives would no longer speak out for the Haitian regime. And even though an occasional voice of enthusiasm for Haiti's experiment in emancipation was raised in antislavery circles, the abolitionists in general were on the defensive over the issue. Southern slaveholders had succeeded in shaping the conventional wisdom, which was that Haiti was the epitome of a vicious, brutal revolt against property and life, a threat to public order, and, since its independence, a slovenly, backward autocracy.

Apathy and hostility, then, became the hallmarks of the American attitude, and subsequently the country's policy, toward Haiti. America had never been comfortable with a black, revolutionary state in its neighborhood, and even those who had promoted trade with Toussaint had been cautious about promoting independence, and insistent on insulating the United States from any spin-off. After the setbacks of the Dessalines massacres, the fateful congressional debates, the trade cutoffs, and the collapse of the trade, no politically meaningful voice spoke for improving relations.

In the circumstance, it is no wonder that hostility won, and that successive American administrations would continue to withhold recognition from the black, revolutionary state.

EPILOGUE

If any good reason exists why we should persevere longer in withholding our recognition of the sovereignty and independence of Hayti and Liberia, I am unable to discern it. . . . It does not admit of doubt that important commercial advantages may be obtained by treaties with them.

—Abraham Lincoln to Congress, December 3, 1861

For over fifty years after the embargo was repealed, Americans continued to conduct a modest trade with Haiti, even while shunning the new nation politically. It was no longer a high-risk, high-profit trade, and it was not without its troubles. King Henri, as General Christophe came to be called, preferred to do business with the British, and in 1811 he became in engaged in a commercial dispute with American traders that spoiled trade with the northern part of the island for years. Pétion, on the other hand, was slightly more ready to encourage Americans, and even made efforts to promote the sale of Haitian products in America. But it was not until Jean-Pierre Boyer ruled over a reunited Haiti in 1820 that the difficulties eased and the level of exchanges began to recover. Modest in scope, the trade all the same employed dozens of small vessels and amounted to 3 percent of total American trade in 1821.[1] In 1860, the trade had grown to approximate that of the United States with Russia, but still accounted for less than 1 percent of total imports and exports. Haiti, which in the prerevolt boom of 1790 had been America's second trading partner, surpassed only by Great Britain, had fallen by 1860 to forty-sixth of the sixty nations with which the Americans traded.[2]

Over the years, different American administrations had even sent commercial representatives to Haiti to monitor the trade and assist American merchant captains. One of them was also given an essentially diplomatic mission, in addition to his commercial duties. He was William Taylor, who was sent to Pétion's Haiti by Secretary of State Monroe, during the War of 1812 with Great Britain. Taylor was entrusted with a mission to negotiate access to southern Haitian ports for American warships during the hostilities, and was successful in his task—except that the success came too late in the war to have much practical effect. Taylor had also been given a reporting task, as President Madison's administration was suspicious of Pétion's pro-British sympathies as well as Haitian efforts to spread anticolonial sentiment in Spain's American colonies. After the war, Taylor returned to Haiti again to try to gain for American traders the same tariff concessions that Pétion had granted the British, but he did not have much success.

A jump from tolerated trading relations, however, to full recognition of Haitian independence was never in the cards during the period. Occasional pro-Haitian petitions were presented to Congress over the years, but they had no political weight behind them and were dead on arrival because of solid southern opposition. That opposition only hardened as the vital national debate over slavery became ever more heated in Washington. Haiti continued to be a convenient rhetorical and tactical whipping boy for southern politicians. The southerners may have exaggerated the threat, but they did have some new reasons for concern. One was Pétion's flirtation with the exportation of revolution. Another was the post-1809 descent on American soil of still another wave of black and white refugees—this time Frenchmen and their slaves who had first gone to Cuba in 1804, and now had to flee again due French-Spanish difficulties in Europe.

The southerners had made it an integral part of their defense of slavery that they would not accept recognition of a free, independent, and black Haiti. And with no interest group that had the clout and determination to storm that particular redoubt, the southern position toward Haiti continued to prevail as the effective national policy.

The French, on the other hand, recognized the reality of Haitian independence in 1825. Their recognition was indirect, masked by a degree of doublespeak that would have made Talleyrand proud, and paid for by a huge Haitian indemnity payment, but it nonetheless opened the way to normal relations between the two aggrieved parties.

The American government still would not, and could not, match the step. The Haitian bugbear was alive and well, impacting on foreign as well as domestic policy. In 1826, for example, the United States was not represented at the Panama Congress of the new Latin American republics, in part because of the opposition of southerners who feared the potential discussion of slavery, and the fact that attendance would have required the American representative to accept the equality of the Haitian. Thus the American position on Haiti, which was born from a legitimate concern about internal security in the South, seemed finally to have ossified into a paranoid and racist travesty of American republicanism.

It took the shock of secession to break the stalemate. With no southerners left in Congress who could block such a proposal, President Lincoln offered to send American diplomatic representatives to both Haiti and Liberia. In the spring of 1862, a short congressional debate ensued over the terms and funding for the proposed missions. A bill was passed, but even then not without objections from senators who opposed elevating the missions to diplomatic rank. To do so, they caviled, would be unacceptable because it would put black ambassadors from those nations, and their families, on a basis of equality with whites. However, the bill passed without their restrictive amendment and was signed into law. Soon the first accredited diplomat since Tobias Lear assumed his duties in Haiti.

The following year, Lincoln formally recognized the independence and sovereignty of Haiti, and two years later a treaty of amity and commerce was signed between the two independent republics. The bridge of recognition had finally been crossed.

Toussaint, however enigmatic he may have been in his public statements, had almost surely dreamed of an independent country, governed by its free black majority and supported by the great republic to the north. American self-interest had for a short time coincided with his, and the proponents of strong relations had had a meaningful voice in shaping America's policy. American assistance, and the first U.S. Navy intervention in Haiti's internal affairs, had allowed Toussaint to defeat his domestic enemies. Later, American inaction had contributed indirectly to the defeat of French efforts to reimpose colonial rule on the island.

But the locus of American political power shifted over time, as did the incentives for close relations with Haiti. In consequence, the key political space came to be occupied by opponents of the black republic. Assistance became inaction, then became enmity. It took six decades and a civil war in the United States to break the stranglehold that Haiti's enemies had on policy. And even then Toussaint's successors had to settle for a grudging acceptance by America, and not much support.

NOTES

INTRODUCTION

1. Jefferson to the mayor and citizens of Alexandria, March 11, 1790, in *The Papers of Thomas Jefferson,* ed. Julian P. Boyd, vol. 16, p. 225.

1. JULY 1790

1. *New York Journal and Patriotic Register,* July 6, 1790.

2. George Washington, The George Washington Papers, Library of Congress, Manuscript Division, Diaries, Jackson and Twohig, vol. 6, p. 85.

3. *New York Journal and Patriotic Register,* July 6, 1790.

4. *Federal Gazette and Philadelphia Daily Advertiser,* August 6, 1790.

5. Washington to Lafayette, August 11, 1790, Washington Papers, Series 2, letterbook 17, image 110.

6. *Gazette of the United States,* September 25, 1790.

7. Washington to Rochambeau, August 10, 1790, Washington Papers, letterbook 22, image 348.

8. *American State Papers, Foreign Relations,* vol. 1, p. 382.

9. Robinson, p. 250.

10. Coatsworth, p. 243.

11. Adams to Robert Livingston, June 23, 1783, in C.F. Adams, *Works,* vol. 8, p. 74.

12. Williams, p. 113; and A. Stinchcombe, p. 120.

13. *Gazette of the United States,* August 6, 1790; *New York Journal and Patriotic Register,* September 7, 1790.

14. Jean Girard to Stephen Girard, from McMaster, p. 99.

2. ST. DOMINGUE

1. McCusker, p. 33.

2. This work will follow the American custom of the time, generally calling the French colony St. Domingo (except when quoting from French sources), and the Spanish part of the island Santo Domingo.

3. Geggus, *Slavery, War and Revolution,* p. 1.

4. Also called Le Cap and, in a more modern spelling, Cap Français. Today, it is Cap Haitien.

5. The "Mount and Cape Trade" involved sailing to Monte Cristi, on the border near Cap François, where Spanish papers and a Spanish flag could be obtained. The ships would regain their American registration, after trading in the French colony, by a return stop at Monte Christi. See Kennedy, p. 19.

6. McCusker, pp. 402, 420.

7. Geggus, ed., *The Impact of the Haitian Revolution,* p. 79.

8. Zuckerman, p. 177.

9. *New York Journal and Patriotic Review,* September 14, 1790.

10. Geggus, "Slavery, War, and Revolution," p. 17.

11. Korngold, p. 21.

12. Fick, *The Making of Haiti,* p. 19.

13. Royal Colonial Administrator Pierre Vaissiere, quoted in Fick, *The Making of Haiti,* p. 19.

14. Garrett, p. 3.

15. Geggus, *Slavery, War and Revolution,* p. 25.

16. Gaspar and Geggus, p. 55.

17. Fick, *The Making of Haiti,* p. 26.

18. Geggus, *Slavery, War and Revolution,* p. 27.

19. Stoddard, p. 64, estimates their number at no more than five thousand.

20. James, p. 60.

21. Cooper, p. 70.

22. Ott, p. 38.

3. WHITE COCKADE, RED COCKADE

1. *Gazette of the United States,* August 24, 1791.

2. It is, of course, an oversimplification to imply that the free men of color were a cohesive political group. They were not. But, for the purposes of this necessarily concise survey of the unfolding events in St. Domingo, it is a satisfactory approximation.

3. Fick, *The Making of Haiti,* p. 240.

4. Fick, "The St. Domingue Slave Insurrection," p. 2.

5. Korngold, p. 72.

6. *New York Daily Advertiser,* October 14, 1791.

7. McMaster, p. 127.

8. Jefferson to Bourne, May 13, 1791, in Thomas Jefferson, The Thomas Jefferson Papers, Library of Congress, Manuscript Division, Series 1, image 478.

9. General Assembly to Congress, French Archives, Ministère des Affaires Étrangères, *Correspondence Politique*, vol. 35, p. 393.

10. *New York Daily Advertiser,* October 7, 1791.

11. Ternant to Montmorin, September 21, 1791, Turner, p. 47.

12. Washington to Ternant, September 24, 1791, Washington Papers, Series 2, letterbook 23, image 162.

13. Ternant to Montmorin, November 17, 1791, Turner, p. 70.

14. Lieutenant General Philibert Blanchelande to Ternant November 29, 1791, French Archives, Ministère des Affaires Étrangères, *Correspondence Politique*, vol. 35, p. 453. Ternant might have not have been relieved had he known that Blanchelande, on his return to France, would be executed.

15. Over a year later, when the revolution had become increasingly brutal—but before the Terror—Jefferson was still sanguine enough to write to the U.S. chargé d'affaires in Paris, "In the struggle which was necessary, many guilty persons fell without the forms of trial, and with them some innocent. These I deplore as much as any body, & shall deplore some of them to the day of my death. But I deplore them as I should have done had they fallen in battle. It was necessary to use the arm of the people, a machine not quite so blind as balls and bombs, but blind to a certain degree. A few of their cordial friends met at their hands the fate of enemies. But time and truth will rescue & embalm their memories, while their posterity will be enjoying that very liberty for which they would never have hesitated to offer up their lives. The liberty of the whole earth was depending on the issue of the contest, and was ever such a prize won with so little innocent blood? My own affections have been deeply wounded by some of the martyrs to this cause, but rather than it should have failed, I would have seen half the earth desolated" (Jefferson to William Short, March 1, 1793, Jefferson Papers, Series 1, image 572).

16. Jefferson to William Short, November 24, 1791, Jefferson Papers, Series 1, image 204.

17. Washington to Pinckney, March 17, 1792, Washington Papers, Series 2, letterbook 18, image 113.

18. Ternant to Foreign Minister Lessart, May 20 and March 9, 1792, Turner, pp. 97, 89.

19. Hamilton argued to the president that the suspension of King Louis's power by the National Assembly, plus the disorder and possible disloyalty of St. Domingo, made further credits unwise, and that the United States should do "as little as possible . . . with the single view of preserving the colony from destruction by Famine—that in all communications on the subject, care should be taken to put it on this footing and even to avoid the explicit recognition of any regular authority in any person" (Hamilton to Washington, November 12, 1792, Syrett, vol. 13, p. 171).

20. Ternant to Ministry, January 1, 1793, Turner, p. 168.

21. *National Gazette,* November 24, 1791.

22. *National Gazette,* May 7, 1792.

23. Fick, "The St. Domingue Slave Insurrection," p. 25.

24. *National Gazette,* May 4, 1792.

25. Jefferson to Lafayette, June 16, 1792, Jefferson Papers, Series 1, image 721. Jefferson's reference to "compounding" with the slaves refers to the agreement the British had reached with runaway slaves on Jamaica in 1739, in which those maroons had been granted a limited local autonomy.

4. THE COST OF NEUTRALITY

1. *American State Papers, Foreign Relations,* vol. 1, p. 21.

2. Jefferson to Monroe, July 14, 1793, Jefferson Papers, Series 1, image 1180. Italics in the original.

3. Genêt spelled his name without the accent over the final e, but we will use the more traditional spelling.

4. Turner, p. 210.

5. Genêt to Ministry, May 15, 1793, Turner, p. 214.

6. Jefferson to Madison, August 11, 1793, Jefferson Papers, Series 1, image 126.

7. Genêt to Ministry, May 31, 1793, Turner, p. 216.

8. Genêt to Ministry, June 19, 1793, Turner, p. 217.

9. Oliver Wolcott to Oliver Wolcott Sr., July 11, 1793, Gibbs, vol. 1, p. 103.

10. Jefferson to Monroe, July 14, 1793, Jefferson Papers, Series 1, image 1180.

11. Bartholomew Dandridge to de Grasse, January 29, 1794, Washington Papers, Letterbook 18, no. 339. The admiral's daughters, Amelie, Adelaid, Melanie, and Silvie, resident in Salem, Massachusetts, also appealed to Congress later in the year, stating they were "destitute of means of support, . . . having no other means of support but in property on the island of St. Domingo, from which in present circumstances no supplies can be drawn." Those were the very properties that their father had offered to mortgage, in 1781, in order to finance the American Revolution. A stingy but nonetheless grateful Congress eventually awarded the admiral's daughters $1,000 each in February 1795, and a further $400 each year for five years in 1797.

12. Jefferson to Thomas Mann Randolph, July 7, 1793, Jefferson Papers, Series 1, image 1099; Jefferson to Monroe, July 14, 1793, Jefferson Papers, Series 1, image 1180.

13. Genêt to Ministry, October 5 and September 5, 1793, Turner, pp. 261 and 259.

14. Genêt to Jefferson, September 6, 1793, *American State Papers, Foreign Relations,* vol. 1, p. 177.

15. *American State Papers, Foreign Relations,* vol. 1, p. 188.

16. Genêt to Ministry, October 8, 1793, Turner, p. 245.

17. Turner, p. 284.

18. *Annals of Congress of the United States,* Journal of the House of Representatives, January 21, 1794, 3rd Cong., 1st sess., p. 36.

19. Genêt to Ministry, October 12, 1793, Turner, p. 277.

5. TROUBLE WITH BRITAIN

1. *New York Daily Advertiser,* March 11, 1794.

2. In 1786, Jay, in abortive negotiations with Spanish minister Diego Gardoqui, had offered to suspend free navigation of the Mississippi River.

3. *New York Daily Advertiser,* June 10, 1794.

4. South Carolina Archives, Series S165009, message 0522, pp. 34 and 1.

5. Jordan, p. 394.

6. Sidbury, p. 540.

7. South Carolina Archives, Series S165009, message 0577.

8. *New York Journal and Patriotic Register,* October 16, 1793.

9. Stoddard, p. 184.

10. Jefferson to William Moultrie, December 23, 1793, Jefferson Papers, Series 1, image 1186.

11. French Archives, Ministère des Affaires Étrangères, *Correspondence Politique,* vol. 41, pp. 316 and 51.

12. Jefferson to Monroe, July 14, 1793, and Jefferson to Thomas Mann Randolph, July 14, 1793, Jefferson Papers, Series 1, images 1180 and 1186.

6. TROUBLE WITH FRANCE

1. The case in fact dragged on, through diplomatic claims and counterclaims, until the resolution of claims following the Louisiana Purchase.

2. Fauchet to Ministry of Foreign Affairs, February 6, 1795, Turner, p. 576.

3. Fauchet to Ministry of Foreign Affairs, May 5, 1794, Turner, p. 330.

4. Randolph to Monroe, December 12, 1794, *American State Papers, Foreign Relations,* vol. 1, p. 689.

5. Syrett, vol. 18, p. 531. Hamilton had retired as secretary of the treasury in January 1795, when a new Republican majority in Congress threatened to reinvigorate attacks against his performance. He still maintained a strong influence in cabinet discussions, though, through his henchman Wolcott and the new secretary of war, Timothy Pickering.

6. Toussaint generally had his sobriquet (technically "L'Ouverture," meaning "the opening") spelled without an apostrophe.

7. Fauchet, p. 23.

8. *American State Papers, Foreign Relations,* vol. 1, p. 731.

9. A fact he admitted to his Federalist confidant, the American minister in London, Rufus King. King, *Life and Correspondence,* vol. 2, p. 29.

10. Pickering to Monroe, June 13, 1796, *American State Papers, Foreign Relations,* vol. 1, p. 738.

11. Hamilton to Washington, June 23, 1796, Washington Papers, Series 4, image 526.

12. *American State Papers, Foreign Relations,* vol. 1, p. 742.

13. Stephen Girard, in the summer of 1797. McMaster, p. 339.

14. Adet to Ministry of Foreign Affairs, May 12, 1796, Turner, p. 983.

15. Fauchet to Committee on Foreign Relations, February 2, 1795, Turner, p. 570.

16. Logan, p. 63.

17. Hamilton to Wolcott, November 22, 1796, Gibbs, vol. 1, p. 398.

18. Jefferson to Gerry, January 26, 1799, Jefferson Papers, Series 1, image 838.

7. TOUSSAINT'S CLAUSE

1. Pickering to Mayer, June 27, 1798, Department of State, *Consular Dispatches, Cape Haitien Series,* vol. 1, no. 0011.

2. *Annals of Congress,* HR, 5th Cong., 2nd sess., p. 1863.

3. Pickering to Mayer, November 30, 1798, *Consular Dispatches, Cape Haitien Series,* vol. 1, no. 0027.

4. *New York Daily Advertiser,* November 20, 1798.

5. James, p. 211.

6. *New York Daily Advertiser,* December 28, 1798.

7. *New York Daily Advertiser,* August 9, 1798.

8. Minister of Marine and Colonies to Talleyrand, July 14, 1798, French Archives, Ministère des Affaires Étrangères, *Correspondence Politique,* vol. 50, p. 57.

9. Dupont to Talleyrand (undated copy) and Talleyrand to Directory, July 27, 1798, French Archives, Ministère des Affaires Étrangères, *Correspondence Politique,* vol. 50, pp. 99 and 131.

10. Toussaint to Adams, November 6, 1798, *Consular Dispatches, Cape Haitien Series,* vol. 1, nos. 0046, 0083, and 0168.

11. Letombe to Talleyrand, December 20, 1798, French Archives, Ministère des Affaires Étrangères, *Correspondence Politique,* vol. 50, p. 361.

12. Toussaint was literate, but he depended on secretaries for his correspondence. He would dictate the text and then revise it several times.

13. *Annals of Congress,* HR, 3rd Cong., 2nd sess., p. 1043.

14. All quotes are from *Annals of Congress,* HR, 5th Cong., 3rd sess., pp. 2742–82.

8. CREATING A QUARANTINE

1. Pickering to Adams, February 1, 1799, in Timothy Pickering, The Timothy P. Pickering Papers (microfilm version) (Boston: Massachusetts Historical Society, 1966), vol. 10, no. 304.

2. Adams to Stoddert, June 7, 1799, and Adams to Pickering, June 15 and 29, 1799, in Adams Family, Adams Family Papers (microfilm version) (Boston: Massachusetts Historical Society, 1954), vol. 119, nos. 78, 90, and 109.

3. Adams to Pickering, April 17, 1799, Adams Papers, vol. 119, no. 17.

4. King to Pickering, July 14, 1797, King, *Life and Correspondence,* vol. 2, p. 147.

5. Pickering to Rufus King, March 12, 1799, King, *Life and Correspondence*, vol. 2, p. 557.

6. Pickering to Hamilton, February 9, 1799, Syrett, vol. 22, p. 474.

7. Hamilton to Wolcott, May 5, 1798, Gibbs, vol. 2, p. 50.

8. Hamilton to Wolcott, May 5, 1798, Gibbs, vol. 2, p. 50; Hamilton to Pickering, February 9, 1799, Syrett, vol. 22, p. 474.

9. Jefferson to Madison, February 5, 1799, Jefferson to John Page, January 24, 1799, Jefferson to Madison, February 12, 1799, Jefferson Papers, Series 1, images 866, 835, and 885.

10. Jefferson to Madison, February 5, 1799, Jefferson Papers, Series 1, image 866. Matthewson has interpreted (correctly) Jefferson's allusions in the last sentence to refer to emancipation ("timely measures") and slavery ("the matter"). See "Jefferson and the Non-Recognition of Haiti," p. 225. Unfortunately, Jefferson never actively pursued the measures he prescribed for reducing the slaveholding South's vulnerability to slave insurrections.

11. Talleyrand to Pichon, September 28, 1798, *American State Papers, Foreign Relations*, vol. 2, p. 239.

12. Adams to Washington, February 19, 1799, C.F. Adams, *Works*, vol. 8, p. 625.

13. Pickering to Hamilton, February 25, 1799, Syrett, vol. 22, p. 500.

14. Hamilton to Pickering, February 21, 1799, Syrett, vol. 22, p. 492.

15. Letombe to Ministry, February 25, 1799, French Archives, Ministère des Affaires Étrangères, *Correspondence Politique*, vol. 51, p. 72.

16. Hamilton to Pickering, February 21, 1799, Syrett, vol. 22, p. 492.

17. Tench Coxe to Madison, May 1, 1801, in James Madison, The James Madison Papers, Library of Congress, Manuscript Division, vol. 2, p. 131.

18. Pickering to Stevens, March 7, 1799, in Pickering Papers, vol. 10, no. 462.

19. Wolcott to S. Smith, March 20, 1799, Gibbs, vol. 2, p. 228.

20. Cabinet memo to President, February 20, 1799, *Consular Dispatches, Cape Haitien Series*, vol. 1, p. 0072.

21. King to Pickering January 10, 1799, King, *Life and Correspondence*, vol. 2, p. 499.

22. Tansill, p. 49.

23. Pickering to Stevens, April 20, 1799, *Consular Dispatches, Cape Haitien Series*, vol. 1, no. 0172.

24. Pickering to Stevens, May 9, 1799, Pickering Papers, vol. 11, no. 69.

25. Pickering to King, April 22, 1799, Department of State, *Diplomatic Instructions, All Countries*, vol. 5, p. 106.

9. THE ST. DOMINGO STATION

1. *Massachusetts Mercury* (Boston), April 19, 1799, quoted in Office of Naval Records, *Naval Documents*, vol. 3, p. 67.

2. Stevens to Pickering, May 3, 1799, *Consular Dispatches, Cape Haitien Series,* vol. 1, p. 181.

3. Pickering to Stevens, December 3, 1799, Pickering Papers, vol. 12, no. 404.

4. Stevens to Pickering, October 26, 1799, Office of Naval Records, *Naval Documents,* vol. 4, p. 326.

5. Adams to Pickering, July 2, 1799, Adams Papers, vol. 119, no. 119.

6. Adams to Stoddert, June 7, 1799, Adams to Pickering, June 15, 1799, Adams Papers, vol. 119, nos. 78 and 90.

7. Adams to Pickering, September 9, 1799, Adams Papers, vol. 120, no. 100.

8. Adams to Stoddert, June 7, 1799, Adams Papers, vol. 119, no. 78.

9. Adams to Stoddert, May 8, 1799, Adams Papers, vol. 119, no. 33.

10. Gibbs, vol. 2, p. 304, Pickering Papers, vol. 12, no. 400.

11. Stevens to Pickering, June 24, 1799, *Consular Dispatches, Cape Haitien Series,* vol. 1, p. 271.

12. Toussaint to Adams, August 14, 1799, Department of State, *Diplomatic Instructions, All Countries,* vol. 5, p. 190.

13. Stevens to Little, December 4, 1799, Office of Naval Records, *Naval Documents,* vol. 4, p. 487.

14. Office of Naval Records, *Naval Documents,* vol. 5, p. 250.

15. Adams to Pickering, August 6, 1799, Adams Papers, vol. 120, no. 53.

16. French Archives, Ministère des Affaires Étrangères, *Correspondence Politique,* vol. 51, p. 389.

17. Stevens to Pickering, February 13, 1800, *Consular Dispatches, Cape Haitien Series,* vol. 2, no. 166.

18. Stevens to Pickering, April 19, 1800, *Consular Dispatches, Cape Haitien Series,* vol. 2, no. 251.

19. Lundahl, p. 125.

20. Dupuy, p. 54. Lundahl (p. 135) estimates that the export levels of sugar and coffee in 1801 reached 13 percent and 57 percent, respectively, of their 1789 levels, and climbed in 1802 to 38 percent and 45 percent.

21. Stevens to Pickerring, May 24, 1800, *Consular Dispatches, Cape Haitien Series,* vol. 2, p. 277.

10. JEFFERSON EQUIVOCATES

1. Letombe to Ministry, March 15, 1801, French Archives, Ministère des Affaires Étrangères, *Correspondence Politique,* vol. 53, p. 42.

2. Pichon to Talleyrand, March 18 and 20, 1801, French Archives, Ministère des Affaires Étrangères, *Correspondence Politique,* vol. 53, pp. 70 and 56.

3. *American State Papers, Foreign Relations,* vol. 2, p. 431.

4. Acting Secretary of State Lincoln to Pichon, April 28, 1801, French Archives, Ministère des Affaires Étrangères, *Correspondence Politique,* vol. 53, p. 111. Pichon to

Talleyrand, April 10, 1801; French Archives, Ministère des Affaires Étrangères, *Correspondence Politique*, vol. 53, p. 105.

5. Lear subsequently had a distinguished diplomatic career in North Africa's Barbary States.

6. Lear to Madison, July 7, 1801, *Consular Dispatches, Cape Haitien Series*, vol. 3, p. 94.

7. Pichon to Talleyrand, October 9, 1801, French Archives, Ministère des Affaires Étrangères, *Correspondence Politique*, vol. 53, p. 324.

8. Lear to Madison, July 20, 1801, *Consular Dispatches, Cape Haitien Series*, vol. 3, p. 97.

9. Pichon to Talleyrand, July 20, 1801, French Archives, Ministère des Affaires Étrangères, *Correspondence Politique*, vol. 53, p. 169.

10. Pichon to Talleyrand, July 22, 1801, French Archives, Ministère des Affaires Étrangères, *Correspondence Politique*, vol. 53, p. 170.

11. Jefferson to Monroe, November 24, 1801, Jefferson Papers, Series 1, image 82.

12. Pichon to Talleyrand, November 25, 1801, French Archives, Ministère des Affaires Étrangères, *Correspondence Politique*, vol. 53, p. 343.

13. Pichon to Talleyrand, December 1, 1802, French Archives, Ministère des Affaires Étrangères, *Correspondence Politique*, vol. 53, p. 432.

14. The Republican activist Tench Coxe, for example, had warned Madison of this threat, arguing that French subversive influence "will come through the strainer of St. Domingo, and will keep up a constant intimate connection with that great Negro state. They are free. They are military. Their habits of subordination and labor are broken. . . . It is impossible to be too much on guard against the consequences of a large detachment of republican blacks from St. Domingo to Louisiana, accompanied by the sudden emancipation of the blacks there. If the French mean to reduce the Islands, they may do it the more easily by sending the most warlike to Louisiana" (Coxe to Madison, November 28, 1801, Madison Papers, vol. 2, p. 281).

15. Pichon to Talleyrand, December 3, 1801, French Archives, Ministère des Affaires Étrangères, *Correspondence Politique*, vol. 53, p. 437.

11. THE LECLERC EXPEDITION

1. Lokke, "The Leclerc Instructions," p. 97.

2. Lokke, "The Leclerc Instructions," p. 93.

3. Lear to Madison, November 11, 1801, *Consular Dispatches, Cape Haitien Series*, vol. 3, p. 230.

4. Lear to Madison, December 11, 1801, and January 17, 1802, *Consular Dispatches, Cape Haitien Series*, vol. 3, no. 281, and, vol. 4, no. 31.

5. *Columbian Centenial*, February 13, 1802.

6. Madison to Lear, January 8 and February 26, 1802, Department of State, *Consular Instructions, All Countries*, vol. 1, pp. 117 and 121.

7. *Annals of Congress*, Senate, 9th Cong., 1st sess., p. 123.

8. Lear to Madison, February 28, 1802, *Consular Dispatches, Cape Haitien Series,* vol. 4, p. 12.

9. Leclerc to Decres, February 9, 1802, cited in Pierre Pluchon, *Toussaint Louverture, de l'esclavage au pouvoir* (Paris: L'École, 1979), p. 196.

10. Hussart, p. 9.

11. *Columbian Centinel,* March 24, 1802.

12. Lieutenant General Baron Amphide de la Croix, as quoted in a letter to the *New York Evening Post,* July 10, 1862.

13. Lear to Madison, March 22, 1802; *Consular Dispatches, Cape Haitien Series,* vol. 4, p. 213.

14. Madison to Livingston, September 23, 1801, and Livingston to Madison, February 26, 1802, *American State Papers, Foreign Relations,* vol. 2, pp. 510 and 513.

15. Livingston to King, December 30, 1801, *American State Papers, Foreign Relations,* vol. 2, p. 512.

16. Madison to Livingston, January 5, 1802, *American State Papers, Foreign Relations,* vol. 2, p. 516.

17. Jefferson to Livingston, April 18, 1802, Jefferson Papers, Series 1, image 131.

12. ST. DOMINGO AND LOUISIANA

1. *Columbian Centenial,* April 17, 1802.

2. Pichon to Talleyrand, April 1, 1802, French Archives, Ministère des Affaires Étrangères, *Correspondence Politique,* vol. 54, p. 265.

3. Livingston to Talleyrand June 15, 1802, French Archives, Ministère des Affaires Étrangères, *Correspondence Politique,* vol. 54, p. 437.

4. Talleyrand to Pichon, July 8, 1802, French Archives, Ministère des Affaires Étrangères, *Correspondence Politique,* vol. 54, p. 432.

5. Pichon to Talleyrand, March 28, 1802, French Archives, Ministère des Affaires Étrangères, *Correspondence Politique,* vol. 54, p. 254.

6. Pichon to Talleyrand, May 10 and 29, 1802, French Archives, Ministère des Affaires Étrangères, *Correspondence Politique,* vol. 54, pp. 324 and 353.

7. Pichon to Talleyrand, February 23, 1802, French Archives, Ministère des Affaires Étrangères, *Correspondence Politique,* vol. 54, p. 162.

8. Toussaint would die in April 1803, an ignored and miserable prisoner in a cold, damp fortress in France's Jura mountains.

9. Leclerc to Bonaparte, August 6, 1802, quoted in Stoddard, p. 335.

10. Jefferson to Thomas McKean, June 14, 1802, Jefferson Papers, Series 1, image 567; Hussart, p. 25.

11. Pichon to Talleyrand, July 7, 1802, French Archives, Ministère des Affaires Étrangères, *Correspondence Politique,* vol. 54, p. 410.

12. *Annals of Congress,* HR, 7th Cong., 2nd sess., p. 385.

13. Jefferson to Monroe, January 13, 1803, Jefferson Papers, Series 1, image 817.

14. Rochambeau to Bernadotte, August 22, 1803, French Archives, Ministère des Affaires Étrangères, *Correspondence Politique*, vol. 56, p. 99. Bernadotte had been named minister to Washington but never assumed his duties, and the letter was received by Pichon.

15. Korngold, p. 232.

16. *New York Evening Post*, July 5, 1805, as quoted in "Hamilton on the Louisiana Purchase: A Newly-Identified Editorial from the New York Evening Post," *William and Mary Quarterly* 12, no. 2 (1955, 3rd series): p. 274.

13. A Risky Trade

1. *Columbian Centinel*, March 31, 1804.

2. Pichon's situation had become increasingly difficult. Quite clear in his dispatches to Paris that he detested Rochambeau's heavy-handed policies, he was nonetheless the general's indispensable backup for procuring and shipping essential supplies to St. Domingo. But he could never procure enough, and his inability to get the American government to guarantee commercial credits, or advance money from debts due as a result of the Louisiana Purchase, led Rochambeau to accuse him of incompetence. The authorities in Paris had already begun to doubt his full commitment to France's agenda, and had nominated Count Bernadotte to replace him in Washington. But the count had in the end not taken up the assignment, and a new representative, nominated in December 1803, did not arrive until February of the following year. Pichon was thus left in a prolonged state of limbo, in which he enjoyed the confidence of Jefferson and Madison perhaps more than that of his own government.

3. Dessalines to Jefferson, June 23, 1803, Jefferson Papers, Series 1, image 667.

4. Pichon to Talleyrand, October 6, 1803, French Archives, Ministère des Affaires Étrangères, *Correspondence Politique*, vol. 56, p. 93.

5. Monroe to Madison, October 20, 1804, Hackett, vol. 5, p. 454.

6. Pichon to Talleyrand, January 17, 1804, French Archives, Ministère des Affaires Étrangères, *Correspondence Politique*, vol. 56, p. 292.

7. Madison to Livingston, January 31, 1804, Department of State, *Diplomatic Instructions, All Countries*, vol. 5, roll 77, p. 192.

8. Jefferson to Madison, February 12, 1799, Jefferson Papers, Series 1, image 885.

9. Pichon to Talleyrand, March 20, 1804, French Archives, Ministère des Affaires Étrangères, *Correspondence Politique*, vol. 56, p. 437.

10. Pichon to Talleyrand, March 9, 1804, French Archives, Ministère des Affaires Étrangères, *Correspondence Politique*, vol. 56, p. 413.

11. Pichon to Madison, May 7, 1804, French Archives, Ministère des Affaires Étrangères, *Correspondence Politique*, vol. 57, p. 9.

12. Jefferson's note on May 26, 1804, cabinet meeting, Jefferson Papers, Series 1, image 820.

13. Pichon to Talleyrand, June 6, 1804, French Archives, Ministère des Affaires Étrangères, *Correspondence Politique*, vol. 57, p. 58.

14. Livingston to Talleyrand, June 27, 1804, French Archives, Ministère des Affaires Étrangères, *Correspondence Politique*, vol. 57, p. 144.

15. Talleyrand to Livingston, August 28, 1804, and Talleyrand to Decres, October 24 and November 2, 1804, French Archives, Ministère des Affaires Étrangères, *Correspondence Politique*, vol. 57, pp. 246 and 352.

16. Talleyrand to Livingston, August 28, 1804, French Archives, Ministère des Affaires Étrangères, *Correspondence Politique*, vol. 57, p. 246.

14. THE CLEARANCE ACT DEBATE

1. Samuel Smith to Madison, May 17, 1804, Madison Papers, Series 1, roll 8.

2. Talleyrand to Turreau, July 26, 1804, cited in Logan, p. 172.

3. C.F. Adams, *Memoirs of John Quincy Adams*, vol. 1, p. 316.

4. Pichon to Talleyrand, November 21, 1804, French Archives, Ministère des Affaires Étrangères, *Correspondence Politique*, vol. 57, p. 400.

5. Livingston, who had asked to be relieved, was being replaced by his brother-in-law, but Armstrong would not arrive until the fall. Madison to Armstrong, July 15, 1804, Department of State, *Diplomatic Instructions, All Countries*, vol. 5, roll 77, no. 246.

6. C.F. Adams, *Memoirs of John Quincy Adams*, vol. 1, p. 314.

7. *Annals of Congress*, Senate Proceedings, 8th Cong., 2nd sess., p. 12.

8. Jefferson's earlier draft had called the armed trade to St. Domingo "an aggression on the rights of other nations, and is *dangerous to the peace of our own*" (italics added) (Jefferson Papers, Series 1, image 628). Pichon to Talleyrand, September 3, 1804, French Archives, Ministère des Affaires Étrangères, *Correspondence Politique*, vol. 57, p. 265.

9. *Annals of Congress*, HR, 8th Cong., 1st sess., February 29, 1804, p. 1070; *Annals of Congress*, HR, 8th Cong, 1st sess., February 4, 1804, p. 996.

10. E. Brown, p. 210; John Lucas, December 13, 1804, *Annals of Congress*, Senate, 8th Cong., 2nd sess., p. 824.

11. *Annals of Congress*, Senate, 8th Cong., 2nd sess., p. 813.

12. *Annals of Congress*, HR, 8th Cong., 2nd sess., pp. 813 and 815.

13. *Columbian Centinel*, December 4, 1804.

14. As run in the Charleston, S.C., *City Gazette*, December 27, 1804. It should be noted that the U.S. Navy was at the time heavily engaged in defending American shipping rights in a war against the predatory states of North Africa, the so-called Barbary pirates. The USS *Philadelphia* had been burned in Tripoli harbor in April, and victory over the Barbary States would not come until the following April.

15. *Columbian Centinel*, January 9, 1805.

16. *City Gazette*, January 21, 1805. *Aurora's* article as re-run in the *City Gazette* of March 8, 1805; *Columbian Centinel*, January 9, 1805.

17. *Charleston Courier*, March 5, 1805.

18. Madison to Armstrong, March 5, 1805, and Madison to Monroe March ?, 1805, Department of State, *Diplomatic Instructions, All Countries*, vol. 5, roll 77, pp. 268 and 274.

15. THE TRADE SUSPENDED

1. Gallatin to Senator Mitchill, January 1, 1805, cited in Hickey, "America's Response," p. 378.

2. Armstrong to Madison, February 15, 1805, Department of State, *Consular Dispatches, France,* vol. 13.

3. Jefferson to Madison, April 11, 1805, Jefferson Papers, Series 1, image 157; Turreau to Talleyrand, April 5 and June 13, 1804, French Archives, Ministère des Affaires Étrangères, *Correspondence Politique,* vol. 58, pp. 113 and 171.

4. *New York Evening Post,* June 16, 1805, cited in Logan, p. 173.

5. *American State Papers, Foreign Relations,* vol. 2, p. 272.

6. H. Adams, p. 89.

7. Talleyrand to Armstrong, August 7, 1805, *American State Papers, Foreign Relations,* vol. 2, p. 726.

8. Armstrong appears to have had no new instructions to deal with the problem caused by the New York convoy. Madison's most recent letter, of June 6, had simply continued to urge him to try to sell the idea of an agreed "innocent trade," as originally proposed by Chancellor Livingston, and to protest the decrees of Governor Ferrand (Department of State, *Diplomatic Instructions, All Countries,* vol. 5, roll 77, no. 304).

9. Armstrong to Talleyrand, August 8, 1805, *Consular Dispatches, France,* vol. 13; Talleyrand to Armstrong, August 16, 1805, *American State Papers, Foreign Relations,* vol. 2, p. 727.

10. Turreau to Madison, November 14, 1805, *American State Papers, Foreign Relations,* vol. 2, p. 726.

11. Jefferson to Madison, August 25, 1805, Jefferson Papers, Series 1, image 475.

12. All quotes from *Annals of Congress,* Senate, 9th Cong., 1st sess., pp. 29–37.

13. Jefferson had once again avoided making an administration case for the bill. He merely forwarded Turreau's note of the previous November, and an additional one dated January 3, 1804, in which Turreau's tone had become even more demanding: "The system of tolerance which produces this commerce, which suffers its being armed, which encourages, by impunity, its extension and excess, cannot longer remain, and the Emperor and King my master expects from the dignity and candor of the Government of the Union that an end be put to it promptly" (*American State Papers, Foreign Relations,* vol. 2, p. 726).

14. *Annals of Congress,* Senate, 9th Cong., 1st sess., pp. 124–32.

15. Citations from *Annals of Congress,* HR, 9th Cong., 1st sess., pp. 512–15.

16. Hickey, "Timothy Pickering," p. 178.

17. Plumer, p. 437.

18. Tolles, p. 268.

19. *Columbian Centinel,* March 5, 1806.

20. H. Adams, p. 700.

21. Plumer, p. 186.

16. EMBARGO AND NEGLECT

1. Jefferson to Armstrong, February 14, 1806, Jefferson Papers, Series 1, image 545; Madison to Armstrong, March 15, 1805, Department of State, *Diplomatic Instructions, All Countries,* vol. 5, roll 77, no. 325.

2. Talleyrand to Bonaparte, May 6, 1806, and Talleyrand to Turreau, June 2, 1806, French Archives, Ministère des Affaires Étrangères, *Correspondence Politique,* vol. 59, pp. 138 and 233.

3. Madison to Armstrong, July 15, 1807, Department of State, *Diplomatic Instructions, All Countries,* vol. 5, roll 77, no. 431.

4. Coradin, p. 53.

5. Hoffman, p. 195.

6. Turreau to Talleyrand, September 4, 1807, cited in H. Adams, p. 1023.

EPILOGUE

1. Montague, p. 47. Haiti was first broken out separately in the trade statistics in 1821.

2. Geggus, *Impact of the Haitian Revolution,* p. 79; *Congressional Globe,* Senate, 37th Cong., 2nd sess., p. 1775.

BIBLIOGRAPHY

Adams, Charles F. *The Memoirs of John Quincy Adams,* vol. 1. Freeport, N.Y.: Books for Libraries Press, 1969.

———. *The Works of John Adams,* vol. 8. Boston: Little, Brown, 1853.

Adams, Henry. *History of the United States of America during the Administrations of Thomas Jefferson.* New York: Library of America, 1986.

Adams Family. Adams Family Papers (microfilm version), vols. 118–20, 194–95. Boston: Massachusetts Historical Society, 1954.

American Minerva (1790).

American State Papers, Foreign Relations, vols. 1–3. Washington: Hein, 1998.

Annals of the Congress of the United States. Library of Congress. http://memory.loc.gov/ammem/amlaw/lwac.html.

Auguste, Yves L. *Haiti et les Etas Unis, 1804–1862* (Haiti and the United States). Sherbrooke, Canada: Editions Naaman, 1979.

Aurora General Advertiser (1793–1802).

Bowman, Albert Hall. *The Struggle for Neutrality.* Knoxville: Univ. of Tennessee Press, 1974.

Branson, Susan. "St. Domingan Refugees in the Philadelphia Community of the 1790's." *Amerindians, Africans, Americans: Papers on Caribbean History.* Mona, Jamaica: University of the West Indies, 1993.

Brown, Evertt S., ed. *William Plumer's Memorandum of Proceedings in the United States Senate, 1803–07.* New York: Da Capo Press, 1969.

Brown, Jonathan. *The History and Present Condition of Haiti.* Philadelphia: William Marshall, 1837.

Cassell, Frank A. *Merchant Congressman in the Young Republic: Samuel Smith of Maryland.* Madison: Univ. of Wisconsin Press, 1971.

Charleston Courier (1805).

Childs, Frances S. *French Refugee Life in the United States, 1790–1800.* Philadelphia: Porcupine Press, 1978.

City Gazette (Charleston) (1791, 1802–1805).

Clarfield, Gerard H. *Timothy Pickering and American Diplomacy*. Pittsburgh: Univ. of Pittsburgh Press, 1980.

Clauder, Anne C. *American Commerce as Affected by the Wars of the French Revolution and Napoleon*. Clifton, N.J.: Augustus M. Kelley Press, 1972.

Clark, Benjamin. *A Plea for Haiti*. Boston: Eastburn's Press, 1853.

Coatsworth, John A. "American Trade with European Colonies in the Caribbean and South America, 1790–1812." *William and Mary Quarterly*, 3rd ser., 24, no 2 (1976): pp. 243–66.

Columbian Centinel (Boston) (1802–1805).

Cooper, Anna J. *Slavery and the French Revolutionists*. Lewiston, N.Y.: Edward Millen Press, 1988.

Coradin, Jean. *Histoire diplomatique d'Haiti* (Diplomatic History of Haiti). Port au Prince: Editions des Antilles, 1988.

Day, Stacey B. *Edward Stevens*. Cincinnati: Cultural and Educational Productions, 1969.

DeConde, Alexander. *The Quasi-War: The Politics and Diplomacy of the Undeclared War with France, 1797–1801*. New York: Scribner's, 1966.

Deerr, Noel. *The History of Sugar*. London: Chapman and Hall, 1949.

Department of State. *Consular Dispatches, Cape Haitien Series*, vols. 1–4. U.S. Archives microfilm record series M9.

———. *Consular Dispatches, France*, roll 1113. U.S. Archives microfilm record series M34.

———. *Consular Instructions, All Countries*, vol. 1. U.S. Archives microfilm record series M78/1.

———. *Diplomatic Instructions, All Countries*, vol. 5. U.S. Archives microfilm record series M28/5, 77/1.

Desrosiers, Toussaint. *Relations d'Haiti aveque Amerique* (Haiti's Relations with America). Port au Prince: Ateliers Fardin, 1980.

Duffy, Michael. *Soldiers, Sugar and Sea Power: The British Expedition to the West Indies and the War against Revolutionary France*. Oxford: Clarendon Press, 1987.

Dupuy, Alex. *Haiti in the World Economy*. Boulder, Colo.: Westview Press, 1989.

Egerton, Douglas R. *Gabriels's Rebellion*. Chapel Hill: Univ. of North Carolina Press, 1993.

———, ed. *Rebels, Reformers and Revolutionaries*. New York: Routledge, 2002.

Fauchet, Joseph. *A Sketch of the Present State of our Political Relations with the U.S.A.* Philadelphia: Benjamin Franklin Bache, 1979.

Federal Gazette and Philadelphia Daily Advertiser (1790).

Fick, Carolyn E. *The Making of Haiti: The Saint Domingue Revolution from Below*. Knoxville: Univ. of Tennessee Press, 1990.

———. "The St. Domingue Slave Insurrection of 1791—A Socio-Political and Cultural Analysis." *Journal of Caribbean Studies* 25, no. 1 (1991): pp. 1–35.

Ford, Worthington C. *The Writings of John Quincy Adams*, vols. 1–2. New York: Greenwood Press, 1968.

French Archives, Ministère des Affaires Étrangères. *Correspondence Politique, Étas-Unis* (Political Correspondence, United States), vols. 35–63. Library of Congress, manuscript collection.

Garrett, Mitchell B. *The French Colonial Question, 1789–1791: Dealings of the Constituent Assembly with Problems Arising from the Revolution in the West Indies.* New York: Negro Univs. Press, 1970.

Garrigus, John D. "Catalyst or Catastrophe? Saint-Domingue's Free Men of Color and the Battle of Savannah, 1779–82." *Revista Interamericana* 22, no. 1 (1992): pp. 109–25.

———. "Redrawing the Color Line: Gender and the Social Construction of Race in Pre-Revolutionary Haiti." *Journal of Caribbean Studies* 30, no. 1 (1996): pp. 28–50.

Gaspar, David B., and David P. Geggus, eds. *A Turbulent Time: The French Revolution and the Greater Caribbean.* Bloomington: Indiana Univ. Press, 1997.

Gazette of the United States (1790–1792, 1802).

Geggus, David P., ed. *The Impact of the Haitian Revolution.* Columbia: Univ. of South Carolina Press, 2001.

———. *Slavery, War and Revolution: The British Occupation of Haiti.* Oxford: Clarendon Press, 1982.

Genovese, Eugene. *From Rebellion to Revolution.* Baton Rouge: Louisiana State Univ. Press, 1979.

Gibbs, George. *Memoirs of the Administrations of Washington and John Adams, Edited from the Papers of Oliver Wolcott.* 2 vols. New York: Burt Franklin, 1971.

Hackett, Mary, et al., eds. *The Papers of James Madison,* vols. 1–5. Secretary of State series. Charlottesville: Univ. Press of Virginia, 1986–2000.

"Hamilton on the Louisiana Purchase: A Newly Identified Editorial from the New York Evening Post." *William and Mary Quarterly* 12, no. 2 (1955, 3rd series): pp. 268–81.

Harper, Robert Goodloe. *Observations on the Dispute Between the U.S. and France.* Boston: privately published, 1798.

Heinl, Robert D. and Nancy G. Heinl. *Written in Blood: The Story of the Haitian People, 1492–1971.* New York: Houghton Mifflin, 1978.

Hickey, Donald R. "America's Response to the Slave Revolt in Haiti." *Journal of the Early Republic* 2, no. 1 (1982): pp. 361–79.

———. "Timothy Pickering and the Haitian Slave Revolt: A Letter to Thomas Jefferson in 1806." *Essex Institute Historical Collections* 120, no. 3 (1984): pp. 149–63.

Hoffman, Leon-Francois. "An American Trader in Revolutionary Haiti: Simeon Johnson's Journal of 1807." *Princeton University Library Chronicle* 49, no. 2 (1988): pp. 182–99.

Hunt, Alfred N. *Haiti's Influence on Antebellum America.* Baton Rouge: Louisiana State Univ. Press, 1988.

Hussart, Mary. *Secret History, Written by a Lady at Cape François to Colonel Burr.* Freeport, N.Y.: Books for Libraries Press, 1971.

Hyslop, Beatrice. "American Press Reports of the French Revolution." *New York Historical Society Quarterly* 42, no. 4 (1958): pp. 329–48.

James, Cyril. *The Black Jacobins.* New York: Vintage Books, 1963.

Jefferson, Thomas. The Thomas Jefferson Papers. Library of Congress, Manuscript Division. http://memory.loc.gov/ammem/mtjhtml/mtjhome.html.

Jordan, Winthrop D. *White Over Black: American Attitude toward the Negro.* Chapel Hill: Univ. of North Carolina Press, 1968.

Kaplan, Lawrence. *Entangling Alliances with None: American Foreign Policy in the Age of Jefferson.* Kent, Ohio: Kent State Univ. Press, 1987.

Kennedy, Roger G. *Orders from France: The Americans and the French in a Revolutionary World, 1780–1820.* New York: Alfred Knopf, 1989.

King, Charles R. *The Life and Correspondence of Rufus King,* vols. 2–4. New York: Putnam, 1895.

King, Stewart R. *Blue Coat or Powdered Wig: Free People of Color in Pre-Revolutionary St. Domingue.* Athens: Univ. of Georgia Press, 2001.

Kline, Mary Jo, ed. *Political Correspondence and Public Papers of Aaron Burr.* Princeton: Princeton Univ. Press, 1983.

Knight, Franklin W. "The Haitian Revolution." *American Historical Review* 105, no. 1 (2000): pp. 105–15.

Korngold, Ralph. *Citizen Toussaint.* New York: Hill and Wang, 1965.

Langley, Lester D. *Struggle for the American Mediterranean.* Athens: Univ. of Georgia Press, 1976.

Laurent, Gerard. *Haiti et l'independence americaine* (Haiti and American Independence). Port au Prince: Seminaire Adventiste, 1976.

Lecorps, Louis Marceau. *La Politique Exterieure de Toussaint Louverture* (Toussaint Louverture's Foreign Policy). Port au Prince. Cheraquit, 1935.

"Letters of Toussaint Louverture and of Edward Stevens, 1798–1800." *American Historical Review* 16, no. 1 (1910): pp. 64–101.

Logan, Rayford W. *Diplomatic Relations of the United States with Haiti.* Chapel Hill: Univ. of North Carolina Press, 1941.

Lokke, Carl L. "Jefferson and the Leclerc Expedition." *American Historical Review* 33, no. 11 (1928): pp. 322–28.

———. "The Leclerc Instructions." *Journal of Negro History* 10, no. 1 (1925): pp. 80–99.

Lundhall, Mats. "Toussaint and the War Economy of St. Domingue." *Slavery and Abolition* 6, no. 2 (1985): pp. 122–38.

Lyon, E. Wilson. *Louisiana in French Diplomacy, 1759–1804.* Norman: Univ. of Oklahoma Press, 1974.

Madison, James. The James Madison Papers. Library of Congress, Manuscript Division.

Matthewson, Timothy M. "Abraham Bishop, 'The Rights of Black Men' and the American Reaction to the Haitian Revolution." *Journal of Negro History* 67, no. 2 (1982): pp. 148–54.

———. "George Washington's Policy toward the Haitian Revolution." *Diplomatic History* 3, no. 3 (1979): pp. 321–36.

———. "Jefferson and Haiti." *Journal of Southern History* 61, no. 2 (1955): pp. 209–48.

———. "Jefferson and the Non-Recognition of Haiti." *Proceedings of the American Philosophical Society* 140, no. 1 (1996): pp. 22–48.

McCullough, David. *John Adams.* New York: Simon and Schuster, 2001.

McCusker, John. *Rum and the American Revolution*. New York: Garland Publishers, 1989.

McKee, Christopher, ed. "'Constitution' in the Quasi-War with France: The Letters of John Roche Jr., 1798–1801." *American Neptune* 27, no. 2 (1967): pp. 135–49.

McMaster, John B. *The Life and Times of Stephen Girard, Mariner and Merchant*. Philadelphia: Lippincott, 1918.

Meadows, R. Darrell. "Engineering Exile: Social Networks and the French Atlantic Community." *French Historical Studies* 23, no. 1 (2000): pp. 67–102.

Miller, John C. *Wolf by the Ears: Thomas Jefferson and Slavery*. Charlotesville: Univ. Press of Virginia, 1991.

Montague, Ludwell L. *Haiti and the United States, 1714–1938*. Durham: Duke Univ. Press, 1940.

Nash, Gary B. "Reverberations of Haiti in the American North: Black Saint Dominguans in Philadelphia." *Pennsylvania History* 65 (supplement) (1988): pp. 44–73.

National Gazette (1790–1792).

National Intelligencer (1801).

Newman, Simon Peter. *Parades and the Politics of the Street*. Philadelphia: Univ. of Pennsylvania Press, 1997.

New York Daily Advertiser (1790–1799).

New York Journal and Patriotic Register (1790–1793).

Office of Naval Records. *Naval Documents Related to the Quasi-War between the United States and France*. 7 vols. Washington, D.C.: Government Printing Office, 1935.

Ott, Thomas O. *The Haitian Revolution*. Knoxville: Univ. of Tennessee Press, 1984.

Padgett, James A. "Diplomats to Haiti and Their Diplomacy." *Journal of Negro History* 25, no. 3 (1940): pp. 265–331.

Pancake, John S. *Samuel Smith and the Politics of Business*. University: Univ. of Alabama Press, 1972.

Pickering, Timothy. The Timothy P. Pickering Papers (microfilm version), vols. 10–13. Boston: Massachusetts Historical Society, 1966.

Providence Gazette and Country Journal (1790).

Robinson, Donald L. *Slavery in the Structure of American Politics, 1765–1820*. New York: Harcourt Brace Jovanovich, 1971.

Rosenfeld, Richard N. *American Aurora*. New York: St. Martin's Press, 1977.

Shulim, Joseph. *The Old Dominion and Napoleon Bonaparte: A Study in American Opinion*. New York: Columbia Univ. Press, 1952.

Sidbury, James. "St. Domingue in Virginia: Ideology, Local Meanings, and Resistance to Slavery." *Journal of Southern History* 63, no. 3 (1997): pp. 531–52.

Smith, Ronald D. "Napoleon and Louisiana: Failure of the Proposed Expedition to Occupy Louisiana." *Louisiana History* 12 (1971): pp. 21–40.

Stephens, James. *The Crisis of the Sugar Colonies*. New York: Negro Univs. Press, 1969.

———. *The Opportunity, or Reasons for an Immediate Alliance with Santo Domingo*. London: C. Whitingham, 1804.

Stinchcombe, Arthur. *Sugar Island Slavery*. Princeton: Princeton Univ. Press, 1995.

Stinchcombe, William C. *The American Revolution and the French Alliance*. Syracuse: Syracuse Univ. Press, 1969.

Stoddard, Theodore Lothrop. *The French Revolution in Santo Domingo*. Boston: Houghton Mifflin, 1914.

Syrett, Harold E., ed. *The Papers of Alexander Hamilton*, vols. 9–26. New York: Columbia Univ. Press, 1961–1987.

Tansill, Charles. *The United States and Santo Domingo, 1798–1873*. Gloucester, Mass.: Peter Smith, 1967.

Taussig, Charles W. *Rum, Romance and Rebellion*. New York: Minton Balch, 1928.

Tolles, Frederick. *George Logan of Philadelphia*. New York: Oxford Univ. Press, 1953

Tucker, Robert W., and David C. Hendrickson. *Empire of Liberty: The Statecraft of Thomas Jefferson*. New York: Oxford Univ. Press, 1980.

Turner, Frederick J. *Correspondence of the French Ministers to the United States, 1791–97*. 2 vols. New York: Da Capo, 1972.

Turnier, Alain. *Les Etas-Unis et le marché Haitien* (The United States and the Haitian Market). Montreal: St. Joseph Press, 1955.

Washington, George. The George Washington Papers. Library of Congress, Manuscript Division. http://memory.loc.gov/ammem/gwhtml/gwhome.html.

Williams, Eric. *Capitalism and Slavery*. New York: Andre Deutsch, 1989.

Wills, Gary. *James Madison*. New York: Henry Holt, 2002.

Weeden, William B. *An Economic and Social History of New England, 1620–1789*. New York: Hillary House Publishers, 1963.

Zuckerman, Michael. *Almost Chosen People; Oblique Biographies in the American Grain*. Berkeley: Univ. of California Press, 1993.

INDEX